Decoding the Egalitarianism of the Qur'an

Lexington Studies in Classical and Modern Islamic Thought

Hussam S. Timani

This series will explore and examine a vast literature on understudied strands in Islamic thought. The series topics include, but not limited to, Qur'an and hadith studies, classical theological and philosophical doctrines, the human knowledge, law and tradition, law and legal reforms, tradition and renewal, Salafi thought, piety movements, neo-traditionalism, neo-liberalism, neo-reformism, neo-Islamism, cultural pluralism, and liberal and ethical humanism. Additional subjects for consideration would be trends in contemporary Islamic thought such as democracy, justice, secularism, globalization, international relations, Islam and the West, and feminism. The volumes in the series would examine, historicize, and analyze Muslim intellectual responses to the various trends of Islamic thought that have been understudied in Western scholarship. This series would make an important and timely literature available to the English reader.

While the series encompasses both classical and modern Islamic thought, a special emphasis will be put on modern and contemporary Islamic reformist thought. In light of radicalism and the rise of violence in the Islamic world today, the expectations of reformist thought in Muslim societies are running high. What are the programs that qualify as reformist, what are the qualities an Islamic reformist is expected to demonstrate, and what does exactly make for Islamic reformist thinking? There are two strands of Muslim reformers in the Islamic world today: those who refer to themselves as Islamic reformers (they are out to reinterpret the Islamic tradition to make it compatible with the current age) and those who are described as reformist but claim that they are not out to reform Islam, but rather only to interpret it in an "Islamically correct" manner. To date, far too little attention has been devoted to the thought of the thinkers in both groups. The volumes in this series would examine contemporary reformist thought as well as its reception in both the Islamic world and the West.

Titles in the Series

Decoding the Egalitarianism of the Qur'an: Retrieving Lost Voices on Gender, by Abla Hasan

Decoding the Egalitarianism of the Qur'an

Retrieving Lost Voices on Gender

Abla Hasan

LEXINGTON BOOKS
Lanham • Boulder • New York • London

Published by Lexington Books
An imprint of The Rowman & Littlefield Publishing Group, Inc.
4501 Forbes Boulevard, Suite 200, Lanham, Maryland 20706
www.rowman.com

6 Tinworth Street, London SE11 5AL, United Kingdom

Abla Hasan, "The Quranic Story of Mary: Does Rethinking the Text Support Women Prophethood?" *Ar Raniry*, 3, no. 1 (2016), pp. 189–204.

Abla Hasan, "The Queen of Sheba: Would rethinking the Qur'anic story support female public leadership In Islam?" *Analize*, 21, no. 7 (2016).

British Library Cataloguing in Publication Information Available

Library of Congress Cataloging-in-Publication Data Available

ISBN: 978-1-7936-0989-2 (cloth : alk. paper)
ISBN: 978-1-7936-0991-5 (pbk : alk. paper)
ISBN: 978-1-7936-0990-8 (electronic)

∞™ The paper used in this publication meets the minimum requirements of American National Standard for Information Sciences—Permanence of Paper for Printed Library Materials, ANSI/NISO Z39.48-1992.

For Hassan

"The Massenger has said, 'Lord, my people treat this Qur'an as something to be shunned'"
(Qur'an 25:30)

Contents

Foreword

Islam and its holy book, the Qur'an, have traditionally been interpreted as being at odds with the egalitarian ideals of feminism. This book argues that, to the contrary, the Qur'an affirms the equal rights and equal value of men and women. It reaches this conclusion on the basis of detailed semantic analyses of the relevant Qur'anic texts. These analyses serve both to refute traditional, anti-feminist interpretations of certain passages and to show how the egalitarian interpretation can be justified.

The first chapter exposes the various fallacies of interpretation that have, historically, led to the systematic misinterpretation of Qur'anic passages about women and their interrelationships with men; the best way to interpret the Qur'an, it suggests, is to pay careful attention to its exact words and to seek an interpretation of the Qur'an as a whole that avoids ascribing any inconsistencies to its divine message.

The second chapter appeals to various passages from the Qur'an, starting with the story of Adam and Eve, to show that the book affirms the equality of men and women and to show that it should not be read as asserting the superiority of males. The last two sections of the chapter support this interpretation by a detailed semantic analysis of two of the Qur'an's key terms.

The third chapter, which deals with marriage, argues that the Qur'an treats marriage as a sacred relationship between equals and refutes various patriarchal misinterpretations of Qur'anic teachings on marriage. It argues that marriage, according to the Qur'an, involves a solemn pledge between two people who commit themselves to treating each other with love and kindness in order to achieve mutual tranquility. Commentaries on the Qur'an that interpret it as endorsing the marriage of underage girls and domestic violence are shown to have no basis in the texts. According to the author's interpretation, verse Q.4:34, which has been interpreted as endorsing wife-beating, is not even about marital conflict at all; no fewer than twenty arguments are adduced in support of this conclusion. Similarly, the traditional interpretation of verse Q.4:128, which has been read as depriving women of some of their rights in marriage, is shown to be a misreading. Finally, the author addresses polygyny in the Qur'an. She distinguishes what she calls "Islamic polygyny"—the traditional polygynous doctrine of Islam—according to which men are allowed to have up to four wives, from what she calls "Qur'anic polygyny," the actual teaching of the Qur'an. She traces how the former came to be confused with the latter, and argues that Qur'anic polygyny applies only to cases in which men marry the mothers of fatherless children, and that even in such cases it is subject to various restrictions.

Chapter four, on female body ownership, interprets the Qur'an as endorsing sexual modesty as an ideal for both men and women. Turning then to the topic of whether Muslim women should wear *hijab*, or the veil, it suggests that *hijab* may be understood as a silent way of communicating the message that a woman is interested only in serious relationships, as opposed to casual sex or aimless dating, and thus as one among many options that women can use in public to convey this message. It also suggests that the wearing of *hijab* can be a way of liberating women from social pressure to encourage their own sexual objectification by displaying their bodies. Wearing *hijab*, the author stresses, is according to the Qur'an a free choice; society has no right to force women to dress in any particular way. Finally, the author maintains that the Qur'an instructs women to liberate themselves not only from social pressures against modesty but also from their own conceptions of themselves as primarily sexual objects. Only by doing so can they come to realize that their true happiness can come only from their development of the full range of their human virtues and their full participation in every aspect of society.

Chapter five maintains that the Qur'an presents women as fully functioning members of society. It appeals to the Qur'anic story of *Maryam* as an instance of the Qur'an's according the status of a prophet to a woman, and to the story of the queen of Sheba as a case of its according a women equal status with men as a political authority. This chapter further argues that the Qur'an grants women the equal right to citizenship (including the right to vote), the equal right to engage in the work of their choice, and the right to be compensated for their domestic labor if they choose to devote their energies to homemaking and caring for their husbands and children.

In her concluding remarks author disclaims any pretense to having provided the last word on Qur'anic interpretation and welcomes further work on the topics treated in her book. She locates her work within the context of contemporary Muslim critiques of heritage-based schools of exegesis and observes that her work is sanctioned by the Qur'an injunction to "reflect" upon its teachings. In her last paragraph she observes that, given the premise that the Qur'an is the word of God, the message of gender equality that she has found in it sharpens our understanding of God's justice.

The foregoing summary is intended only to provide readers with a preview of the book's conclusions. Reading it is, of course, no substitute for reading the book, whose primary value lies in its mastery of the Qur'anic texts and in the careful and detailed arguments with which it defends its conclusions. Only readers who have studied those arguments will be in a position either to agree intelligently with its conclusions or to argue convincingly against them.

Edward F. Becker
University of Nebraska

Acknowledgments

I am grateful to the University of Nebraska for supporting the writing of this book via the ENHANCE research grant. A special word of thanks goes to Patty Simpson and all my colleagues in the Department of Modern Languages and Literatures for their support and encouragement. I thank Michael Gibson, Tarek Ghanem and Edward Becker. I thank my parents and my father-in-law. I am also thankful to Valerie Joy Turner for the professional and thorough editing of the manuscript. In addition, I have to acknowledge all the valuable discussions with my students at the University of Nebraska, Rutgers University, Maryland University, University of Nizwa in Oman and the Osher Lifelong Learning Institute at the University of Nebraska. Finally, I am thankful to an anonymous reviewer for a valuable suggestion of a chapter restructure.

Introduction

How can a book that—allegedly—openly advises husbands by saying, "Strike them" (Q.4:34) in cases of marital conflict have any possible egalitarian interpretation with regard to gender? Does the Qur'an really reflect a misogynist ideology? Was the Qur'anic message misunderstood by medieval scholars, jurists, and their modern followers, who interpreted the Qur'an through patriarchal lenses? What can an analytical, linguistic, and critical approach to the Qur'anic text reveal in relation to women's issues? Is there any reason to believe that there have been systematic manipulative readings of the Qur'an that resulted in a gender-biased understanding of the divine text? Can rethinking the original text unearth inconsistencies or even contradictions caused by a long history of an androcentric interpretative tradition?

This book is an academic, yet a theologically oriented hermeneutical approach to the Qur'an. It aims to rethink women's status in the Qur'an by unlocking its philological character. By allowing the Qur'anic text to speak for itself, instead of following inherited exegeses, which "turned into a yardstick and a lens to reshape and redefine the Qur'anic text,"[1] we seek to gradually unearth an unknown gender-egalitarian face of the Qur'an.

In this book, my careful hermeneutical investigation challenges a long history of normalizing patriarchal approaches to the Qur'an and calls for a questioning of the interpretive credibility of many inherited Qur'anic commentaries. The research ends with the rediscovery of a lost humanitarian and gender-egalitarian textual richness that has been poorly and loosely handled for centuries. As Asma Barlas (b. 1950) argues, "The problem is not inherent in the text 'itself,' but in the relationship between knowledge and the means of its production."[2]

Roughly speaking, this book stresses the importance of reviewing the interpretive linguistic choices that jurists and exegetes over the last fourteen centuries have adopted to semantically reshape the Qur'anic text. My research concludes by questioning the credibility of many of these choices and the so-called unconditional validity of many of them, which stretched the applicability of many interpretations beyond the limited time frame of their production. In fact, the vigilant reading I provide of some carefully chosen commentaries suggests that many interpretive approaches of the Qur'an were dominated by sociopolitical factors alien to the intrinsic semantic values of the text itself. More importantly, as we see, inconsistencies across putatively sound books of *tafsīr* indicate that the Qur'anic text might have suffered from a historical and systematic drainage of its humanitarianism, gender egalitarianism, and religious pluralism. As a result, I argue that the text has, in various ways, lost its flexibility and the outcomes its humanitarian upheaval was supposed to bring about. Therefore, any possible potential of reading this book as a universal religious revelation—at least as the majority of Muslims believe it to be—has been drastically reduced.

This book is, in short, an invitation to read the Qur'an in isolation from any previously held prejudices, and without presupposing any meaning other than what the Qur'anic text entails, in order to reassess the lost humanitarian and gender-egalitarian richness of the Qur'an. In this book, I seek to reveal a more authentic humanitarian face of the Qur'an, after centuries of marginalizing women's interpretations of the Qur'an. The hermeneutical methodology I adopt in the book is not developed ex nihilo; rather it is inspired by what the Qur'anic text asserts when it repeatedly refers to itself as a "clear book."[3] In this work, I seek to recognize and implement the inimitable internal interpretive capacity of the Qur'anic text—a text that holds all the keys to its own decoding—as these are essential tools to reconnect with the Qur'an. The methodology I refer to as the "semantic completeness of the Qur'anic language," is inspired by what the Qur'anic language itself indicates: "We have sent the scripture down to you explaining everything" (Q.16:89). The methodology is also supported by a growing literature that supports interpreting the Qur'an by using the Qur'an itself (*tafsīr al-Qur'an bi al-Qur'an*) to free its message from cultural, traditional, and judicial preferences. Historically speaking, in the conflict over who has the right to interpret the divine text, traditionalists or proponents of *tafsīr bi-l-ma'thur* (tradition-based exegesis) attempted to curb rationalists or proponents of *ra'y* (reason, personal judgment, and opinion) who relied on linguistic aspects of the Qur'an, by labeling them audacious and sometimes blasphemous. Nasr Abū Zayd (1943–2010) refers to a decisive split between two different interpretive modes of the Qur'anic text, what he calls the "heritage interpretive mode,"[4] and the "opinion interpretive mode."[5] The first aims at semantically unlocking the Qur'anic text by gathering historical as well as linguistic evidence to understand the text the way it was understood by the contemporary recipients of that text; the second starts from the interpreter's current intellectual attitude, and does not involve a study of historical accounts. He describes how the first interpretive mode was received with respect, while supporters of the interpretive mode were often met with suspicion and even faced, "accusations of blasphemy and book-burning."[6]

By the "semantic completeness of the Qur'anic language"[7] which I introduce as a strict application of using the Qur'an to interpret the Qur'an, I refer to the unmatchable sufficiency of the Qur'anic language, which makes all external semantic investigation of the meanings of words, terms, and expressions complementary in nature; these can come only second to the "best explanation" (Q.25:33) that the Qur'anic text provides exclusively. According to the "semantic completeness of the Qur'anic language," the self-interpretive capacity of the Qur'anic text can be accessed as the most basic interpretive and epistemic tool to unlock the philological and the sematic nature of the Qur'anic text—a tool that derives its validity from God's commitment in the Qur'an itself to make reading and understanding the Qur'an accessible, as we read in: "We have made it easy to learn lessons from the Qur'an" (Q.54:17) and "it is up to Us to make it clear" (Q.75:19). Therefore, the only resource I use in this book is the Qur'anic text itself. I have not sought support from other sources, such as the *sira* (prophetic biography), hadith, or Islamic jurisprudence. I believe the main hindrance to understanding the Qur'an is the dominance of a juxtapositional method, one that does not seek a textual understanding of the Qur'an without appealing to other sources—historical, cultural, ethnic, political, and even local sources. I tried to avoid biased perspectives in reading the Qur'anic text, in an effort to purify my reading and to ensure the sincerity of my commitment to understanding the meaning of the Qur'anic text.

In my hermeneutical investigation of the Qur'anic text, I tried to stay faithful to a strictly internal interpretational methodology. Throughout the book, I reinterpret and ultimately retranslate some of the most controversial verses in the Qur'an, and base my arguments on linguistic evidence from the Qur'an. I have not allowed myself to borrow and insert elements from later lexical developments of the Arabic language, hadith, *sira*, variable Islamic judicial attitudes, and exegetical elaborations, particularly because these are proven to have a distorting or alienating impact on the semantic authenticity of the Qur'anic text. In rethinking a Qur'anic word or term I use only the Qur'anic text itself as a valid hermeneutic reference.

I use one academic translation of the Qur'an, that of Muhammad Abdel Haleem (Oxford University Press, 2010). On occasion, I provide my own translation, based on my interpretation of certain problematic verses. As the reader will notice, the introduction of the new translation is piecemeal, as I gradually move forward with my arguments. Therefore, while I eventually provide a final translation of full verses, a step by step, initial and even an intermediary translation is provided in the text according to a comprehensive logical plan, purposefully and carefully designed to make sense of every translation choice I take in this arduous journey to reinvestigate every expression, every term, and even every preposition in the verses in question.

The book is divided into five chapters. In chapter 1, I provide a general elucidation of some exegetical deficiencies that ended in this alienation of the Qur'anic text from its rich gender-egalitarian message. In the book, I apply these deficiencies to verses in question to clarify their real and most authentic Qur'anic meaning. Chapter 2 discusses gender egalitarianism in the Qur'an. In this chapter I demonstrate, first, a gradual but a slow, progressive exegetical evaluation of the role Eve allegedly played in what is commonly known as the story of creation. While the Qur'anic text itself provides clear-cut support for Eve's innocence, I argue that early exegetes used uncited biblical narratives as an excuse to demonize Eve and shift the blame to her. Also, in this chapter, I provide new linguistic evidence from the Qur'an that supports Eve's innocence. The chapter, next, explains the Qur'anic undeniable confirmation of gender egalitarianism and discusses in detail the concept of male guardianship or *qiwāma*. I argue that this concept, which can be linguistically proven to refer to the responsibility of men, in fact does not exceed the financial duty to provide . It was culturally reconstructed and used as the basic foundation for men's ethical and intellectual superiority to women. The chapter provides a detailed linguistic investigation of what this concept stands for. Chapter 3 provides a full Qur'anic-based discussion of the meaning and purpose of marriage in the Qur'an, and the Qur'anic guidance for healthy marital sexuality. I prove that controversial questions like the permissibility of minor marriage, domestic violence, and polygyny have totally different Qur'anic answers than what traditional Islamic schools of exegeses have presented for more than fourteen centuries. Chapter 4 explains women's modesty from a Qur'anic perspective, both in behavior and in appearance. Finally, chapter 5 proves that the Qur'an fully endorses women's three-dimensional agency: religious, political, and economic agency. In this chapter I argue that *ajr* is a lost Qur'anic right for women in marriage.

In short, this book provides strong linguistic evidence to support the existence of a lost gender egalitarian voice in the Qur'an, one that has been both deliberately and unintentionally defaced in the history of overt exegetical–biased studies of the Qur'an. The conclusions I reach in this book came about as a result of intense academic effort, during which I sought objectivity by depending only on the Qur'anic text. I humbly bring my new reading of the divine text to the table for discussion, with full acknowledgment of those who did their best according to the best of their knowledge at their time, but who, as Abou-Bakr states, "were products of their own eras and cultures, naturally not aware of or interested in establishing equal status for men and women."[8] To avoid presentism let me explain my project via drawing a simple analogy: while al-Zahrāwī's (936–1013) *Zaraqa*[9] was a scientific revolution at his time, when Muslim scientists moved forward, dismissing it did not provoke feelings of guilt in the Islamic world; likewise, scholars of the Qur'an should feel the same about moving on with our understanding of the Qur'anic text, beyond the spatiotemporal limitations of inherited exegetical corpora.

NOTES

1. Jasim Sultan, *al-Turāth wa-ishkaliyyathu al-kubrā* (Beirut: Arab Network for Research and Publishing and Tamkin, 2015), 156.
2. Asma Barlas, "Qur'anic Hermeneutics and Sexual Politics," *Cardozo Law Review* 28, no. 1 (2006), 144.
3. As in Q.5:15.
4. Naṣr Ḥāmid Abū Zayd, *Ishkāliyat al-qirā'a wa-āliyyat al-ta'wīl* (Beirut: al-Markaz al-Thaqāfī al-'Arabī, 2005), 15.
5. Abū Zayd, *Ishkāliyat al-qirā'a wa-āliyyat al-ta'wīl.*
6. Ibid.
7. The completeness of physics is a philosophical thesis which claims that physics is causally closed. Here, I borrow the term with an alteration; I use the "semantic completeness of the Qur'anic language" to indicate that the Qur'an is semantically closed. That is, we do not need any external resource other than the Qur'an to understand the Qur'an.
8. Omaima Abou-Bakr (ed.), *Feminism and Islamic Perspectives: New Horizons of Knowledge and Reform* (Cairo: Women and Memory Forum, 2013), 4.
9. A surgical instrument invented by al-Zahrāwī.

Chapter 1

Decoding the Egalitarianism of the Qur'an

Overcoming Deficiencies

How did widely accepted interpretations of the Qur'an lose the connection—as I argue in this book—with the Qur'an's clear humanitarian and gender-egalitarian richness? What motivated many exegetes, both traditionalists and modernists, to read the Qur'anic text in ways that we can, more or less, describe today as ambiguous or misleading? If linguistic evidence—as I prove in this book—support a gender-egalitarian interpretation of verses related to women in the Qur'an, how can we explain the dominant patriarchal tendencies—easily observed—in almost all traditional and most modern approaches to Qur'anic exegeses? Is it the ambiguity of the Qur'anic text itself or is it the lens many of these mainstream exegetes borrowed to read the text, such that they reached conclusions that correspond to their assumptions. In addition to examining, in detail, the issue of how and in what ways the Qur'anic exegetical tradition deviated from the Qur'an's gender-egalitarian message in the remainder of this book, I briefly describe the historical roots of the debate in which Muslim feminists find themselves today.

In the following, I provide a general elucidation of some systematic deficiencies that I believe actively and instrumentally contribute to what I call the disabling of Qur'anic gender egalitarianism. We find that understanding these deficiencies gives us a better chance of understanding the alienation of the Qur'anic text from its rich gender-egalitarian and human-focused message. In the book, I variably apply these deficiencies to specific verses to explain the reason/reasons why many of these verses have lost their real meaning.

EXCESSIVE EXEGETICAL NARRATIVIZATION OF THE QUR'AN

The first deficiency of the exegetical approaches to the Qur'anic text is what I refer to as "excessive exegetical narrativization." This desire to fill in details that are absent from the Qur'anic narratives was extended to cover specific issues related to Qur'anic teachings of duties and obligations. This perplexing epistemic behavior of many exegetes was mostly based on the use of obsolete details (both authentic and inauthentic) from vaguely transmitted religious myths, preserved prophetic sayings, biblical narratives, and folk wisdom. Many times, this conglomeration of information was used to construct lengthier, more vibrant and entertaining Qur'anic commentaries. However, as expected, this behavior resulted in exegeses that were not fully reliable or authentic.

To avoid unjust generalizations, however, I would note that some approaches to *tafsīr* were made by those with good intentions, to convey a clear and vividly described message, but they borrowed details, both authentic and unauthentic, and added them to the original body of information (that is, the Qur'an), while in fact what they added is not Qur'anic. However, in doing this, these commentators violated two intrinsic Islamic theological claims: first, the Islamic consensus that the Arabic of the Qur'an is a sacred language, or the argument for the inimitability, or wondrous nature, of the Qur'anic Arabic, known as the *i'jāz* doctrine. Muhammed Abdel Haleem (b. 1930) rightly described this: "Theologically, it is the Arabic version that is considered the true Qur'an, the direct word of God, and read in acts of worship,"[1] where all words and even all letters are believed by Muslims to have been purposely, eloquently, and divinely chosen to serve an irreplaceable semantic task. Second, it violated the consensus concerning the universality of the Qur'anic message, because adding too many details to the concise text of the Qur'an leads to a culturally constructed version of the text that could no longer be considered universal. The Qur'anic message, in theory and from the point of view of Muslim theologians, is supposed to be "flexible enough to accommodate cultural situations being universally beneficial for all."[2]

As Ṭāriq al-Bishrī (b. 1933) makes clear, the occasions that accompanied the revelation of the religious text are better understood as mere correlations and as opportunities to apply the text and not as the active causes of the text, "otherwise the text will not be described as general and abstract."[3] Therefore, this excessive exegetical narrativization undoubtedly formed a departure from this well-established Islamic theological argument that the Qur'an is a universal revelation and has a general guidance for humanity that is consistent with all possible and all potential traditions, nationalities, communities, and ethnicities. That is, "It was only as a mercy that We sent you [Prophet] to all people" (Q.21:108).

In contrast to this tendency, the Qur'anic message was purposefully structured as an open-ended revelation that included no more than "generalizations and major objective values."[4] The Qur'anic text offers only general guidance (this is particularly true in terms of legal guidelines): "Its method of guidance for practical Islamic life does not consist of laying down minutely detailed laws and regulations."[5] Qur'anic stories, for example, do not provide details of the chronological order of events. In addition, in many cases, Qur'anic stories appear like scattered scenes, in which names of people, places, and dates are seldom mentioned. Even in relation to rules and commandments, it is easy to see that the Qur'an keeps the door widely open to follow Qur'anic commands if adopted by any congregation, anywhere and anytime. For example, as I explain in detail, in relation to women's modesty, the general principles of Qur'anic commands make it flexible for any woman, living in any community and leading any lifestyle, to commit herself to a general type of Qur'anic modesty, without any obligation to give up fashion, her own dressing style or custom, as long as the general Qur'anic requirements of modesty are fulfilled. In fact, understanding modesty in a narrow way, in a way that led to a single culturally preferred "uniform," like a black dress or abaya, is a trend that has only recently been suggested, and even required, by conservative interpretations that narrowed the Qur'anic view of modesty to such a degree, without realizing that details were intentionally left out. As I explain, the Qur'anic text systematically utilizes abstract language that is broad enough to accommodate human advancement and what modesty means for each community, generation, and tradition.

To avoid oversimplifying the impact of this exegetical tendency to localize the Qur'anic message, we must note that there were reasons for overlooking this basic Qur'anic generalization. At various times in Islamic history, religion was the main or only tie unifying the expanding Islamic empire. Arabs had learned from their pre-Islamic enmity that it was necessary to unite and cooperate under the umbrella of their new religion, which they used as a political focal point and foundation of legislation. This unity meant that all laws should be derived from the Qur'an or at least linked to the Qur'an in a way that early Muslim authorities could claim that the laws were derived from it; this was true even in cases in which the Qur'anic text did not specifically reveal a law.

That said, any approach to understanding the Qur'anic text today should start by isolating the text from the history of its sociopolitical interpretive discourse. Acknowledging the pragmatic and even the authoritative need to translate the general language of the Qur'an into a set of rules, regulations, and laws, which took place during the early history of Islam, can be a key to understanding how the generality of the Qur'anic text was transformed into a fixed set of rigid rules and strict regulations. Much of what is believed to be Islamic today can be easily proven to have no Qur'anic roots at all. For example, in this book, I distinguish between what can be referred to as Qur'anic polygyny and what is practiced and known as Islamic polygyny. While one might assume that "Qur'anic" is synonymous with "Islamic," in fact, studying what the Qur'an says about polygyny reveals how Muslims' practice of it has deviated from the essential Qur'anic idea. It is critical to identify this disconnection between modern exegetes and legal applications and the Qur'anic text itself. If we fail to do this, we will make the same mistakes that Salafis and even radical movements make when they resurrect obsolete local interpretations of the Qur'an and claim that they are Islamic and therefore should be followed by all Muslims. Therefore, at this early stage, let me draw attention to a conclusion that I assert in the book: the abstract open-ended textual style of the Qur'an does not allow for narrowly constructed cultural normativity. The semantic style of the Qur'an is purposefully structured to allow for an open-ended interpretive capacity. For example, as I make clear in the book, *ma'rūf*[6] is mentioned in the Qur'an as a rule, sufficient to regulate the marital relationship (e.g., Q.4:19 and Q.2:229); however, the definition of *ma'rūf* was never spelled out. I argue that this was intentional. It was done to allow various and successive interpretations of the meaning of *ma'rūf*, that is, it allows this meaning to vary from time to time and from one culture to another. Another example is the word *'adl*, which means justice, as in (Q.4:58). This word was used in the Qur'an to indicate the general Qur'anic criterion of sound political rulings, which as the generality of the word indicates, allows for an almost endless number of human legal choices, provided that justice is sought. As Kecia Ali (b. 1972) argues, our modern understanding of justice would cease to have any straightforward meaning if medieval interpretations of the Qur'an are all what we have, because our modified concepts vary substantially from their culturally preferred sets of plausible choices. She writes,

> Today, when we speak of the ethical with regard to gender in Islamic law, we often mean egalitarianism. It is vital to recall that these jurists did not idealize an egalitarian order. Instead, they believed that some people were, though not inferior as believers, properly subordinate to others in the life of this world.[7]

As Khaled Abou el Fadl (b. 1963) rightly observes, "The Qur'an itself doesn't specify a particular form of government,"[8] therefore, the generality of the Qur'anic text is purposefully designed to allow that ample room for successive human legislative efforts to reshape and refine what justice means. In other words, I argue that when the Qur'anic text refers to abstract concepts like *'adl*, *ma'rūf*, *iḥsān*, etc., these concepts should always be comprehended via readings that allow room for an open interpretation, contrary to the exegetical tendency I refer to as "excessive exegetical narrativization of the Qur'an."

THE USE OF HADITH TO INVALIDATE THE QUR'ANIC TEXT

The second deficiency in reading the Qur'anic text comes from the use of hadith to weaken or undermine the Qur'anic text. While interpreting the Qur'an, some exegetes tried a strategy of inserting more details borrowed from the prophetic tradition. However, this strategy resulted in problematic outcomes, because "even if one contends that the problematic elements are only a small part of the "Sira," one's ability to rely on it is undermined, because there is as yet no generally accepted and foolproof method for distinguishing what might be true from what might be false."[9]

Hadith was supposed to play only a minor role in terms of explaining the Qur'an. The Qur'an itself indicates this by describing the Qur'anic text as "clear" (Q.2:99), consistent, "if it had been from anyone other than God, they would have found much inconsistency in it" (Q.3:82), and as fully explained, "we have explained it on the basis of true knowledge" (Q.7:52). Unfortunately, the unjust categorization of the Qur'anic text as a profoundly abstruse text, allowed scholars to use hadith as a necessary tool to unlock its ambiguities, until it gained a prioritized status almost equal to the Qur'anic text itself, while in fact, as Ayman El-Desouky observes, in the Qur'an, there is no report of the prophetic encounter, rather the emphasis is on "the direct voice."[10] Unfortunately, pre-modern and even modern exegetical understanding of the Qur'anic text came to be increasingly reliant on elements borrowed from "highly contested"[11] prophetic sayings. This entanglement between the Qur'an and hadith included not only cases in which the hadith seems to affirm the meaning in the Qur'an but extended to cases of hadiths that assert the opposite meaning or negate a Qur'anic verse. Jonathan Brown (b. 1977) rightly asserts the prioritized status of hadith by saying, "Partisans of hadith scholars did not treat the Qur'an as categorically epistemologically superior to reliable hadiths."[12]

But more importantly, prioritizing hadith over the Qur'anic text sometimes went beyond the mere desire to explain the Qur'an, and became an active effort to falsify Islamic history and provide the struggling political powers that emerged shortly after the death of the Prophet with the ideological support they needed in their conflicts. In addition to the realistic concern that "we are unable to ascertain that the Prophet played the primary role in the authorial enterprise that generated these traditions,"[13] as Fatima Mernissi argues, "political adventures and economic conflicts motivated hadith fabrications"[14] which seemed, at the time, as the only available option, since "every authority, starting from the seventh century was justifiable only via religion."[15]

Convoluted contradictions between the Qur'anic text and the hadith made any possible reconciliation a difficult task that caused many to make choices that were not necessarily faithful to the Qur'anic text. For example, Layla

Ramī provides an interesting reading of the status of women in public leadership positions by rethinking the Qur'anic story of the Queen of Sheba. However, while Ramī clearly concludes by acknowledging the Qur'an's unconditional support for female leadership, since, as she comments, "had the position assigned to that woman been prohibited, God would have mentioned that even if by way of using a small reference, as when he described the Pharaoh as a tyrant";[16] paradoxically, she unexpectedly moves from using her conclusions to challenge the mainstream "elusive"[17] image of the Queen of Sheba, and instead adopts a defensive position that denies even the intention to reclaim public leadership as a right for women. She writes,

> This does not mean I argue [in favor of] assigning public authority positions to women . . . I do not think our problem lies in assigning authority to women as much as it is the need to engage women in making different types of decisions that run the society. The Prophet (PBUH) dismissed assigning women public authority positions but he did not reject women's participation in political, intellectual, and legislative decisions.[18]

This flaw is exacerbated by the many undeniable difficulties related to the process of hadith collection and the many questions about the reliability of what scholars classified as weak and sound (*ṣaḥīḥ*) hadith. Those who insist on understanding the Qur'an via hadith face a number of obstacles: First, what are considered canonical collections of hadith, for example, those collected by al-Bukhārī (810–870) are still his evaluations of hadith, which were based on his individual efforts to eliminate all those he considered fabricated. His undeniably great effort does not change the fact that he was one individual human, inevitably subjective in some of his choices. Second, the historical gulf between the time the Qur'an was collected and recorded in writing by the companions during the lifetime of the Prophet[19] or shortly after, as many believe, and the later process of writing the hadith "in the middle of the ninth century."[20] Third, it is noteworthy that the writing of hadith was discouraged by the Prophet himself, who asked his companions to burn anything they write after him, except the Qur'an.[21] As Jamāl al-Bannā (1920–2013) argues, the specificity of the hadith was meant to serve the temporal needs of the emerging community; therefore, the validity of using the hadith traditions was restricted to the minimum, in contrast to the Qur'anic text, which alone had the right to "immortalization."[22] Fourth, even if we consider a broader role for hadith in understanding the Qur'an, this view should be seen in light of the cumulative nature of scholarship and should encourage and not prohibit later and modern hadith scholars from re-examining hadith. In other words, those scholars who followed in the footsteps of al-Bukhārī, and even modern scholars, should not be denied the right to authenticate, refine, and even rethink the authenticity of canonical hadith collections.

Undoubtedly, the hadith comprise a bold challenge to any feminist approach to rethinking women's status in the Qur'an. Aysha A. Hidayatullah was right when she criticized the way feminist readings of the Qur'an have dealt with hadith as she wrote,

> The uneven use and scrutiny of the Hadith demonstrates a methodological inconsistency across the collective body of feminist tafsir works . . . the successful use of the feminist method of historical contextualization will require that scholars of feminist tafsir more carefully clarify their positions on the Hadith tradition as a whole in part by treating the Hadith more systematically in all their readings of the Qur'an rather than referring to Hadith in selected cases when it is convenient to support or defend their interpretations.[23]

However, in addition to the full acknowledgment of this flaw—the use of the hadith to invalidate the Qur'anic text—we must still assert that, in interpreting the Qur'anic text, it is necessary to prioritize the Qur'an over any other resource, especially in cases of contradictions. While this mission might sound impossible for some, it should be pursued for two reasons. First, in the long run, it saves time which might otherwise be spent reconciling antithetical contradictions between the hadith and the Qur'an, and even between different hadiths. Second, and more importantly, the solidly grounded hermeneutical structure of the Qur'an forms the necessary and the sufficient condition for its own decoding. As we see in this book, the semantic comprehensiveness of the Qur'an makes any attempt to interpret it by anything other than the Qur'an itself redundant and superfluous. For those who might find the invitation to interpret the Qur'an by the Qur'an (*tafsīr al-Qur'an bi al-Qur'an*) and to prioritize the Qur'an over all other resources in an attempt to rethink gender egalitarianism in the Qur'an an unconventional proposal, I invite them to think of the proposal as a thought experiment, as such a nontraditional route might help us uncover new unexplored horizons that we cannot see now, given the distraction of other resources. Likewise, the disconnection I propose to make from the historical, judicial, and traditional data has a huge impact in eliminating self-contradictions, logical inconsistences, and theological dilemmas that those engaged in Qur'anic studies have been trying, unsuccessfully, to rationalize and even normalize. My project should not be seen as a call to belittle or question other approaches as much as it should be considered a new window through which we might view the same scene.

THE ABROGATION FALLACY

Despite the fact that the Qur'anic text was described by the Qur'an itself as a book that, "falsehood cannot touch from any angle" (Q.41:42), the allegation of abrogation makes a problematic case for the Qur'an as an unfinished project and as an inchoately edited book. According to many traditional scholars, abrogation can be divided into two types: the first refers to the belief in the existence of some verses that, while they remain in the Qur'an, they have no practical application. Their later abrogation made these verses void of any intrinsic value, except for their value as a form of worship, that is, reciting them remains a blessed activity. The second refers to lost verses that clerics continued referring to, despite their absence. However, as Oliver Leaman (b. 1950) argues, "The Qur'an nowhere specifies which Qur'anic verses are abrogated by which other verses or which passages from Jewish or Christian scriptures are superseded by which Qur'anic verses. Therefore, there was never any agreement among exegetes on these matters."[24]

Abd al-Salam Figo,[25] like many others, argues that the two verses in the Qur'an—commonly interpreted as supporting and asserting abrogation—use the word *aya*, which can simultaneously mean a "miracle" or a "verse." For example, in Q.26:7–8, as in many other verses, the term is used to refer to miracles: "Do they not see the earth, and what noble kinds of things We grow in it? There truly is a sign (*aya*) in this, though most of them do not believe." This means that the replacement of some *ayat* by others, as mentioned in both verses, does not essentially and necessarily refer to the replacement of verses, rather it might refer to the replacement of miracles. But even beyond the linguistic analysis of the Qur'an, the concept of abrogation does not make sense to many people, because "the thesis that a human being can modify or repeal portions of a divine text is fundamentally contrary to the notion of God's authority."[26]

Abrogation is without a doubt a challenge for any approach to the Qur'an as "the only authority" or even as "the authority," since some later judicial and exegetical opinions had no textual support of any kind. Some of those opinions were considered sound even in cases in which the Qur'anic text seems to disprove the judicial interpretation. One clear example is the punishment of stoning for publicly witnessed adultery or *zinā*; this is supported by many mainstream schools of jurisprudence, though it has no Qur'anic textual support of any kind. Broadly speaking, while the Qur'anic punishment for publicly witnessed *zinā* was limited in the Qur'an to 100 lashes (Q.24:2), later jurists replaced this ruling—for the married—with one that calls for stoning.[27] The so-called lost stoning verse is believed to be an abrogated verse that was revealed but then went missing, when the page on which the verse was written, and which was kept under *'Ā'isha's* bed, was eaten by a goat![28] Unfortunately, the story of the missing verse was used not only to challenge the overt Qur'anic elaboration, but to ignore it as well. In the current context, we must note the way in which abrogation was/is used as another tool to eliminate the Qur'anic gender-egalitarian message.

THE AUTHORITARIAN APPROACH TO THE QUR'AN

Mohammed Arkoun (1928–2010) argues that the historical political-religious alliance caused a "divorce from the beginning"[29] between religions as they were revealed to prophets and laws that were constituted and crystallized later. Ziba Mir-Hosseini (b. 1952) rightly observed the same, by making a distinction between "faith (and its values and principles) and organized religion (institutions, laws, and practices)."[30] Unequivocally, the political pressure from authorities that variably favored more amenable religious views paved the way for some views, but not others, to find their way to the surface. Since this political-religious alliance did not and could not change the Qur'anic text itself, authorities were compelled to use other less obvious tools; and eventually they succeeded in imposing interpretations that seemed more feasible, pragmatic, and politically advantageous. In times of conflict, only the voices of the elite and the religious authorities were heard, while the religious opposition, which was unheard of, was persecuted, or totally excluded.

But thinking of the political elite as the only social strata that helped marginalize the more liberal content of the Qur'an is an oversimplification of a convoluted process that in fact only started with the political elite and went on from there. For example, women's voices are seldom included in the exegetical efforts of premodern scholars to translate the abstract language of the Qur'an into concrete judicial laws and standards. As we might expect, the result was a gender-biased Islamic jurisprudence that seldom addressed women's best interests. More importantly, debates among scholars themselves concerning whose interpretation should be given precedence were sometimes resolved by a partial or even a complete marginalization of many linguistic based exegeses, and were never fully recovered. The Sunnis' fundamental claim to authority was based on their claim to *tafsīr* and they were, in times of conflict, as Walid Saleh explains, "ultimately willing to discard any philological reading (although it had always maintained that philology was the way to understand the Qur'ān) whenever it threatened to undermine a Sunni theological reading not supported by philology."[31]

In addition, we should also keep in mind the premodern and even the modern politicization of education, which altered and radically transformed the motivations and goals of religious teaching. Theological schools did not encourage critical thinking the way they encouraged the reassertion and glorification of already existing theological arguments. This observation can be better understood if we examine the evaluative criteria and standards used to accept or reject scholarly works. With the exception of the Arabic golden age (prior to the collapse of the 'Abbāsid caliphate), religious scholarship seemed to stress the need to support theologically well-established arguments more than innovation, which was always treated as suspicious. This tendency increased notably over time throughout Arabic history and was one of the main concerns of the Arab renaissance in the late 19th.[32] Jamāl al-Bannā, who personally suffered from the institutional tyranny of some in al-Azhar when many of his views and some of his books were banned, refers to "one thousand years of imitation ended by rust in the Islamic mind."[33]

THE MALE ADDRESSEE FALLACY

An overwhelming cultural-based patriarchal reading of the Qur'anic text dominated almost all available pre-modern commentaries and schools of jurisprudence. With the exception of *'Ā'isha* bt. *Abī Bakr*, who Geissinger describes as "the most commonly cited female figure by far in Sunni classical tafsir works,"[34] all major premodern exegetes were male. Gender was "central to their visions of a divinely-mandated social order"[35] and this left a clear and undeniable imprint. As I show in this book, the careful analytical reading of the Arabic of the Qur'an exposes a biased masculine reading of some scholars who "[forged] the Qur'an and projected their concepts on it."[36] As Aisha Geissinger rightly observes, "in medieval biographical dictionaries of exegetes, Quran reciters, and other specialists of various aspects of Quranic study, entries for women are virtually absent."[37] In many cases, as I note in this book, exegetical attempts to masculinize the Qur'anic text lack logical consistency, not only by different exegeses, but also within the same commentary. As I discuss in the book, the same Qur'anic terms were interpreted in different ways by the same commentaries when they are used to describe men and women. For example, the same term, when used in relation to the Queen of Sheba, is interpreted differently when it is used (in the same chapter of the Qur'an) to refer to Soloman. More importantly, earlier exegetes "keen on preserving male authority"[38] interpreted the Qur'an as a book that exclusively addresses men. The masculinization of the religious text and the biased treatment of issues related to women is a natural result of the voluntary and involuntary absence of the feminine voice, a phenomenon that still defines Arabic cultural life, not only in religious studies but in all other areas of processing or producing knowledge. 'Alī Ḥarb (b. 1941) comments on this serious deficiency by saying, "The majority of those who speak about women and their rights, and those who seek women's liberation from male authority, are men or women who—except for a few—merely echoed men, and this is sufficient by itself to invalidate their attempts."[39]

As we see in this book, the majority of verses that use the masculine plural subject pronoun, which is used in Arabic to address both a group of men or a mixed group, or to address the believing community or even to address the human community in general, were commonly interpreted one way: to suggest an exclusively male audience. An understanding of this fallacy of the masculine addressee—as we see in this book—solves the difficulties of interpreting what is commonly considered the most controversial verse in the Qur'an, namely, Q.4:34.

Clearly, the patriarchal monopoly on reading the Qur'an, which is the most basic foundation for understanding Islam, has, historically at least, allowed interpretations biased toward a more masculine view.

However, it is very important, not to allow ourselves to go too far in terms of scandalizing some systematically sexist behavior of medieval exegetes. As Ayesha S. Chaudhry explains,

> The fact that the pre-colonial Islamic tradition was patriarchal is unsurprising, given the socio-historical context of that time. Nor was patriarchy unique to Islam; adherents of all living religious traditions rooted in patriarchal social and historical contexts struggle to find ways to reconcile gender-egalitarian values with religious traditions that primarily served the interests of men.[40]

Ultimately, premodern exegetes studied every expression and every letter, establishing and enhancing *tafsīr* to the best of their knowledge, and according to the highest possible scholarly standards of their time. What deserves criticism though is the reliance of some modern scholars on the medieval Islamic exegetical heritage. This modern scholarly insistence on extending the epistemic validity of medieval exegeses beyond their spatiotemporal legal functionality limits the textual flexibility of the Qur'an.

THE FALLACY OF EXEGETICAL SEMANTIC SATIATION

Many times—as I argue in this book—repeated words, phrases and scenes, or what might sound like repeated scenes in the Qur'an are commonly treated as indicating the same exact meaning. However, in a book like the Qur'an, believed by Muslims to be a literal miracle, rethinking repetition can unearth many hidden messages that have been gone inaccurately interpreted for so long. Since I am limiting myself in this book to women-related verses, I will be discussing only two places in which unlocking the repetition can be proven to have a huge impact on the way the Qur'anic message can be understood. The two places I am addressing is the scene in Q.3:45 of Mary meeting a group of angles, which is usually wrongly mixed with another scene in Q.19:18 when she meets Angel Gabrile. The second place I address deals with the repetition of the expression "has chosen you" in Q.3:42. In verse Q.3:42 unlocking why the expression "has chosen you" was repeated twice will lead to proving woman's right to prophethood as a solid Qur'anic argument that challenges centuries of denying women the right to prophethood.

THE SO-CALLED AUTHORITATIVE ASCENDANCY OF EARLY RELIGIOUS SCHOLARS

The alleged authoritative ascendancy of the early religious scholars has meant that Muslim feminists, or even reformists, are challenged by the religious dominance of pre-modern scholars, who came to be idolized by many ordinary Muslim readers.[41] Even beyond this extremism, the belief that early scholars of Islam and pioneer commentators had an advantage in reading and understanding the Qur'anic text has long blocked attempts to claim any new authentic contribution to Qur'anic studies, which, by definition, should be ongoing, as it "can't be arrested."[42] This challenge, which has been used in the ideological battle against based on opinion- interpretation has been used, increasingly, to challenge pioneers of Islamic feminism in the Arab world in an attempt to stop the progressiveness of their significant contributions to the Islamic gender-egalitarian scholarship. For example, while "Women and Memory Forum[43] scholars have been making efforts to engage with religious scholars through conferences and workshops,"[44] unfortunately, "these efforts have not led to any fruitful discussions. Often the position of religious scholars has been one of rejection, claiming that those producing this new knowledge are not trained in traditional religious education; and their work seeks to undo the whole Islamic tradition."[45]

Unfortunately, many traditional interpretations of the Qur'anic text continue to hinder more dynamic readings. As Yvonne Haddad (b. 1935) and John L. Esposito (b. 1940) rightly observe,

> Compared to the classical tradition, modern and contemporary tafsir works generally dwell more on the ethical issues in culture, society, politics, and economics and less on points of theology or aspects of language (grammar and rhetoric) in the Quranic text. Nevertheless, most of these works are still "traditionalist" in nature in that they echo their predecessors' conclusions, especially on gender issues where the latter have been enshrined in sharia law.[46]

Undoubtedly, medieval scholars made countless valuable contributions, but their opinions are just a part of the cumulative human effort to comprehend the divine text, and this effort will remain relative and insufficient. In addition, ascribing sanctity to the views of those scholars reveals nothing but a problematic type of "appeal to authority logical fallacy" and ignorance of the fact that these scholars' "formulations and interpretations must be seen in the sociological perspective of their time."[47]

Despite the overwhelming belief to the contrary—especially as advocated by traditionalists and the Salafi movement—premodern scholars did not necessarily understand the revealed text better than modern scholars; in fact, advocating such a claim contradicts one of the most prominent arguments widely supported by mainstream Islamic scholars, which is the argument that the everlasting, evolving, and miraculous nature of the Qur'an effectively echoes the needs of all generations.

It may be useful to elaborate a little more on the nature of the Prophet's message. The Prophet is believed by Muslims to be the Messenger of God—the one who was entrusted to convey the divine message. He is also believed—according to Islamic theology—to have conveyed a message that he literally and verbally received. This means that the Prophet is supposed to have conveyed a message in a way that was completely independent from the message and regardless of the content of the message. It was clear that this is what happened. For example, there were cases in which the Qur'anic text reproached the Prophet for certain decisions; this and similar incidents assured Muslims of the Prophet's complete independence from the text. Now, highlighting the Prophet's role as a Messenger and not as an author means that neither the Prophet himself nor his immediate companions could have fully understood the Qur'anic text more than others; therefore, the belief that earlier scholars were better able to understand the text as a universal message that holds true in all times and cultures is a relative argument that does not apply equally to all of the Qur'anic revelation. For example, they may have better understood some verses related to contemporary events. But, in relation to verses that some modern scholars believe are related to recently discovered scientific phenomena, I argue that we cannot claim that early scholars were more capable of understanding these verses than scholars today are.[48]

We can easily understand the fear of change and the resistance to any attempt to rethink the Qur'an. However, this fear doesn't have any solid ground since confusing the project of rethinking the Qur'an and the fear of changing the Qur'an depends only on the myth that by rethinking the Qur'an modern scholars are changing the unchanged meaning of the text. While what they do in fact is nothing but changing a meaning that has already been changed. Or to put it another way, they replace others' proposed and adopted understandings by their own proposed understanding. To make myself clear, reading the Qur'an or any religious text for the purpose of understanding it can't be done without an actual human interact with the divine text. This interact by definition would and should include all kinds of human-based epistemic efforts to unlock the transcendental abstractness of the text. This applies to understanding the context of the text, interpreting the semantics of the text, inferring laws and regulations, moving from generalizations to specificities and vice versa. This means that reading the text—and I mean by reading here the active reading that goes beyond the mere ritualistic recitation—would necessarily involve changing that text from an abstract into a humanly accessible and applicable one. First recipients of the revelation and pre-modern scholars did exactly what modern scholars are trying to do. They interpreted the text and changed its abstractness by making it a humanly processed text. Therefore, the false accusation that any new attempt to reinterpret the text will lead to changing it doesn't apply to modern scholars more than it applies to premodern ones.

In addition, we can easily understand the psychological and even the pragmatic appeal of keeping things as they are and the temptation to resist any demand for a change in the interpretation of the religious text, especially if the consequences of this demand will topple the patriarchal system that elites have long advocated. Catharine MacKinnon (b. 1946) and Andrea Dworkin (1946–2005) clearly explain this mentality:

> People seem to resist change and to defend the status quo whatever it is. Sometimes the defenses are bigoted and violent. Sometimes they are sophisticated and intellectual. If the status quo is endangered, both kinds of defenses are called into play. Inequality is made to seem normal and natural, whatever social form it takes.
>
> When some people have power and some people do not, creating equality means taking power from those who have too much and giving power to those who have too little. Social change requires the redistribution of power. Those who have power over others tend to call their power "rights." When those they dominate want equality, those in power say that important rights will be violated if society changes.[49]

Therefore, in an attempt to escape any confrontation with the past, which is generally viewed as a glorious lost utopia, many Arab Muslim feminists have long sought reforms through secular routes. But this strategy has meant that they have lost their connection to the Qur'anic text, which is supposed to be their main framework of female liberation. For example, attempts to end minor marriage in the Arab world did not and could not succeed in rethinking the Qur'anic text to reinvestigate the issue of whether or not the text supports minor marriage;[50] rather, reformers turned to new legal methods—inspired by Western modernity, secularism, or even socialism—to bring about changes in minor marriage laws. As a result, legal reform took place in the Arab and the Muslim world in isolation from religious reform, but more importantly it left behind an excess baggage of untouched obsolete religious heritage. Unfortunately, this systematic avoidance of any confrontation with the past ended with the complete alienation of these committed Muslim reformers from the religious text, which ceased being a source that they could use in their struggle for a real sense of liberation.

THE ANTAGONISTIC APPROACH TOWARD WESTERN-ORIENTED QUR'ANIC STUDIES

This postcolonial political reaction that takes a defensive attitude toward what is considered by some as Western "imposed"[51] values, including but not limited to gender egalitarianism, religious tolerance, and religious pluralism is a flaw that must be remedied. To understand this defensive attitude, we should keep in mind the historical fact that the adoption of what we might refer to today as universal values, was not, for many in the Arab world, a free choice as much as it was the humiliating surrender of some Muslim jurists who first "opposed the importation of foreign laws, but they were too weak and marginalized to offer any meaningful resistance."[52] In the modern Arab world, largely formed by countries formerly colonized by Europeans, collective religious consciousness came to view religion as the only and last way to reassert independence and reclaim identity. One way or another, preserving traditional religious identity became the last face-saving strategy against the West, which continued to "drag the societies into the political, ideal and commercial system established by it."[53] In addition, the fact that European colonialists—armed with their critical intellectual orientalist approach to the Middle East—used labels advocating liberality, freedom of speech, and democracy, and even women liberation has undoubtedly created a close association between those values and the colonial West, especially among conservatives, who took "a defensive stand against modernity."[54] For many Muslims, feminism turned into the "a final frontier,"[55] and was, early on, destined to attract more negative than positive attention. Western-inspired feminist values were variably treated by some Muslims as "an attempt to alienate Muslims and destroy their historical identity"[56] and "as an encroachment upon their faith tradition and as a foreign Western import";[57] as Mir-Hosseini puts it, these values were seen as "a Western plot to undermine the Muslim way of life."[58] For example, Sahar Amer elaborates on the different ways Muslims interpreted Western calls to unveil Muslim women: "So while for some Muslims, unveiling Muslim women meant liberation and progress, for others, it meant the exact opposite—the loss of cultural identity and surrender to Western domination."[59]

Others rejected borrowed European values because they lost efficacy[60] when estranged from the conditions of their initial emergence. For many, as Abū Zayd reminds us, the European Enlightenment and its liberation of women is considered a mere "conspiracy against Islam and Muslims."[61] Therefore, when the American armed involvement in the Middle East, in Afghanistan, and in Iraq took place, it was more or less understood by many as more of the same intellectual strategy to establish a one-dimensional imperial tyranny.

Since "both international human rights and feminist ideals are open to manipulation . . . there is a huge gap between these ideals and the practices of their proponents."[62] Many in the Arabic and the Islamic world were and still are caught in the middle, this is especially true of traditionalists who were unable to decide where to draw a line between inherited values and globally shared values. Hassan elaborates more on this cultural struggle:

> Unable to come to grips with modernity as a whole, many contemporary Muslim societies make a sharp distinction between two aspects of it. The first—generally referred to as "modernization" and largely approved—is identified with science, technology, and a better standard of life. The second—generally referred to as "Westernization" and largely disapproved—is identified with emblems of "mass" Western culture such as promiscuity, breakup of family and community, latchkey kids, and drug and alcohol abuse. Many Muslims see "emancipated" women not as symbols of "modernization" but as symbols of "Westernization." The latter is linked in Muslim minds not only with the colonization of Muslim people by Western powers in the not-too-distant past, but also with the continuing onslaught on "the integrity of the Islamic way of life" by Westerners and Westernized Muslims who uphold the West as a model for intellectual and social transformation of Muslim communities.[63]

As a result, many Muslims clung to their traditional heritage, as this appeared to be the safest strategy to deal with the threat that the West would swallow their sense of uniqueness and cultural independence. Very soon, religion "along with all its rituals and rites turned into a fence and a cage"[64] to protect the Muslim identity. Even the need to reform religious thinking itself, as ʻAbd al-Sattar Fatḥallāh Saʻid (b. 1931) argues, came to be increasingly viewed as "one of the worst outcomes"[65] of this Western "intellectual invasion"[66] because it was considered responsible for motivating some Muslim scholars to reconcile Islamic teachings with Western values and theories. Many Westernized Arab intellectuals were believed to have been recruited as local agents for the imperial Western ideology, because of their ability to "negotiate with customers in their own language."[67] For many, "resisting Islamic feminism suggests an anticolonial politics and a refusal to be circumscribed within hegemonic Western constructs";[68] likewise, many feminist arguments, like the argument against men's right to guardianship (*qiwāma*) as based on a sexist misunderstanding of the Qur'an, are often viewed as "founded by colonialism."[69]

The postcolonial intellectual reaction in the Arab and Islamic would leave its clear imprint on Qur'anic studies. Gradually, an excessive unconscious usage of Strawman arguments to discredit Western values and a blind defense of tradition, as a strategy for freeing it from the unpredictable expansion of the Western civilization, grew until they became a way of life. Jasim Sultan describes this attitude as a natural psychological reaction that, at least initially, took place alongside European colonialization,

> Many stopped asking questions, canceling them in a defensive attitude, out of fear of the outcomes of these questions. This is a natural psychological reaction that probably could be excused, especially during critical times of European colonial arrogance. At those times, people faced the imbalance of power, psychological humiliation, and the overwhelming presence of colonialists by reverting to mechanisms of self-glorification, by blaming colonialism for the reason of degradation, and by blaming people for not applying Islam the way it was applied during the glorious past.[70]

Even when, in the second part of the twentieth century, scholars began to reprocess the tradition in isolation from orientalist assessments, some Islamists felt the need to "bring the classical *fiqh* books out of the closet"[71] in an attempt to maintain consistency in defending traditionally agreed upon *fatwa*s against any criticism. Thus, it became common to accuse those attempting to reinterpret the divine text as inspired by or even connected to conspiracy theories. Not surprisingly, feminism is "consistently seen as a threat and an indirect way to colonize this part of the world"[72] as, in the eyes of traditionalists, it only serves to disrupt the established female submission imposed by the patriarchal system in the Middle East.

For example, like many other prominent Arab intellectuals, ʻAbd al-Wahhāb al-Miṣrī (1938–2008) provides what can be best described as an attempt to expose an alleged dark side of Western feminism,

> The women-centered intellectual approach is a deconstructive one that declares the necessity of female-male struggle and the necessity of ending patriarchal history and starting our human experience without any memory. It aims to create anxiety, narrowness, boredom, and insecurity in women by redefining her and by making her identity conditional on what she does outside the family.[73]

Moreover, in his analysis he presents Western feminism as the modern reincarnation of colonialism, "this [is the] way the new global system can—via deconstruction—reach the goals which the old colonial system was unable to reach through immediate confrontation."[74]

Furthermore, Western media complicated things more when viewed women's status in the Arab and Islamic world "through a lens constructed by Western patriarchy colored by imperial desires."[75] The inherent contradiction between the Western fascination in women's rights in the Arab and Islamic world and the West's indifference to bloodshed in the Arab world caused feminism to be viewed by many as an imperial hypocrisy. Leila Ahmed (b. 1940) was one of the earliest to elaborate on this point:

> For many of us, particularly those who have worked for years on issues of women's rights in Islam and in Muslim societies, these glaring disparities in our times between the notion of purported concern for the suffering of Muslim women commonplace in our public conversation and the simultaneous seeming indifference and unconcern among many Americans and Europeans to the mounting death counts, maiming and trauma suffered by mostly Muslim women and children was a sobering experience.[76]

Today, Muslim feminists are unfortunately still trapped in the middle, and still have a long way to go, with no hope of being granted the luxury of choosing their battles. Accusations and *ad hominem* attacks come from everywhere: The Western media accuses them of secretly supporting traditionalist agendas; Muslim traditionalists accuse them of betraying the values of their own heritage and use a "hasty generalization" of "imperial feminism" to reject all feminism and deny all Western attempts (both imperial and humanitarian) to reform the status of women in the Arab world; authoritative male strata claim that they are disturbing the order; and Arab nationalists allege that they promote postcolonial plans. But perhaps the worst accusations are those from the majority in the Arab world who—largely driven by wishful thinking and dogmata—claim that Muslim feminists are a mere distraction and an obstacle to the bright future of the Arab and the Islamic world. As a result, the majority of the most promising efforts, led by Islamic feminists like Ziba Mir-Hosseini (b. 1952), Leila Ahmed (b. 1940), Riffat Hassan (b. 1943), Fatima Mernissi (1940–2015), Amina Wadud (b. 1952), Kecia Ali (b. 1972), and many others were and are still "met with staunch opposition from traditionalist scholars, men and women alike."[77] This repeated scenario often results in the shunning of Islamic feminists, and their struggle to provide alternative Qur'anic interpretations fails, after they are accused of promoting anti-Islamic hate speech and postcolonial agendas, and focusing on unorthodox trivialities. Although the entrenched attitude toward many of these feminist contributions was based on accusations that they were promoting suspicious theological interpretations, these contributions were also grouped into a category of "women-led movements," an attitude that overlooks the fact that "feminists are made, not born. One does not become an advocate of feminist politics simply by having the privilege of having been born female."[78] In a simple, yet meaningful answer, when asked whether she feels threatened, in her native Pakistan, for speaking to women, Riffat Hassan answers sarcastically, "I am a woman. Nobody takes me very seriously!"[79]

THE WIDENING GAP BETWEEN THE TWO TRADITIONS OF MUSLIM AND WESTERN SCHOLARSHIP

Unfortunately the increasingly adopted Western- centered approach to Qur'anic studies in Western academia fueled the previously explained postcolonial antagonistic attitude by insisting on a partial, or even sometimes, on a total marginalization of studies produced outside the narrow Western -centered Qur'anic studies. This Western academic hegemony over Qur'anic studies is deeply rooted in a way or another in the inherited Orientalist claim to intellectual superiority that Edward Said (1935–2003) famously argued for,

> In a quite constant way, Orientalism depends for its strategy on this flexible positional superiority, which puts the Westerner in a whole series of possible relationships with the Orient without ever losing him the relative upper hand. And why should it have been otherwise, especially during the period of extraordinary European ascendancy from the late Renaissance to the present? The scientist, the scholar, the missionary, the trader, or the soldier was in, or thought about, the Orient because he could be there, or could think about it, with very little resistance on the Orient's part. Under the general heading of knowledge of the Orient, and within the umbrella of Western hegemony over the Orient during the period from the end of the eighteenth century, there emerged a complex Orient suitable for study in the academy, for display in the museum, for reconstruction in the colonial office, for theoretical illustration in anthropological, biological, linguistic, racial, and historical theses about mankind and the universe, for instances of economic and sociological theories of development, revolution, cultural personality, national or religious character. Additionally, the imaginative examination of things Oriental was based more or less exclusively upon a sovereign Western consciousness out of whose unchallenged centrality an Oriental world emerged, first according to general ideas about who or what was an Oriental, then according to a detailed logic governed not simply by empirical reality but by a battery of desires, repressions, investments and projections.[80]

Today, many in Western academia adopt traditional translational choices without revising the gap that keeps widening not only between the Qur'anic text and its original interpretation/interpretations but also between the Arabic interpretation and its translation/translations. Like many other Muslim scholars who specified that mastering Arabic must be a condition, among other conditions for sound *tafsīr*,[81] Muḥammad al-Jabrī (1935–2010) emphasizes the fundamental nature of the Arabic language as an essential semantic tool, and asserts the requirement that one have proficiency in Arabic, as a prerequisite for productive Qur'anic studies; he states that "the Qur'anic phenomenon—even if spiritual in its essence—as it forms a type of prophethood and messengerhood, still constitutes, linguistically, culturally, and socially, an Arabic phenomenon."[82] The Western academic approach to studying the Qur'an through translations, even while it freed it from apologetic and dogmatic pitfalls, was and is still challenged by the inscrutable nature of Arabic, a language that "absolutely defies translation, because the multiple meanings tend to vanish as soon as the translator tries to fix them semantically into a foreign language."[83] Likewise, in his interesting theory, Arkoun suggests three interactive reading protocols essential for any persuasive textual approach to the Qur'anic text: a historical-anthropological reading, a semantic-linguistic reading, and a theological-interpretive reading. But more importantly, he concludes that "the theological-interpretive reading shouldn't be sought unless the first two readings are completed."[84] Similarly, Naṣr Abū Zayd describes the linguistic analysis of the Qur'anic text as "the only possible methodology, in terms of its appropriateness and suitability to the studied subject."[85] As Oddbjørn Birger Leirvik (b. 1951) asserts, "The search for a critical scriptural hermeneutics, seems to be intimately wedded to modernist values";[86] because, once "a comprehensive study of the gender fluidity of the Qur'anic Arabic with respect to statements regarding the Divine and human subjects"[87] is accomplished, and once a means to overcome the way critical Qur'anic concepts like *qiwāma* (male guardianship of women) are traditionally understood by "using the primary text,"[88] then, "the path to transforming both the ethics and the politics of gender hegemony and all other forms of oppression is made transparent."[89] Therefore, in an acknowledgment of these difficulties Joseph Lumbard (b. 1969) stresses the need to embrace a greater epistemological diversity that can "allow for epistemic transformations that follow scripts outside those developed by Western centric critical theories."[90]

It is not difficult to register the many problems that any serious academic scholar encounters when approaching Qur'anic studies; first, the commentaries are, for the most part, "unedited . . . unstudied . . . and in many cases they are not even cataloged."[91] For some scholars these commentaries are even, "unhelpful for the modern-day reader, especially in terms of their methodology."[92] In addition, Qur'anic studies are "still very much wrestling with the issues of the Qur'an's formation and its relationship to the larger scriptural milieu of the Near East."[93] For the purpose of this book, what matters is not a critique of traditional commentaries, or even a criticism of modern scholarship on Qur'anic hermeneutics, rather, what concerns us is the necessity of dealing with the unfortunate and the unjust outcomes caused by the linguistic ambiguities of these commentaries, which enabled religious authorities to use "views patriarchal and patronizing"[94] to "the disadvantage of female believers."[95]The majority of the new feminist readings of the Qur'anic text in the West today are initiated by non-native speakers of Arabic, by Islamic scholars in the diaspora, orientalists, new orientalists, new converts to Islam, and second-generation immigrants. This turns the linguistic re-examination of traditionally circulated views that were assumed to be Qur'anic into a challenge. But more importantly, all these challenges mean that pre-modern Islamic readings and interpretations still dominate the way the Qur'an is understood and used in the field of modern Qur'anic studies, even in the West.

THE FALLACY OF RELATIVE REFORM

This comparative approach—commonly seen in introductions or first chapters of books on women in Islam—uses the degraded status of women in pre-Islamic Arabia to argue that Muslim women already have a progressive status and require no reform of any kind other than to properly apply traditional interpretations of that status. This approach to the Qur'anic text is particularly popular in homiletics, which claim that Qur'anic teachings on women-as currently understood and preached—especially teachings that deal with social and gender reform are sufficient. Many scholars, consciously and subconsciously, still use some pre-Islamic historic practices like female infanticide, wife beating, unlimited pre-Islamic polygyny, and other pre-Islamic misogynist practices to draw a hyperbolic contrast with the later Islamic reforms, and to conclude—by way of depending on this "relative privation" fallacious argument—that Muslim women's current status is advanced. Many traditional scholars adopt this comparative methodology or approach, which can be considered successful only in terms of drawing attention to the improvements that Islam brought to women of the seventh century, but ultimately only helped those who sought to disavow social and gender reform as an independent ongoing liberal movement. The extension of this comparative approach and overuse of it to conclude a flawless current status of Muslim women, who should feel fortunate that their status is better than that of pre-Islamic women, relieved many scholars of any obligation to rethink the justice of traditional Islamic teachings, or whether or not they should be improved, re-evaluated, or adapted to the modern world.

In contrast to this approach, which is satisfied by merely scratching the surface of the Qur'anic ongoing plan for women's liberation a more serious approach must be considered. This more serious approach would objectively evaluate the current status of Muslim women and find improvement in modern and continuous interpretations of the Qur'anic text itself.

EXEGETICAL CONTEXTOMY FALLACY

Many rulings related to women that I discuss in this book and explain in detail, and many widely circulated public opinions, and even some scholarly arguments are based on extracting conclusions from fragments of chapters and scattered verses. Reinvestigating the original meaning of these arguments, many of which have been lost in the process of extracting quotes, proves effective, not only in terms of reconciling many of the unresolved contradictions that we find in conflicting Qur'anic messages but also in terms of providing a holistic reading to the Qur'anic text. This holistic reading is intended to explore new semantic dimensions by relating verses to those that precede and follow them, and unifying meanings and references across different passages. For example, I prove that many Qur'anic expressions that have been extensively quoted have in fact a different meaning once they are analyzed in their original context. "Marry those who please you" (Q.4:3) and "men have a degree above them" (Q.2:228) are just two examples in which we can see the problems that have arisen as a result of exegetical contextomy. In the following chapters I variably apply the previously discussed deficiencies to clarify the real meaning of some carefully selected verses related to the Qur'anic gender egalitarian message.

NOTES

1. Muhammad Abdel Haleem, *Understanding the Qur'an: Themes and Style* (London: I.B. Tauris, 2011), 201.
2. Shahzadi Pakeeza and Chishti Asghar, "Critical Study of the Approaches to the Exegesis of the Holy Qur'an," *Pakistan Journal of Islamic Research* 10 (2012), 23.
3. Ṭāriq al-Bishrī, *al-Tajadd al-ḥaḍārī* (Beirut: Arabic Network for Research and Publishing, 2015), 138.
4. Jamāl al-Bannā, *Jawāz imāmat al-mar'a li-l-rijāl* (N.p.: Dār al-Shurūq, 2010), 67.
5. Tarik Maudoodi, *Four Key Concepts of the Qur'an* (Leicester: Kube Publishing, 2013), 26.
6. Explained in chapter 3.
7. Kecia Ali, *Marriage and Slavery in Early Islam* (Cambridge, MA: Harvard University Press, 2010), 190.

8. Khaled Abou el Fadel, Deborah Chasman, and Joshua Cohen (eds.), *Islam and the Challenge of Democracy* (Princeton, NJ: Princeton University Press, 2004), 5.
9. Fred Donner, "The Historical Context," in *The Cambridge Companion to the Qur'an*, ed. Jane McAuliffe (Cambridge and New York: Cambridge University Press, 2007), 34.
10. Ayman El-Desouky, "Between Hermeneutic Provenance and Textuality: The Qur'an and the Question of Method in Approaches to World Literature," *Journal of Qur'anic Studies* 16, no. 3 (2014), 27.
11. Marion Katz, *Women in the Mosque* (New York: Columbia University Press, 2014), 8.
12. Jonathan Brown, "Did the Prophet Say It or Not?" *Journal of the American Oriental Society* 129, no. 2 (2009), 270.
13. Khaled Abou El Fadl, *Speaking in God's Name: Islamic Law, Authority and Women* (New York: Oneworld, 2014), 120.
14. Abou El Fadl, *Speaking in God's Name*, 19.
15. Fatima Mernissi, *al-Harīm al-siyāsī* (Damascus: Dār al-Hasad, 1987), 19.
16. Layla Ramī, *Mawqi' al-mara' al-nakhbayi fī mujtama' al-risāla. Kitāb al-Umma*, vol. 141 (Doha: Idārat al-Buḥūth al-Dirāsāt al-Islāmiyya, 2011), 66.
17. Barbara Stowasser, *Women in the Qur'an, Traditions and Interpretation* (New York: Oxford University Press, 1994), 62.
18. Ramī, *Mawqi' al-mara' al-nakhbayi fī mujtama' al-risāla. Kitāb al-Umma*, 69.
19. Malik Ibn Nabī, *al-Ẓāhira al-qur'āniyya* (Damascus: Dār al-Fikr, 1979), 104.
20. John L. Esposito, *Women in Muslim Family Law* (Syracuse University Press, 1982), 6.
21. Abū l-Ḥusayn 'Asākir al-Dīn Muslim, *Saḥīḥ Muslim* (Riyadh: Dār Ṭayyiba, 2006), hadith number 3004, 1366.
22. Al-Bannā, *Jawāz imāmat al-mar'a*, 96.
23. Aysha Hidayatullah, *Feminist Edges of the Qur'an* (Oxford: Oxford University Press, 2014), 86.
24. Oliver Leaman, *The Qur'an: An Encyclopedia* (London: Routledge, 2006), 3.
25. 'Abd al-Salām Figo, *al-Qir'a al-mu'aṣira li-l-nuṣūṣ al-shar'iyya* (Cairo and Mansoura: Dār al-Kalīma, 2016), 90.
26. Liaquat Ali Khan, "Jurodynamics of Islamic Law," *Rutgers Law Review* 61, no. 2 (2009), 292.
27. In addition to the lack of any textual evidence to support the existence of stoning as a punishment in the Qur'an, Q.4:25 logically falsifies stoning as a possible punishment for publicly witnessed *zinā* for married couples, since this verse indicates that the adultery punishment for married believing slaves should be half the punishment for free women. This suggests the question: How can a punishment of stoning to death be divided! This logical contradiction limits our options to the only option mentioned in the Qur'an which is one hundred lashes that can be brought down in our specific case to fifty lashes.
28. Abū 'Abdallāh Muḥammad b. Yazīd Ibn Māja, *Sunan Ibn Māja* (Cairo: Dār Iḥyā' al-Kutub al-'Arabiyya, n.d.), 626, hadith no. 1944.
29. Mohammed Arkoun, *Ayna huwa al-fikr al-Islāmī l-mu'aṣir* (Beirut: al-Saqui, 1995), 127.

30. Ziba Mir-Hosseini, "Muslim Women's Quest for Equality: Between Islamic Law and Feminism," *Critical Inquiry* 32, no. 4 (2006), 632.

31. Walid Saleh, "Hermeneutics," in *The Wiley Blackwell Companion to the Qur'an*, ed. Andrew Rippin and Jawed Mojaddedi (Hoboken, NJ: Wiley-Blackwell, 2017), 393.

32. I am grateful to my student Nadir Kharusi for a valuable conversation in a class discussion.

33. Jamāl al-Bannā, *al-Mar'ā bayn taḥrīr al-Qur'ān wa-taqīd al-fuqaha'* (Cairo: Dār al-Fikr al-Islāmī, 1998), 176.

34. Aisha Geissinger, *Gender and Muslim Construction of Exegetical Authority: A Rereading of the Classical Genre of Qur'an Commentary* (Leiden: Brill, 2015), 257.

35. Geissinger, *Gender and Muslim Construction*, 2.

36. al-Bannā, *al-Mar'ā bayn taḥrīr*, 14.

37. Geissinger, *Gender and Muslim Construction*, 16.

38. Nasr al-Joueli, "Contemporary Interpretations of Qiwamah," in *Feminism and Islamic Perspectives: New Horizons of Knowledge and Reform*, ed. Omaima Abou-Bakr (Cairo: Women and Memory Forum, 2013), 175.

39. 'Alī Ḥarb, *al-Ḥub wa-l-fanā'* (Beirut: Dār al-Manāhil, 1990), 14.

40. Ayesha Chaudhry, *Domestic Violence and the Islamic Tradition* (Oxford: Oxford University Press, 2013), 19.

41. Riffat Hassan, *Her Voice Her Faith*, ed. Arvind Sharma and Katherine K. Young (Boulder, CO: Westview Press, 2003), 225.

42. Abdolkarim Soroush, "The Changeable and the Unchangeable," in *New Directions in Islamic Thought: Exploring Reform and Muslim Tradition*, ed. Kari Vogt, Lena Larsen, and Christian Moe (New York: I.B. Tauris, 2011), 14.

43. The Women and Memory Forum (WMF) was founded in 1995 by a group of women academics, researchers, and activists concerned about the negative representations and perceptions of Arab women in the cultural sphere. See https://www.wmf.org.eg.

44. Mulki al-Sharmani, "Islamic Feminism: Transnational and National Reflections," *Approaching Religion* 4, no. 2 (December 2014), 91.

45. al-Sharmani, "Islamic Feminism: Transnational and National Reflections".

46. Yazbeck Haddad and John L. Esposito, *Islam, Gender, and Social Change* (New York and Oxford: Oxford University Press, 1998), 33.

47. Asgharali Engineer, *The Rights of Women in Islam* (New York: Sterling Publishers, 1992), 3.

48. An example is the well-known "rivers under the sea" phenomenon, which is believed to be described in the Qur'an (25:53).

49. Andrea Dworkin and Catharine MacKinnon, *Pornography and Civil Rights: A New Day for Women's Equality* (Minneapolis, MN: Organizing Against Pornography, 1989), 17.

50. As I make it clear in the book, the Qur'an does clearly oppose minor marriage.

51. Malise Ruthven, *Islam in the World* (Oxford and New York: Oxford University Press, 1984), 387.

52. Ali Khan, "Jurodynamics of Islamic Law," 283.

53. Sehmus Demir, "On Modernity, Islamic World and Interpretation of Qur'an," *Ekev Academic Review* 12, no. 37 (September 2008), 100.

54. Stowasser, *Women in the Qur'an, Traditions and Interpretation*, 6.

55. Haddad and Esposito, *Islam, Gender, and Social Change*, 7.

56. Khadīja al-'Azīzī, *al-Usūs al-falsafiyya lī-l-fikr al-nasawī l-gharbī* (Beirut: Bisan, 2005), 11.

57. Aysha Hidayatullah, "Muslim Feminist Birthdays," *Feminist Studies in Religion* 27, no. 1 (March/April 2011), 120.

58. Ziba Mir-Hosseini, "Beyond 'Islam' vs. 'Feminism,'" *IDS Bulletin* 42, no. 1 (January 2011): 67–77.

59. Sahar Amer, *What Is Veiling*? (Chapel Hill: University of North Carolina Press, 2014), 5.

60. Malik Ibn Nabī, *Mushkilat al-afkār fī l-'alām al-Islāmī* (Damascus: Dār al-Fikr, 1979), 160.

61. Naṣr Ḥāmid Abū Zayd, *Dawa'ir al-khawf* (Beirut: al-Markaz al-Thaqāfī l-'Arabī, 2004), 98.

62. Jana Rumminger, Mulki al-Sharmani, and Ziba Mir-Hosseini, *Men in Charge: Rethinking Authority in Muslim Legal Tradition* (London: Oneworld, 2015), 20.

63. Riffat Hassan, "Feminism in Islam," in *Feminism and World Religions*, ed. Arvind Sharma and Katherine K. Young (Albany: State University of New York Press, 1999), 251.

64. 'Isā, Ibrāhīm, *Afkār muhadada bi-l-qatal* (Cairo: Maṭāba' Sitār bi-Ras li-l-Ṭibā'a wa-Nashr, 1993), 165.

65. 'Abd al-Sattar Fatḥallāh Sa'īd, *al-Ghazū l-fikrī wa-l-ṭayarāt al-mu'adiyya lī-l-Islām* (Mansoura: Dār al-Wafa, 1988), 98.

66. Sa'īd, *al-Ghazū l-fikrī wa-l-ṭayarāt al-mu'adiyya lī-l-Islām.*

67. Mamdūḥ al-Shaykh, *al-Islāmiyyūn wa-l-'ilmāniyyūn* (Beirut and Amman: Dār al-Bayyāriq, 1999), introduction.

68. Fatima Seedat, "Islam, Feminism, and Islamic Feminism: Between Inadequacy and Inevitability," *Journal of Feminist Studies in Religion* 29, no. 2 (2013), 40.

69. Muḥammad al-Bahi, *al-Fikr al-Islāmī l-ḥadīth wa-ṣilathu bi-ista 'mār al-gharbī* (Cairo: Wahba, 1964), 50.

70. Sultan, *al-Turāth*, 33.

71. Ziba Mir-Hosseini, "Classical Fiqh, Contemporary Ethics and Gender Justice," in *New Directions in Islamic Thought: Exploring Reform and Muslim Tradition*, ed. Kari Vogt and Christian Larsen (New York: I.B.Tauris, 2011), 78.

72. Abeer al-Sarrani and Alaa Alghamdi, "Through Third World Women's Eyes: The Shortcomings of Western Feminist Scholarship on the Third World," *Analize* 2 (2014), 5, online: http://www.analize-journal.ro/library/files/alaa.pdf. Accessed April 9, 2018.

73. 'Abd al-Wahhāb al-Miṣrī, *Qadiyyat al-mar'a* (Giza: Nahḍat Miṣr, 2010), 37.

74. al-Miṣrī, *Qadiyyat al-mar'a.*

75. Robin L. Riley, *Depicting the Veil: Transnational Sexism and the War on Terror* (London: Zed Books, 2013), 20.

76. Leila Ahmed, *Quiet Revolution: The Veil's Resurgence, from the Middle East to America* (New Haven, CT and London: Yale University Press, 2011), 228–9.

77. Abdullah Saeed, *The Qur'an: An Introduction* (London: Routledge, 2008), 213.

78. Bell Hooks, *Feminism is for Everybody* (Cambridge, MA: South End Press, 2000), 7.

79. Riffat Hassan, "What Islam Teaches about Ethics and Justice," An Interview with Riffat Hassan, *U.S. Catholic* 61, no. 5 (1996), 19.

80. Edward Said, *Orientalism* (New York: Vintage Books, 1979), 8.

81. Ahmad von Denffer, *'Ulum al-Qur'ān: An Introduction to the Sciences of the Qur'ān* (Leicestershire: Kube Publishing, 2011), 96.

82. Muḥammad al-Jābirī, *Madkhal ilā al-Qur'ān al-karīm* (Beirut: Markaz Dirasāt al-Wiḥda al-'Arabiyya, 2006), 1:27.

83. Ruthven, *Islam in the World*, 91.

84. Mohammed Arkoun, *al-Qur'an: min al-tafsīr al-mawrūth ilā tahlīl al-khiṭāb al-dīnī* (Beirut: Dār al-Tali'a, 2005), 39.

85. Naṣr Ḥāmid Abū Zayd, *Mafhūm al-naṣṣ* (Beirut: al-Markaz al-Thaqāfī l-'Arabī, 2014), 25.

86. Oddbjørn Leirvik, "Modern Islamic Approaches to Divine Inspiration, Progressive Revelation, and Human Text," *Studia Theologica* 69, no. 2 (2015), 103.

87. Yasiin Rahmaan, "Feminist Edges of Muslim Feminist Readings of Qur'anic Verses," *Journal of Feminist Studies in Religion* 32, no. 2 (2016), 146.

88. Amina Wadud, "Can One Critique Cancel All Previous Efforts?" *Journal of Feminist Studies in Religion* 32, no. 2 (2016), 134.

89. Wadud, "Can One Critique Cancel All Previous Efforts?".

90. Joseph Lumbard, "Decolonizing Quranic Studies," online: YouTube https://www.youtube.com/watch?v=5hZWGdP_hfs, May 21, 2018.

91. Walid Saleh, *The Formation of the Classical Tafsir Tradition* (Leiden: Brill, 2004), 3.

92. Salwa al-'Awa, "Linguistic Structure," in *The Wiley Blackwell Companion to the Qur'an*, ed. Andrew Rippin and Jawid Mojaddedi (Chichester, W. Sussex, UK: Wiley-Blackwell, 2017), 56.

93. Travis Zadeh, "Quranic Studies and the Literary Turn," *Journal of the American Oriental Society* 135, no. 2 (April 2015), 338.

94. Saeed, *The Qur'an*, 15.

95. Barlas, "Qur'anic Hermeneutics," 143.

Chapter 2

Gender Egalitarianism in the Qur'an

THE STORY OF ADAM AND EVE: THE INNOCENCE OF THE QUR'ANIC EVE

This section provides a full investigation of the story of Adam and Eve from a Qur'anic perspective. As we see in this section, the carefully considered hermeneutical analysis of the Qur'anic story of Adam and Eve reveals a great deal about the real role Eve played in the story. According to my analysis in this section, Adam is proven to be responsible for the act of disobedience that eventually caused both Adam and Eve to lose their right to live in the garden. I focus on clarifying Eve's role in the act of disobedience that has been widely associated with the traditional understanding of what is known as the story of creation and the fall. To avoid the manifold complications of reintroducing this story, I deal with the accounts of the traditional and the mainstream narrative that presuppose that Adam and Eve were expelled from a heavenly dwelling.[1] The reading I provide supports a new understanding of the role Eve played in the Qur'anic story; a role that was misinterpreted by traditional readings of the story. In this section, the deficiency I refer to as the "excessive exegetical narrativization of the Qur'an" plays a major role in terms of shifting the blame to Eve, as exegetes continually borrowed and added biblical details—without citations—to their commentaries on the main body of the Qur'anic story, to end up with a story that, despite being similar to the original Qur'anic story in its overall structure, is radically different in terms of its moral lessons and in its potential social impact.

Let us view the way the story was exegetically reconstructed before we reinvestigate the real role Eve played in the story according to the Qur'anic narrative. In regard to the story of Adam and Eve, the exegetical approaches unfold gradually and progressively but still do not address the philological details of Eve's role. On the contrary, biblical narratives and ancient Arabic myths were used to argue that Eve was "the source of the ultimate evil."[2] For example, Burhān al-Dīn al-Biqā'ī (1406–1480) added a misogynistic message to his interpretation of the story by asserting that if women were obeyed it would only lead to more distress and more harm. While interpreting Q.20:117, "so We said, 'Adam, this is your enemy, yours and your wife's: do not let him drive you out of the garden and make you miserable,'" he says,

> When God included Eve in the exile it was known that she will be included in the consequences of that exile. Also, since women follow men, Adam was the one who was exclusively mentioned when referring to worldly hardship. A great deal of his [Adam's] weariness relates to women. This specific kind of weariness was therefore mentioned individually, and therefore woman's weariness was not mentioned because it means nothing when compared to that of Adam.[3]

In addition, he uses his interpretation to argue for woman's subordination to man, who can "forcefully lead her to good, or can otherwise be led by her to harm."[4]

The extensive use of biblical narratives (without citation) is seen in most premodern interpretations of the story of Adam and Eve, which many male-centered medieval Muslim exegeses used to interpret or add more detail to the Qur'anic narrative. In the *tafsīr* of Jalāl al-Dīn al-Suyūṭī (1445–1505), we find an example of this uncited reference to the biblical narrative:

> Satan approached Eve with a fruit and said: "Look at this tree. What a nice smell! What a delicious taste and what a beautiful color!" Then Eve took it and ate from it and went with the fruit to Adam to say: "Look at this tree. What a nice smell! What a delicious taste and what a beautiful color." Then Adam ate of it, and their private parts appeared to both of them. Adam hid inside a tree and was called by God who said: "Where are you?" Adam said: "Here I am." Then God said: "Come out." Adam said: "I am ashamed of myself." God said: "Get down to the earth" and then said, "Oh, Eve you seduced my servant. Therefore, you will suffer in pregnancy and in giving birth, and often will die doing this." Then God said to the serpent: "You are the one whom the cursed entered into to trick my servant. You will be cursed so your ends will be in your belly and you will never get any food other than dust. You and the offspring of Adam will be mutual enemies, wherever you find anyone of them you will chase [them] and wherever one of them finds you they will cut [off] your head."[5]

It is clear that the previous interpretation has completely replaced the Qur'anic text with a hybrid story that was borrowed, without citation, from a biblical narrative. While in the *tafsīr* of Ibn Kathīr (1300–1373), it is not clear to whom Satan spoke first: "God made it permissible to eat from all the trees of the garden except for this particular tree, but Satan continued to persuade both of them until they both ate from it,"[6] in the *tafsīr* of Ibn 'Ajība (1747–1809), we read a comment loosely ascribed to unidentified sages, who indirectly accuse Eve of distracting Adam and thereby causing him to sin.

> Some sages said, Adam forgot the covenant because when his wife was created for him, God made her love resonate in his heart and he was captivated by desire for her, then he saw the beauty of her face and was overwhelmed by his desire to make love to her.[7]

In short, the majority of premodern exegetical readings of the Qur'anic story of Adam and Eve are dominated by a clear tendency to blame Eve for the act of disobedience. As Naṣr Abū Zayd rightly observes in his elaboration on the story, "the image of the innocent Adam is in its reality a mere reflection of a society in which man is the symbol of goodness and innocence, while the female is a representation of sin and evilness. The story refers to the society more than it explains the religious text."[8]

In modern Qur'anic commentaries we are more likely to find a more progressive and liberal reading of the role played by Eve. 'Ā'isha 'Abd al-Raḥmān (1913–1998), who was the first female scholar to teach in al-Azhar, asserts Adam's responsibility as the "one who forgot and went astray."[9] This emphasis on Adam's responsibility was well addressed by Amina Wadud, who rightly explains the importance of the dual form in the Qur'anic story of creation by saying,

> In maintaining the dual form, the Quran overcomes the negative Greco-Roman and Biblical-Judaic implications that woman was the cause of evil and damnation. Moreover, it signifies the Quranic emphasis on the individual responsibility. . . . The one exception to the Quranic use of the dual form [in Q.20:115–121] to refer to the temptation and disobedience of Adam and Eve in the Garden singles out Adam.[10]

In addition to Q.20:115-121 and the crucial role using the dual form plays in terms of asserting the shared responsibility, more linguistic observations came to assert Adam's greater share of responsibility. In chapter 2, Adam and Eve were both warned by God not to approach one tree, as we find in this verse: "We said, Adam, live, with your wife in this garden. Both of you eat freely there as you will, but do not go near this tree, or you will both become wrongdoers" (Q.2:35). The dual form of the verb is extensively used to show that responsibility was shared equally by Adam and Eve. However, in verses Q.2:36 and Q.2:37, there is a shift from the dual form that refers to both Adam and Eve to a reference made to Adam alone. We read,

> But Satan made [both of] them slip, and removed [both of] them from the state they were in. We said, "Get out, all of you! You are each other's enemy. On earth you will have a place to stay and livelihood for a time" (Q.2:36). Then Adam received some words from his Lord and He accepted his repentance: He is the Ever Relenting, the Most Merciful. (Q.2:36–37)

This unexpected switch in Q.2:37 in the midst of a text that refers to both Adam and Eve equally can be interpreted in a variety of ways. However, one plausible argument is that this switch indicates that forgiveness is given to whoever bears the heaviest burden of responsibility, namely, Adam. The *tafsīr* of Ibn 'Āshūr (1879–1973) provides a confirmation of Adam's responsibility: "Eve's repentance was not mentioned here [in chapter 2] although it was mentioned in other places in a clear indication that Eve followed Adam in everything and that he guided her to what he was guided to."[11] According to Ibn 'Āshūr, "Adam was the role model whom Eve followed in eating from the tree. When he ate she followed him."[12]

In addition to this switch, I argue for another neglected linguistic evidence which supports the same argument that Adam bears the larger share of responsibility. Let us consider the difference between the way the verb *waṣwaṣ*, which means "to whisper,"[13] was used in verses Q.7:20 and Q.20:120. First, in Q.20:120, we read, "But Satan whispered to Adam, saying, 'Adam, shall I show you the tree of immortality and power that never decays?'" In Q.7:20 we see that "Satan whispered to them so as to expose their nakedness, which had been hidden from them: he said, 'Your Lord only forbade you this tree to prevent you becoming angels or immortals.'" Unfortunately, the translation of *waṣwaṣ* as "whisper" in both verses neglects the fact that this same Arabic verb was followed by different prepositions in the two verses; therefore, it clearly has two distinct meanings. In Q.20:120 the verse uses the Arabic preposition *ilā* after the verb *waṣwaṣ* to say that Satan whispered to Adam. While when Satan whispered to both Adam and Eve, the verb *waṣwaṣ* is followed by the preposition *li* as in Q.7:20. This should lead us to question the difference between the two prepositions and ask why these two different prepositions are used after the same verb, one when the verb refers to Adam alone and the second when it refers to both Adam and Eve.

While no sufficient explanation was provided for the change between prepositions after *waṣwaṣ*, Maḥmūd b. 'Umar al-Zamakhsharī (1075–1144) acknowledges the difference between the ways the verb *waṣwaṣ* is used in these two verses: "(*waṣwaṣ*) as followed by (*ilā*) means whispering to someone specific as a final destination."[14] Muḥammad al-Khudarī provides an explanation for this switch between *li* and *ilā* based on the peculiar linguistic difference between the two prepositions. However, while he starts by acknowledging the sound linguistic difference between the two prepositions, he ends up by proposing that referring to Adam as the final destination was due to using Eve in the process. In doing that he was clearly motivated by the (already mentioned) biblical image of Eve as a conspirator—the view that I have already dismissed for not having any Qur'anic support of any kind. He says, "It is possible that Satan was able to seduce Adam through his wife, therefore the Qur'an did not use the phrase *waṣwaṣ* followed by *li* for Adam, as if [to mean that] Satan's whispering was first in Eve's ear, and from there eventually reached Adam."[15]

In fact, an investigation of the ways the two prepositions are used in Arabic and in the Qur'an in isolation from the biblical image of Eve reveals, contrary to what al-Khudarī argues for, a meaning consistent with Adam's larger share of involvement with Satan. Because in Arabic the preposition *ilā*, which was used to describe how Satan whispered to Adam alone, indicates a "final destination."[16] By contrast, the use of the preposition *li* after the verb *waṣwaṣ*, when Satan whispered to both Adam and Eve (as in Q.7:20) indicates "specification."[17] This means that when Satan whispered to Adam, Adam was his primary intended addressee, his final goal, and destination. This also indicates that Satan knew that convincing Adam and not Eve to eat from the tree was the necessary step to reach his goal.

However, since I am committed to using the Qur'an as my primary resource, investigating the way both prepositions are used in the Qur'an is a necessary step for finalizing our linguistic findings. Using *ilā* to indicate a finale destination in place is clear in Q.17:1 as we read, "Glory to Him who made His servant travel by night from the sacred place of worship to the furthest place of worship, whose surroundings We have blessed, to show him some of Our signs: He alone is the All Hearing, the All Seeing." Using *ilā* to indicate final destination in time can be found in "Then fast until nightfall" (Q.2:187). More importantly and clearly though, the idea of God as the final destination was stressed by way of using *ilā* in "How can you ignore God when you were lifeless and He gave you life, when He will cause you to die, then resurrect you to be returned to Him?" (Q.2:28). Also, the ultimate authority the Queen of Sheba had as the final decision maker was made clearer by using *ilā* in Q.27:33. "They replied, 'We possess great force and power in war, but you are in command, so consider what orders to give us.'" Giving money back to its owners as the final destination that can't be replaced by anything or anyone else was made clear by using *ilā* in Q.3:75. "There are People of the Book who, if you[Prophet] entrust them with a heap of gold, will return it to you intact." Finally, comparing two verses in which the exact same Qur'anic expression conveys two different meanings *via* switching from using *ilā* to *li* can be very helpful in terms of highlighting the semantic difference the Qur'an makes by using the two prepositions. These two verses are Q.39:5 "He has subjected the sun and moon to run their courses for an appointed time," which uses *li*, and Q.31:29 "that He has subjected the sun and the moon, each to run its course for a stated term," which uses *ilā*.[18] In Q.31:29 using *ilā* comes to stress a final destination—unlike what we have in Q.39:5. This is done as Fāḍil al-Sāmarā'ī (b. 1933) explains to fit the context of Q.31:29 which indicates "the end, the final gathering and the resurrection."[19] This context is clear from the preceding verse Q.31:28: "Creating and resurrecting all of you is only like creating or resurrecting a single soul [*nafs*]: God is all hearing and all seeing."

> To sum up, the linguistic investigation of the way *ilā* and *li* were used in describing the story of Adam and Eve indicates that it was Adam and not Eve whom Satan had in mind as his goal and as his final destination. Contrary to the traditional biblical narrative, in which seducing Eve was the (first) essential step to seduce Adam, who only followed Eve and did what she did, the Qur'anic narrative reveals that Satan acted in exactly the opposite way. It was Adam whom Satan seduced first and he was the one Satan had in mind first. Probably Satan knew that the easier step was for Eve to follow Adam in disobeying God[20]. In the Qur'an addressing both Adam and Eve by using *li* indicates no more than a specification of a dual addressee for the purpose of ending with the final destination, Adam.

The exegetical tendency I refer to as 'the excessive exegetical narrativization of the Qur'an' is what made the effect of the Qur'anic story of Eve, which should have been enormous, almost invisible. As we have seen in this chapter, many traditional interpretations of the divine text turned into a field to promote concepts that unfortunately failed to capture the deep semantic dimensions of many Qur'anic verses.

As we have seen in the story of Adam and Eve, mixed elements alien to the Qur'anic story have long been present in commentaries that have, in large part, marginalized critical details, like the meaningful repetition of the dual form, the occasional switch from the dual form to the singular form, and the precise usage of prepositions. Although this prejudice seems to have faded gradually, with the advent of new commentaries of the text, the potentially powerful gender-egalitarian impact of the Qur'anic story of Eve is still largely neglected, even in the majority of modern readings.

Unfortunately, as we have seen in the detailed analytical reading of the way various exegetes commented on the Qur'anic text, certain interesting details of the story of Adam and Eve were either neglected or worse yet, ignored or falsified. As a result, a number of key exegetes presented a version of the story less connected to the Qur'anic text and more faithful to traditional commentaries.

WOMEN AS EQUAL HUMAN BEINGS

In pre-Islamic Arabia, women "did not enjoy much freedom and social equality."[21] With the exception of the elite in large cities like Mecca, women were viewed and treated as mere "tools of reproduction and sexual pleasure."[22] The main purpose of marriage was to ensure a sufficient number of male offspring; this was the only factor that guaranteed the survival of the tribe in what was certainly a difficult life. The continuous tribal struggles over scarce resources, combined with a culture in which tribes regularly raided and kidnapped those from rival tribes (and brought humiliation to the tribe when women were captured) "entrenched misogyny . . . and caused [some tribes to practice] female infanticide as a way to escape the shame the capture of women can bring."[23] This practice was mentioned in the Qur'an and was severely condemned:

> When one of them is given news of the birth of a baby girl, his face darkens and he is filled with gloom. In his shame he hides himself away from his people because of the bad news he has been given. Should he keep her and suffer contempt or bury her in the dust? How ill they judge! (Q.16:58–59)[24]

The Qur'anic text successfully launched an important basic change that was desperately needed. It elevated the status of women and acknowledged them as real human beings and equal life partners. The Qur'an as we have seen in the previous section started from the very beginning by announcing Eve's innocence in the famous story of Adam and Eve. Then repeated affirmations of fundamental gender equality came to play an indispensable role that was supposed to pave the way for later improvements to the status of women. Niaz A. Shah asserts that the Qur'an indeed played an important role in elevating women's status:

> The position of women in Arab society before the emergence of Islam was not as deplorable as some Muslim scholars describe but was not as good as some Western writers would make us believe. It was worse for women belonging to a lower social stratum and to nomadic tribes. Women of high social class were able to choose their spouses on an equal basis and to own and run their businesses in contrast to women from lower strata and nomadic tribes. The position of women also varied from tribe to tribe and region to region. The Koran eliminated all these distinctions and introduced egalitarianism for all segments of society, specifically women. Some harmful traditions were abolished outright, such as infanticide, while others were approved after some modification.[25]

In addition to Eve's innocence in the act of disobedience I have previously discussed, the Qur'anic elevation of women's status starts from the story of creation itself.[26] The Qur'an, in contrast to traditional biblical and hadith-based narratives, never asserts that Eve was created from Adam's rib, nor is she described as created after Adam. In place of this exegetical attempt of "ascribing maleness to the primordial human creation,"[27] the Qur'an describes the creation of women from the same soul (*nafs*) men themselves were created from: "Another of His signs is that He created spouses from among yourselves for you to live with in tranquility" (Q.30:21). Amina Wadud makes an important observation about this verse of a genderless creation that "does not even state that Allah began the creation of humankind with the *nafs* of Adam, the man. This omission is noteworthy because the Qur'anic version of the creation of humankind is not expressed in gender terms."[28] And, as she rightly observes, this genderless creation process does not specify gender roles, at least at the moment of creation,

> Although the male and female are essential contingent characters in the creation of humankind, no specific cultural functions or roles are defined at the moment of creation. At that moment, Allah defines certain traits universal to all humans and not specific to one particular gender nor to any particular people from any particular place or time.[29]

In addition, while women's souls (*nufūs*) were not treated as less original than men's souls (*nufūs*), in the Qur'an we do not find a delay in creation that might suggest that the creation of the female took place after and not simultaneously with the creation of men's souls (*nufūs*), as we can find in the verse, "People, be mindful of your Lord, who created you from a single soul [*nafs*], and from it created it's mate" (Q.4:1). This is clear from the conjunction (*wa*) "and"; if the first creation involved a delay of any kind, this conjunction would have been (*thuma*) "then." The same Qur'anic denial of any male prioritization in creation is asserted in Q.78:8 as we read, "Did We not create you in pairs." The juxtaposition of these two observations together clarifies that the Qur'an does not suggest ontological male prioritization in the process of creation.

In addition to this genderless, simultaneous male–female creation process, even a quick reading of the Qur'anic text easily reveals the genderless tone with which the Qur'an addresses both men and women as a human community, both locally and globally. Clarifying the fallacy I refer to as the "male addressee fallacy" enables us to see the true meaning of verses that were misunderstood as addressing men only.

In Arabic, the subject pronoun used to address an audience like the community of believers applies to a group of three or more men or a group of both genders. Reading the Qur'anic dialogue as solely addressing men was a later patriarchal projection that resulted from centuries of exclusively male-dominated exegetical scholarship. In this book, I thoroughly explain this "male addressee fallacy," especially as it concerns verses in which this fallacy results in radical semantic deviations. For now, I address the following examples of genderless dialogue as a basic linguistic structure in the Qur'an; this genderless dialogue constitutes the rule, with the exception of occasions in which a specific group of men and women was intentionally addressed, as in the verses below:

> but if any of you is obedient to God and His Messenger and does good deeds, know that We shall give her a double reward and have prepared a generous provision for her. [31] Wives of the Prophet, you are not like any other woman. If you are truly mindful of God, do not speak too softly in case the sick at heart should lust after you, but speak in an appropriate manner; [32] (Q.33:31–32)

The genderless Qur'anic dialogue is present in numerous places. Consider the following verses:

> "People, worship your Lord, who created you and those before you, so that you may be mindful [of Him]." (Q.2:21)

> "You who believe, fasting is prescribed for you, as it was prescribed for those before you, so that you may be mindful of God." (Q.2:183)

> "You who believe, fair retribution is prescribed for you in cases of murder." (Q.2:178)

The practical application of this equality between men and women that is asserted in the Qur'anic text, at the ontological and the hermeneutical level, is legal and judicial equality without regard to gender. In the Qur'an, men and women are equal in their responsibilities with regard to religious duties, as we read in the following verses:

> "To whoever, male or female, does good deeds and has faith, We shall give a good life and reward them according to the best of their actions." (Q.16:97)

> For men and women who are devoted to God—believing men and women, obedient men and women, truthful men and women, steadfast men and women, humble men and women, charitable men and women, fasting men and women, chaste men and women, men and women who remember God often—God has prepared forgiveness and a rich reward. (Q.33:35)

Gender equality is also required and asserted in worldly punishments and before the law: "Cut off the hands of thieves, whether they are man or woman, as punishment for what they have done—a deterrent from God: God is almighty and wise" (Q.5:38).

In addition, men and women are equally accountable for what they do in their worldly lives and will be rewarded equally in the afterlife: "Whoever does evil will be repaid with its like; whoever does good and believes, be it a man or a woman, will enter Paradise and be provided for without measure" (Q.40:40).

The same message can be found in these two verses:

> "Anyone, male or female, who does good deeds and is a believer, will enter Paradise and will not be wronged by as much as the dip in a date stone." (Q.4:124)

> "Their Lord has answered them: 'I will not allow the deeds of any one of you to be lost, whether you are male or female, each is like the other' [in rewards]." (Q.3:195)

As Syed Mohammed Ali states, verses Q.4:124 and Q.3:195 are "the strongest support for the equality of men and women in the Qur'an [and] even the most conservative Islamic jurist is unable to question the clarity of these verses in their equal treatment of men and women."[30]

THE MYTH OF THE QUR'ANIC MALE SUPERIORITY

Unfortunately, these repeated assurances of full gender equality in the Qur'an are commonly contrasted with the verse that refers to *qiwāma*, which is generally understood to promote male superiority and men's right to guardianship over women. This right is commonly portrayed as being based on men's financial responsibility for women but can also indicate moral and ethical guardianship. In fact, a misunderstanding of *qiwāma* brought about a resurgence of pre-Islamic male chauvinism, using religion to facilitate misogyny.

As we see, the Qur'anic text initiated a paradigm shift in the way women were portrayed before Islam. However, the misinterpretation of *qiwāma* set in motion a regression in the understanding of this full acknowledgment of women's humanity and dignity. Gradually, a gap between the divine text and its later exegetical and judicial application emerged. Eventually this gap opened the door for a new era of misogynist ideology that partially, or fully, revived many pre-Islamic social sexist norms, which were presented to the community as religiously based norms[31]. This time, those so-called religious claims were used to justify the regression to obsolete pre-Islamic ways that were denounced by the Qur'an. In the following, we see the extent of this tendency toward regression—a tendency that was first initiated by elite male religious scholars who dominated the interpretation of the *qiwāma* verse.

In his interpretation of the following beautiful and romantic verse—which I explain in detail in the chapter on marriage in the Qur'an—Muḥammad b.

'Umar al-Razī (1149–1209) inserts an offensive misogynist comment in his interpretation of Q.30:21: "Another of His signs is that He created spouses from among yourselves for you to live with in tranquility: He ordained love and kindness between you." He says,

> The meaning of "He created for you" indicates that women are created the same way animals, plants, and other beneficial objects [are created]. . . .; this means that women were not created for worship in the first place. Therefore, we say, creating women is a kind of a gift to us, since they were created for us. Asking them to worship is one way of making this gift complete, and does not mean that women are to be considered responsible the way men are. Therefore, women were not required to do as much as men. This is because women are weak in their manners and silly. They are more like children. But while children are not accountable for what they do, women are accountable for their deeds for our sake, because this will make every woman fear torment and will motivate her to submit to the husband; otherwise corruption will prevail.[32]

Even in modern interpretations of *qiwāma*, we still find this regression in the acknowledgment of women's full humanity and full right to social, economic, and academic participation. Ḥasan al-Bannā (1906–1949) suggested that women's rights to some academic disciplines should be reevaluated,

> It might be said that Islam made a distinction between men and women in many aspects and perspectives, and did not fully make them equal, which is true. But what should be noticed is the fact that when Islam took some women's rights, these rights were compensated for differently. Probably, this deprivation of some women's rights is for their benefit in the first place. Could anyone claim that women's spiritual as well physical structure is like men? Can anyone say that the role women play in life is like the role of men, as long as we believe in motherhood and fatherhood?[33]

Now, gender-based physical differentiation between men and women cannot justify the extension of this concept to a gender-based spiritual distinction; furthermore, this argument goes beyond what can be considered Qur'anic, especially when it leads to a proposal to ban women from certain careers or academic fields of study.

> Women do not need to excel at different languages. They do not need special esthetic studies, because you know sooner or later that women are for homes. Women do not need to study regulations and laws, it is enough for them to know what ordinary people know. . . . Teach women what they need according to their duty and the role they are created for; namely, housekeeping and taking care of children.[34]

According to this line of thinking, *qiwāma* also applies to levels of education. In the following, Munīr al-Ghaḍbān (1942–2014) argues for women's education but not higher education:

> Higher education is not necessary for women. Since at that age, ideally speaking, women should be married and should already have families. Using higher education as an excuse to increase the age for marriage is abnormal and inconsistent with the core of Islam and its recommendations for marriage at an early age.[35]

Similarly, building on interpretations of the verse on *qiwāma* to assert a gender-based male superiority, 'Abdallāh Maḥmūd reaches the following slippery slope set of conclusions:

> Some scholars said that [the verse on *qiwāma*] is explained by the woman's weakness and the insufficiency of her opinions, as is the case for the majority of women. However, this statement does not exclude the existence of some intelligent, wise women, since many women can excel over their husbands in knowledge, intelligence, and wisdom. But this exemption is only a rare case that cannot be considered a rule; because exceptional cases do not count, what counts is the predominant cases [that are] applicable to the majority of women . . .; therefore, this argument among pseudo supporters of women went too far in terms of asking women to go out of their homes to work, regardless of what every sage person already knows, since this might end with the spread of harm, major social corruption, and the neglect of husbands' rights and parenting responsibilities. By asking women to go out and work, they harm women while thinking they are doing the best for them, and they turn women into unbridled animals that can do whatever they want, like western women. While we seek life for those women, they seek their end.[36]

The verse in question is known as the *qiwāma* verse (Q.4:34). Given the many problematic issues concerning this verse, I begin my analysis of this verse with a general translation in which I leave many terms untranslated. For a full examination of the meaning of each term, I gradually introduce my translation of the verse and eventually provide a full translation, but only after all the inscrutable points are cleared up. Verse Q.4:34 says, "Men are *qawammūn* over women, *bimā* God has preferred some of them to some others, and *bimā* what they spend out of their money" (Q.4:34).[37]

In explaining this part of the verse, the first crucial term is *qawammūn*. Unfortunately, in many interpretations of this verse, we see a tendency to twist the meaning, which is essentially gender neutral, and interpret it under the patriarchal umbrella of male scholars. As Wadud rightly notes, this verse has been "classically viewed as the single most important verse with regard to the relationship between men and women . . . however, it cannot be overlooked that many men interpret the above passage as an unconditional indication of the preference of men over women."[38] As Wadud rightly adds, in "what God has given some of them over some other"; the first "them" uses the masculine plural *ba'ḍahum* and the second "some other" in "over some other" uses *ba'ḍ* and does not use the feminine plural *ba'ḍahunna*, which limits the right of *qiwāma* or the so-called male guardianship, as she argues, to some men over other men and does not mean that all men have the right of *qiwāma* over all women. Since the right of guardianship is conditioned by the ability to spend, she explains, *faddala* (preferred) cannot be unconditional because verse Q.4:34 does not read 'they (masculine plural) are preferred over them (feminine plural). According to Wadud, this means that *qiwāma* is a right of guardianship given only to some men; also, according to her interpretation, the preference (*faḍḍala*) is not given comprehensively to men over women, as it is commonly misunderstood; rather, preference is made to some men over some other men.

But what motivated so many interpreters to understand the verse as an implicit assertion of male superiority over women, despite the fact that this conclusion is not supported by the verse itself? We can suggest two reasons: first, the gender bias caused by the predominance of male exegetes, and second, the interpretation of the verse on *qiwāma* depends on the incorrect interpretation of a previous verse, namely, Q.4:32. I argue that the misinterpretation of verse Q.4:32 to suggest a gender-based divine bias led the majority of exegetes to believe that verse Q.4:34 was a repetition of or a reaffirmation of the meaning of Q.4:32. To eliminate the confusion caused by the misinterpretation of verse Q.4:32, we must reconsider verses Q.4:29–32.

> You who believe, do not wrongfully consume each other's wealth but trade by mutual consent. Do not kill each other, for God is merciful to you. [29] If any of you does these things, out of hostility and injustice, We shall make him suffer Fire: that is easy for God. [30] But if you avoid the great sins you have been forbidden, We shall wipe out your minor misdeeds and let you in through the entrance of honor. [31] Do not covet what God has given to some of you more than others—men have the portion they have earned, and women the portion they have earned—you should rather ask God for some of His bounty: He has full knowledge of everything. [32] (Q.4:29–32)

In contrast to many widely accepted interpretations of Q.4:32, which generally state that this verse is addressed to women and commands them not to envy men for their divinely granted superiority, I provide evidence to the contrary, that this verse was revealed in the context of promising divine justice as a reward for the community, both men and women, who can—because of their different natures—lead different lives, and yet still receive equal rewards. I argue that the verse does not reveal gender privileges, or grant exclusive rights to men.

The "male addressee fallacy" is the key to unlock the semantic mystery of Q.4:32. Only one crucial question can change the way Q.4:32 is understood, namely, who is this verse addressed to? To answer this question, we must begin from Q.4:29, where the text addresses the community of believers, both men and women, without gender specification of any kind. In verse Q.4:32 the addressee remains the same, without interruption; it is preceded by the conjunction *wa* (and), where [the whole community] is commanded to avoid major sins. In particular, in Q.4:32 there is a promise of forgiveness and the command not to wish for what God "has given to some of you more than others." This is still addressed to the community, both men and women, since the dialogue from the beginning addresses both men and women, and since the verse was preceded by "and," and finally, because there is no logical reason to say that the dialogue of the text has suddenly switched from including both men and women to exclusively addressing women. In Q.4:32, the expression "has given to some of you more than others" is used consistently with the way the expression is used in Q.4:34; this is an indication that the addressees referred to in both verses must be the same, since the text was not interrupted in a way that would justify any assumption that the addressee has changed.

In verses Q.4:32 and Q.4:29, the command states that neither men nor women should wish for what God has "given to some of you more than others." This interpretation, which seems to be more faithful to the text, does not fit the dominant modern exegetical view, which insists on the belief in a male superiority, and assumes that the verse makes a sudden switch in the addressee, and thus only addresses women with a reminder not to envy men for their God-given privileges.

The issue of who is addressed in Q.4:34, and my assertion that it is addressed to the community of believers—as the Qur'an clearly and literally says—has a huge impact on the interpretation of the verse as it relates to the Qur'anic so-called permissibility of wife beating which I explain in this book. However, even here, apart from traditional interpretations, which cannot be said to have any textual support, Q.4:32 seems to be an assurance of God's inclusive justice and not God's support of male superiority. As the verse in question asserts, while men's and women's lives might differ and they may vary in their religious approaches, God will judge their efforts equally and justly.

My interpretation of Q.4:32 is further supported by the clear evidence that what is mentioned here is not a worldly preference. This is clear for the reasons outlined below:

(1) The context of the verse assures believers that the preference is not related to worldly affairs. It comes immediately after a promise of forgiveness to the community of believers who avoid major sins. "But if you avoid the great sins you have been forbidden, We shall wipe out your minor misdeeds and let you in through the entrance of honor" (Q.4:31).

(2) There is a meaningful and precise use of the form of the verb *iktsaba* that means "to earn" in the expression, "men have the portion they have earned (*iktasabu*), and women the portion they have earned (*iktasbna*)" (Q.4:32). Note that the Qur'anic expression does not use form I (*fa'ala*), *kasaba*, which means "to earn something," rather it is more specific, and uses the verb *ikatsaba*, which follows form VIII (*ifta'ala*). Why is this specific verb form used? In the Qur'an, switching from the form I of the verb (*fa'ala*) to form VIII (*ifta'ala*), means that additional effort and intentionality is involved. In the case of the verb in question, the root *kasaba* means "to earn," but using the form *iktasaba* indicates an additional meaning, namely something beyond earning—such as earning as a result of great effort or clear intentionality, that is, not something that can be earned accidentally, or be given.

Before moving on to explain the impact of switching to this form of the verb in this specific verse, we should consider the Qur'anic usage of the two forms of the verb in order to further clarify their meanings and to prove that the semantic impact I refer to has solid roots in the Qur'an. To explain the semantic impact in Q.4:32 of using the form *iktasaba* instead of *kasaba*, consider the way the two verbs are used in verse Q.2:286, "God does not burden any soul [*nafs*] with more than it can bear: each gains whatever good it has done (*kasabat*), and suffers its bad (*iktasabat*)" (Q.2:286). This verse uses the two forms: first *kasaba*, to refer to the merit or the reward that a soul (*nafs*) can gain, and second, *iktasaba*, to refer to the punishment a soul (*nafs*) will deserve as a result of its actions in this world. There is a precise switch here from *kasaba* which positively indicates reward and follows the preposition *li* to mean "to this soul (*nafs*) belongs the reward," to *iktasaba*, which indicates a punishment and follows preposition *'alā* to mean "on this soul (*nafs*) falls the burden of what it did." In addition, this switch from *kasaba* to *iktasaba* refers to what can be earned accidentally (*kasaba*) and what only counts if it is earned intentionally (*iktasaba*). From a Qur'anic point of view, people can get credit for the good things they do, but they can also get credit from what accidentally benefits them, or what others can do for them like someone praying for them[39] or even from the legacy they leave behind[40]. By contrast, no one will be punished for a sin unless he or she intentionally and personally chooses to commit that sin[41]. Therefore, the change from *kasaba* to *iktasaba*, which indicates intentionality, is a critical change to the criteria.

Many other examples from the Qur'an affirm intentionality as an essential meaning of *iktasaba*, as in this verse: "and those who undeservedly insult believing men and women will bear the guilt of slander and flagrant sin" (Q.33:58). This verse uses *iktasaba* to refer to an intentional act. There are numerous similar examples that demonstrate that *iktasaba*, unlike *kasaba*, involves intentionality and effort-based merit.

This clarification affects my proposed understanding of Q.4:32 because this form of the verb indicates the meaning of the verse. "Do not covet what God has given to some of you more than others—men have the portion they have earned, and women the portion they have earned," (Q.4:32) cannot apply to the rights given to men and women by virtue of having been born as men or women; rather, the verse refers to the rewards or punishments men and women will receive as a result of their actions and their intentional efforts to earn those rewards. The verse cannot possibly be applied to gender-based rights, as it is commonly misunderstood to mean. One's gender is not a result of effort, but one's rewards (or punishments) are a result of the efforts men and women make in this worldly life and they can—as the verse asserts—hope for rewards equal to their efforts, regardless of their gender. In short, Q.4:32 refers to a reward based on intentionality and hard work and does not mean and should never be interpreted as a reference to gender-based rights, since those rights are given and do not include or require hard work or intentionality.

(3) The word *naṣīb*, which means "portion" and which preceded the reference to rewarding men and women in the expression, "men have the portion they have earned, and women the portion they have earned" (Q.4:32) also clearly indicates that the verse refers to God's rewards, and can never refer to gender-based rights. In the verse, the word *naṣīb* (portion) is accurately used to express men's and women's efforts. While men and women will be rewarded equally, the Qur'an does specify that the reward is only applicable to a portion of the worldly actions of men and women. The precise use of "portion" here is another clear assurance that the verse refers to a reward for worldly efforts undertaken to gain God's forgiveness in the afterlife, and these cannot possibly refer to gender-based worldly rights. First, because in the Qur'an the acceptance of any good deed is based on a number of factors other than the actual deed itself. For example, an act of charity that is undertaken solely to show off and gain social recognition is not accepted and rewarded the same way an act of charity undertaken with the pure intention of helping people in need is rewarded. In other words, the verse means that the deeds of believers, both men and women, will be accepted—in part or in full, based on a number of factors—including sincerity and intentionality. Therefore, men will have a portion of what they strive to earn, and the same applies

to women. We can cite the following examples from the Qur'an: "and We shall turn to the deeds they have done and scatter them like dust" (Q.25:23). This verse confirms that some deeds will be totally dismissed. The same can be found in this verse: "Solomon smiled broadly at her words and said, 'Lord, inspire me to be thankful for the blessings You have granted me and my parents, and to do good deeds that please You; admit me by Your grace into the ranks of Your righteous servants'" (Q.27:19). What Solomon says clarifies that the truly good deeds are those that are accepted by God. This clearly indicates that some deeds might be considered good, yet will not satisfy God.

Second, the word "portion" would not fit the verse if the high rank men are granted is due to their natural biological status as men and if the lower status assigned to women is due to their inferior biological status as women. There would be no point in using the word "portion." That is, if a man is given a high rank because he is male, then he would be granted a full set of rights based on this biological status; nothing would be deducted from these rights because of any partial element. The same applies to women: if they are inferior based on their biological status, then there is no point in saying that this rank will be assigned to them partially or fully. Biological masculinity and femininity are not dividable qualities. Thus, Q.4:23 clearly elaborates not on what men and women are granted for being born as men and women but on divine justice in rewarding believers, which takes into consideration first, the varied approaches of both men and women to righteousness and, second, it reminds believers that God will reward deeds, partially or fully, according to the sincerity and faithful intentions of believers.

(4) Another linguistic proof that Q.4:32 is not related to gender-based rights is the command, "and you should rather ask God for some of His bounty" (Q.4:32). Again, why would God command the community of believers to ask him for his bounty if the verse refers to gender-based rights? If men and women are granted rights or deprived from rights solely for being born male or female, then the criterion is final and definitive. The expression begins with "and" and follows "men have the portion they have earned, and women the portion they have earned" (Q.4:32), therefore, if it refers to gender-based rights, we would expect a commandment to accept or to be satisfied by what God has given them, not a commandment to ask for even more bounty. In fact, this part of the verse adds to the proofs I have provided, that the verse is not related to rights based on gender.

(5) Even the assertion mentioned at the end of Q.4:32 supports God's justice in rewarding both men and women as the main topic of the verse. "He

has full knowledge of everything" comes to remind believers—both men and women—that their deeds will be evaluated by God who knows everything and therefore assures them that they will be judged justly depending on God's divine knowledge.

(6) Finally, the Qura'nic promise of equality between genders in rewarding is not unique to Q.4:32. The same recurring theme can be found in so many other places. Some examples are like in Q.3:195, 4:124, 16:97, 40:40, 9:71, 9:72, 33:35, 33:73, 48:5, and 57:12.

In short, Q.4:32 is directed to the community of believers and states that both men and women will be rewarded for their righteous deeds. The verse assures both men and women that for those who ask God for more, there is hope beyond this lifetime. Interpreting the verse this way maintains the continuity and the logical consistency of the addressee in the previous verse (the community of believers, as indicated in Q.4:29); in addition, it maintains the consistency of the same topic.

To sum up what I have mentioned so far, we see that Q.4:31 states that forgiveness is granted to men and women equally, provided they avoid major sins. In Q.4:32, the text continues with the same topic and commands the community of believers, both men and women, to trust that God will reward them justly. God's favor is not related to worldly affairs; rather, it is related to reward in the next life and to forgiveness in the hereafter. We know this, first, because of the context of the verse, and second, because the verb form that is used indicates something earned by intentionally making an effort. This cannot be applied to one's status as a man or a woman. Third, it refers to a reward that will variably, yet fairly, be given to both men and women for their good deeds during this life. Fourth, the verse commands believers to ask God for more bounty; this would not make sense if the request is based on fixed gender rights. Fifth, the verse ends by a reminder of God's divine knowledge of everything believers say or do and finally, the repetition of the same idea in so many other Qur'anic verses asserts its authenticity. Therefore, Q.4:32 is specifically addressing a question regarding God's justice and the criterion by which God evaluates and grants rewards in the hereafter. The verse sends a message of hope to both men and women and puts an end to sexist arguments by reminding the community of believers that God's justice and knowledge will be equally and fairly applied to both men and women, based on their efforts.

WHAT DOES THE *QIWĀMA* VERSE REALLY MEAN?

Next, I apply this new understanding of Q.4:32 to Q.4:34, what is known as the *qiwāma* verse. But before I do this, we must consider the way *qiwāma* has been variably, yet misleadingly, interpreted in many Qur'anic commentaries. There are evidence of serious flaws in the mainstream understanding of *qiwāma*. Many exegeses consistently interpret Q.4:32 as a gender-based preference for men over women, and interpret Q.4:34 with the same meaning. Undoubtedly, the misinterpretation of *qiwāma* we have seen in Q.4:32 has led to the same pattern we see in the interpretation of Q.4:34, which I discuss in detail in this book.

The *tafsīr* of Muḥammad b. Jarīr al-Ṭabarī (839–923) asserts men's right to "discipline"[42] their wives because of God's preference for them and because they spend on women from their money. In the commentary (*tafsīr*) of al-Zamakhsharī (1075–1144), the reason for the revelation of the verse is connected with men's saying, "God has preferred us to women in the worldly life and we wish for double the reward as well in the afterlife. Then some women wished they could go to jihad like men."[43] In the commentary (*tafsīr*) of 'Abd al-Raḥmān b. Nāṣir al-Sa'dī (1889–1956), we read, "Women should not wish for what God has granted men, likewise, the poor should not wish for what the rich have . . . because this is envy."[44] Al-Sa'dī's interpretation of Q.4:34 reads as below:

> Men are *qawammūn* means that they have the responsibility of guiding women to keep the duties of God and preventing them from corruption. They are also responsible for providing for women, providing clothing for them, and providing a home for them. The reason [for this] is because men are preferred to women. Some ways in which men are preferred to women include governance, which is exclusive to men, and prophethood. In addition, some ways of worship are exclusive to men, like jihad, attending Friday prayers, and Eid prayers. Also, men are special because of what God has given them, in terms of being patient, wise, and balanced, all of which [characteristics] women do not have.[45]

For Ibn Kathīr (1300–1373), *qiwāma* is interpreted as a gender-based right for men; he justifies this by saying that "men are better than women . . . , and therefore, prophethood was given exclusively to men, the same applies to ruling."[46]

As we have seen in the previous section, Wadud disagreed with this traditional view of *qiwāma* that applies to all men over all women. Although I agree with the reading of the verse Wadud provides, I propose, in addition to her argument to limit the application of *qiwāma* to some men, a fundamental change in the way *qiwāma* itself should be understood, before we move on to who has the right to *qiwāma*. The various patriarchal readings of verse Q.4:34—regardless of the variations in the degree of tolerance implied—consistently agree on and take for granted one point, namely, that *qiwāma* is a privilege and a higher rank, a divinely granted right. Sometimes, *qiwāma* is understood as an exchange of women's obedience for men's financial support. But this understanding is extremely problematic, because once *qiwāma* is understood as a right given to men, the rest of the discussion relates to just one question, namely, why do men or even some men have this right over women? In other words, the essential question is, what is *qiwāma*? This seems to have been taken for granted rather than thoughtfully considered as a point of discussion; what mattered for the majority of related discussions was the question of who has the right to *qiwāma*. Given that the majority of premodern commentators[47] were men (as are the majority of modern commentators), the gender-biased interpretation seems to have offered an answer to the question of who has this right to *qiwāma*? Therefore, in the following pages, I reconsider the interpretation of *qiwāma* based on the Qur'an itself. I move even beyond arguing for *qiwāma* as a right that can be given to specific qualified men (and not to any men), and suggest a new understanding of *qiwāma*, not as a right but as a duty.

In my approach to reinterpreting the *qiwāma* verse Q.4:34, I argue that it is necessary to interpret it in connection with Q.4:32. I argue that reading verse Q.4:34 in isolation from verse Q.4:32 is what led to the various observable problems. If we take into consideration that Q.4:32 addresses both men and women equally, though they are rewarded by God differently—as I argued in the previous section—with the promise that they will be rewarded equally, then Q.4:34 cannot contradict the affirmed meaning in Q.4:32. In my interpretation, I propose that the right of *qiwāma*, which I have been referring to, loosely, as a right, is in fact a duty. Wadud is right in observing that *qiwāma* is limited to some men and cannot be equally ascribed to all men; but we still lack an understanding of *qiwāma* not as a right that excludes some unworthy men, but as a duty that only some men are properly suited to manage.

My understanding of *qiwāma* as a duty is more consistent with Q.4:32. As noted in Q.4:32, God commanded that men and women should not envy each other, because, regardless of the differences in their lives, each gender has a fair share of God's blessings and forgiveness. This meaning continues in Q.4:34, which specifically refers to one way in which men can undertake a duty that might bring them a divine reward.

Furthermore, my interpretation of *qiwāma* as a duty and not a right is supported by the way *bimā is used in* the verse. I have intentionally left the word *bimā* without translation so far. In Q.4:34, some men are named *qawammūn* over women, then the verse continues, not to provide reasons for this *qiwāma*, as is commonly believed, but to provide explanations of how can this duty be fulfilled. We must read the verse again and examine the role of the word *bimā*: "Men are *qawammūn* over women, *bimā* God has preferred some of them to some others, and *bimā* they spend out of their money" (Q.4:34).[48] As noted, reading the rest of the verse as a justification of why men are preferred over women or why do men have *qiwāma* (as a "right") over women requires a word that can be translated as "because." But in this case, *bimā* cannot possibly mean "because." A clear example, one that proves that *bimā* is not necessarily used in the Qur'an to mean "because,"[49] can be found in Q.4:155, where *bimā* is used again in a context that cannot logically mean "because." The verse in question is "And so, *bimā* their breaking of their covenant, and their disbelief in God's miracles, and their killing prophets without justification, and their saying 'Our hearts are enveloped,' God has marked their hearts by their disbelief, in a way that they do not fully believe" (Q.4:155).[50] As we see in the previous verse, *bimā* cannot mean "because." Interpreting *bimā* as "because" interrupts the logical semantic continuity of the verse. In Q.4:155, if *bimā* is interpreted as "because," it would form a clause without a main clause to continue or to finish the meaning. Instead, I argue that *bimā*, in both Q.4:34 and Q.4:155, should be interpreted as the relative pronoun *alladhī* (who). Based on this interpretation, a better translation for Q.4:155 is "And so, those who break their covenant, and those who disbelieve in God's miracles, and those who kill prophets without justification, and those who say 'Our hearts are enveloped,' God has marked their hearts by their disbelief, in a way that they do not fully believe" (Q.4:155).[51]

Based on the premise that nothing can explain the Qur'an like the Qur'an itself, I outline the use of *bimā* in Q.4:155 and Q.4:34. In both places, *bimā* explains what follows it—it does not justify what follows it. In Q.4:155, *bimā* explains what the people mentioned in the verse did to deserve the divine punishment of having their hearts sealed; likewise, in Q.4:34, *bimā* explains how men should fulfill their role as righteous men by spending. Therefore, a more refined translation of Q.4:34 would read: "Men are financial guardians of women, [men] whom God has preferred some of them to some others, and those who spend out of their money" (Q.4:34).[5253]

In sum, my interpretation directly contradicts the common conclusion that men are preferred to women. My interpretation is based on the following:

(1) *Qiwāma* is not a gender-based male right; it is a duty and a religious responsibility. Men have the duty to provide for specific women related to them. The fulfillment of this duty in marriage is *ajr*, which wives should be paid as a financial compensation for this indoor labor as I discuss in detail in the last chapter. However, like all other religious duties and commandments that bring reward, only those who understand it as a responsibility can successfully fulfill its requirements. The argument is applicable only to those who want to implement the meaning of *qiwāma* in their lives.

(2) The addressee in the verses from Q.4:29 to Q.4:34 is the community of believers, as these verses clearly say; therefore, there is no reason to believe that verse Q.4:32 refers exclusively to men. On the contrary, the verse asserts that both men and women are given different but equal opportunities to earn reward from God.
(3) *Qiwāma* is not an exchange of women's obedience for men's support, as is commonly believed. It is better understood as a religious duty and opportunity for men to earn reward.
(4) The verse does not use *li'anna* (because), rather it uses *bimā* (who); I argue that the verse is meant to provide a description of those men who fulfill the duty of *qiwāma* by taking care of specific women related to them. The verse makes two assertions: first, not all men are able to fulfill this responsibility of being providers, and second, male guardianship is a financial duty, performed by providing for the women under their financial care. It cannot and should not be understood as a gender-based superiority or as a moral, ethical, or legal guardianship.
(5) The concept of "preference" given in Q.4:34 should be explained in relation to the preceding Q.4:32 and not the opposite. We should pay particular attention to the order of these verses, as this is not coincidental.
(6) The preference in Q.4:32 does not indicate worldly preference; rather, it relates to rewards from God in the hereafter. In verse Q.4:31, the initial promise is given to both men and women, that by avoiding major sins, both men and women can be saved. Then, in the same context, this confirmation is followed by a command for both men and women, that they should not wish for what others are given. The context is still the reward from God; this interpretation is supported by the change in verb form to form VIII (*ifta'ala*, like *iktasaba*), not form I (*fa'ala*, as in *kasaba*), which indicates something earned through intentional effort. As noted, using this form of the verb means first, that the whole conversation concerns worldly deeds for which both men and women can earn rewards from God; it cannot possibly mean biological nature that people are born with. Second, the assurance of divine justice addresses both men and women, who should not wish for the rewards of the other gender, rather, God reminds us that everyone is rewarded with justice.
(7) This reading of *qiwāma* does not assign the Qur'an a message of misandry. First, because the *qiwāma*-based financial rights given to women in case of marriage—as I discuss in the last chapter in this book—are a just compensation for women's indoor unpaid labor and devotion, and second, because acknowledging that women have a right to financial support is more consistent with the Qur'an's clear and unconditional support of the poor, orphans, and those in need.

(8) By saying, "men are *qawammūn* over women, those [men] whom God has preferred some of them to some others" (Q.4:34),[54] the verse alludes to a preference among specific men and not among men over women, since it did not say, "over them" (using the feminine "them"). The verse asserts two facts, first, *qiwāma* can only be rightly handled by righteous men—a fact that has been proven by a long history of the abuse of Muslim women's financial rights. Second, *qiwāma* is limited to the financial support of women.

(9) The concept of *faḍl* in the Qur'an, as we see in Q.4:32 and again in Q.4:34, is not applicable to gender-based bias in this world; rather, this concept refers to reward from God based on effort, or merit.

Qiwāma then, as we see, is a financial duty (primarily in relation to marriage but can include other women as well). *Qiwāma* does not indicate gender-based superiority; rather, it confirms God's acknowledgment of the rights and duties of men and women—duties that differ but are fair and equal.

MISINTERPRETING THE QUR'ANIC CONCEPT OF *DARAJA*

Another verse that has been interpreted as supporting a meaning similar to *qiwāma* (in its traditional sense) is verse Q.2:228:

> Divorced women must wait for three monthly periods before remarrying, and, if they really believe in God and the Last Day, it is not lawful for them to conceal what God has created in their wombs: their husbands would do better to take them back during this period, provided they wish to put things right. [Divorced] women have [rights] similar to their obligations, according to what is fair, and [ex-] husbands have a degree [of right] over them: [both should remember that] God is almighty and wise. (Q.2:228)

In fact, the problematic part does not include the full verse but is limited to the concept of *daraja* (degree) that is often extracted from the rest of the verse. Unfortunately, the way this verse has been commonly interpreted allows for many gender-based generalizations and misunderstandings related to the concept of "degree." This misinterpretation of the concept of "degree" is a clear example of what I refer to as the flaw of "exegetical contextomy." However, once we re-contextualize the issue in question, in this case, the concept of "degree," a new understanding of the verse reveals itself. Some observations can be very helpful in terms of clarifying the concept of "degree." First, the verse here deals exclusively with divorced women; it begins by making a clear reference to new rulings specific to divorced women. The verse starts with the word, "divorced women"; therefore, any conclusions we draw from the verse should relate exclusively to divorced women and cannot be generalized to apply to all women. Second, interpreting the word "men" in the verse as a reference to all men, instead of interpreting the term as referring to "ex-husbands," as the context clearly asserts, is a mistake that has caused some to conclude, as in Q.4:34, that men have a gender-based merit over women.

Wadud elaborates on the importance of limiting our interpretations of the verse to divorce by saying, "This verse has been taken to mean that a *darajah* exists between all men and all women, in every context. However, the context of the discussion is clearly with regard to divorce."[55] Interpreting the word "men" in the verse as referring to all men instead of limiting it to divorced men can be found in many interpretations, like those of al-Razī, al-Ṭabarī, al-Qurṭubī, al-Alūsī, al-Sha'rāwī, Ibn 'Āshūr, and many others. Third, reinvestigating the concept of *daraja* can be extremely helpful in understanding the verse in question. In my discussion of Q.4:32 I conclude that both men and women are granted divine justice in the afterlife. In the Qur'an, both men and women are promised to be equally justly rewarded, despite the ways in which their lives and responsibilities differ. In addition, I note that *qiwāma* is a financial duty for men as providers—one duty that will be rewarded. In Q.2:228, like the concept of *qiwāma* discussed in the interpretation of Q.4:34, the concept of *daraja* supports a man's financial responsibility in the case of divorce—a responsibility that, if fulfilled, allows for him to be granted an additional reward or rank. Reinvestigating the way *daraja* is used in some other Qur'anic verses supports my argument for *daraja* in Q.2:288 as a divine reward and a high rank that divorced men can be granted for fulfilling their commitment to support their divorced wives according to the Qur'anic commandments.

While the concept of *daraja* is used in various ways in the Qur'an, it is clear that in the Qur'an "An individual or group can earn or be granted a *darajah* over another."[56] It is also clear that the Qur'an "distinguishes on the basis of deeds."[57] In Q.4:95 *daraja* refers to a higher rank and a reward given to those who fight and strive in the cause of God, versus those who stay at home. In Q.9:20, the verse refers to a reward for those who believe in God, those who immigrate and strive for the sake of God. In Q.57:10 the same concept of a divine reward acknowledges that those who spent and fought before the conquest of Mecca are not equal to those who joined Islam after the conquest of Mecca. All these Qur'anic references indicate that the concept of *daraja* is used to refer not only to worldly preference but also to a divine rewarding system.

Divorced men can have a higher rank over divorced women because of the men's financial duty—which continues even after divorce takes place. This understanding is more plausible given the lack of supporting evidence in the Qur'an that divorced men are granted more rights than divorced women. On the contrary, we find in Q.2:233, Q.65:1, and in other Qur'anic verses references to obligations that require men to support their divorced wives; therefore, the high rank given to divorced men in Q.2:228 is likely a duty-based religious reward. In another verse, we read,

> Mothers suckle their children for two whole years, if they wish to complete the term, and clothing and maintenance must be borne by the father in a fair manner. No one should be burdened with more than they can bear: no mother shall be made to suffer harm on account of her child, nor any father on account of his. The same duty is incumbent on the father's heir. If, by mutual consent and consultation, the couple wish to wean [the child], they will not be blamed, nor will there be any blame if you wish to engage a wet nurse, provided you pay as agreed in a fair manner. Be mindful of God, knowing that He sees everything you do. (Q.2:233)

In Q.65:1 we read, "Prophet, when any of you intend to divorce women, do so at a time when their prescribed waiting period can properly start, and calculate the period carefully: be mindful of God, your Lord. Do not make them leave their homes—nor should they themselves leave—unless they commit a flagrant indecency."

This interpretation of the concept of degree in Q.2:288 as a duty rewarded to men, specific to divorce, matches the interpretation I provide for Q.4:32 which views the provision for and responsibilities related to *qiwāma* as a duty that can earn men a divine reward. Divorced men who continue to support their divorced wives (as they are ordered to do) then continue to be rewarded for their devotion, the same way men who provide for their wives can be rewarded. The higher degree or *daraja* granted to divorced men is conditional on their fulfillment of these responsibilities and it acknowledges, first, their larger share of the responsibility, and second, their willingness to respond to the Qur'an's guidance.

NOTES

1. I do not agree with the traditional and even mainstream readings of the story; therefore, I limit myself to what I refer to as the "act of disobedience," loosely known as the "fall" and to what I refer to as "the garden." In this chapter, I only rethink the role Eve played in the story (as it is widely understood). The reconstruction of the full story is another project that I do not address in this book.

2. Ibrāhīm al-Ḥaydarī, *al-Niẓām al-abawī wa-mushkilat al-jins 'inda al- 'arab* (Beirut: Dār al-Sāqī, 2011), 131.

3. Burhān al-Dīn al-Biqā'ī, *Naẓm al-durar* (Cairo: Dār al-Kitāb al-Islāmī, 1984), 12:357.

4. al-Biqā'ī, *Naẓm al-durar*.

5. 'Abd al-Raḥmān b. al-Kamāl al-Suyūṭī, *al-Durr al-manthūr* (Cairo: Markaz Ḥajar, 2003), 10:253.

6. Ismā'īl b. 'Umar Ibn Kathīr, *Tafsīr al-Qur'ān al-'aẓīm* (Riyadh: Dār Ṭayyiba, 1999), 5:321.

7. Aḥmad b. Muḥammad Ibn 'Ajība, *al-Baḥr al-madīd fī tafsīr al-Qur'ān al-majīd* (Cairo: Maṭāba' al-Miṣriyya al-'Āmma li-Kitāb, 1999), 3:427.

8. Abū Zayd, *Dawa'ir al-khawf*, 22.

9. 'Ā'isha 'Abd al-Raḥmān, *al-Qur'ān wa-qaḍayā al-insān* (Cairo: Dār al-Ma'ārif, 1999), 43.

10. Amina Wadud, *The Qur'an and Women* (New York: Oxford University Press, 1999), 25.

11. Muḥammad b. al-Ṭāhir Ibn 'Āshūr, *al-Taḥrīr wa-l-tanwīr* (Tunis: al-Dār al-Tunisiyya, 1984), 1:438.

12. Ibn 'Āshūr, *al-Taḥrīr wa-l-tanwīr*.

13. This is a loose translation that I am using here only to clarify the real role Eve had. As I mentioned before, the full reconstruction of the story is a project that I am not dealing with in this book.

14. Maḥmūd b. 'Umar al-Zamakhsharī, *al-Kashāf* (Beirut: Dār al-Ma'rīfa, 2009), 668.

15. Muḥammad al-Khudarī, *Min asrār ḥurūf al-jar fī l-dhiki al-ḥakīm* (Cairo: Wahba, 1989), 228.

16. al-Khudarī, *Min asrār ḥurūf al-jar fī l-dhiki al-ḥakīm*, 222.

17. Ibid., 227.

18. While the English translation is slightly different, the Arabic is the same in both verses.

19. Fāḍil al-Sāmarā'ī, *al-Ta'bīr al-Qur'ānī* (Amman: Dār 'Ammār, 2006), 209.

20. As based on the way the Qur'anic text uses *ilā* and *li*.

21. Al-Ḥaydarī, *al-Niẓām al-abawī wa-mushkilat al-jins 'inda al-'arab*, 115.

22. Buṭrus al-Bustānī, *Udabā' al-'Arab fī l-jāhiliyya wa-ṣadr al-Islām* (Beirut: Dār Ṣādir, 1953), 23.

23. Hādī al-'Alawī, *Fuṣūl 'an al-mar'ā* (Beirut: Dār al-Kunūz al-Adabiyya, 1996), 21.

24. While this verse might sound as addressing an obsolete pre-Islamic local Arabian tradition, its modern applicability can be extended to rebut sex-selective abortion.

25. Niaz Shah, *Women, the Koran and International Human Rights Law: The Experience of Pakistan* (Leiden: Brill, 2006), 42.

26. The two stories, I mean the story of creation and the act of disobedience, are not the same as mainstream Islam adopts and as many might think. However, as mentioned previously I do not discuss the details of the two stories in this book.

27. Nimat Hafez Barazangi, *Woman's Identity and the Qur'an: A New Reading* (Gainesville: University Press of Florida, 2004), 38.

28. Wadud, *The Qur'an and Women*, 20.

29. Ibid., 26.

30. Syed Mohammed Ali, *The Position of Women in Islam: A Progressive View* (Albany: State University of New York Press, 2004), 16.

31. Islamic polygyny which I discuss in details in this book and distinguish from what I call Qur'an polygyny is one example.

32. Fakhr al-Dīn Muḥammad b. 'Umar al-Razī, *al-Tafsīr al-kabīr* (Beirut: Dār al-Fikr, 1981), 111.

33. Ḥasan al-Bannā, *al-Mar'a al-muslima* (Cairo: Dār al-Kutub al-Salafiyya, 1986), 7.

34. al-Bannā, *al-Mar'a al-muslima*, 11–12.

35. Munīr al-Ghaḍbān, *Aḍwa' 'alā tarbiyyat al-mar'a al-muslima* (Cairo: Dār al-Kutub al-Salafiyya, 1986), 126.

36. 'Abdallāh Maḥmūd, *Nihayat al-mar'a al-gharbiyya: bidayat al-mar'a al-'arabiyya* (Cairo: Dār al-Kutub al-Salafiyya, 1986), 72.

37. Translated by Abla Hasan. Although I use Abdel Haleem's translation of the Qur'an for the majority of this book, I make some exceptions, for example, in this verse, he does not provide a literal translation. One striking mistake, for example, is the translation of *rijal* as "husbands" instead of "men."

38. Wadud, *The Qur'an and Women*, 70–71.

39. Like in the Qur'an: 47:19, 3:159, 60:12, 71:28, 14:41 and many other places.

40. Like in the Qur'an 36:12.

41. As it is made clear in many places in the Qur'an, including but not limited to 35:18.

42. Muḥammad b. Jarīr al-Ṭabarī, *Jāmi' al-bayān* (Beirut: Mu'assasa al-Risāla, 1994), 2:451.

43. Al-Zamakhsharī, *al-Kashāf*, 234.

44. 'Abd al-Raḥmān b. Nāṣir al-Sa'dī, *Taysīr al-Karīm al-Raḥmān* (Beirut: al-Risāla, 2002), 176.

45. al-Sa'dī, *Taysīr al-Karīm al-Raḥmān*.

46. Ibn Kathīr, *Tafsīr*, 2:292.

47. With the exception of 'Ā'isha 'Abd al-Raḥmān.

48. Translated by Abla Hasan.

49. The verse is commonly interpreted by adding a semantically alien element as a main clause: (we cursed them) in order to complete the meaning.

50. Translated by Abla Hasan.

51. Translated by Abla Hasan.

52. Translated by Abla Hasan.

53. The verse by using "men" not "husbands" include more than husbands as possible financial guardians of women.

54. Translated by Abla Hasan.

55. Wadud, *The Qur'an and Women*, 68.

56. Ibid., 66.

57. Ibid.

Chapter 3

Marriage in the Qur'an

Marriage in the Qur'an is strictly identified as a sacred relationship between two equal human beings and as a miracle that believers are urged to reflect on, to lead them to the full realization of God's might. As I explain in this chapter, the Qur'an rejects the pre-Islamic vision of marriage, and provides guidance to marital happiness. In contrast to the view of mainstream exegetes, the Qur'an rejects the marriage of minors and any kind of violence in marriage. In the following, I present arguments that support a new reading of the verses related to marriage and show an alternative interpretation of these verses, in contrast to widely circulated traditional views.

In this analysis of the status of women as wives, and the many deviations between the traditional interpretation and the Qur'an's guidance, it is difficult to pinpoint a singular deficiency that is solely responsible for preventing the success of the Qur'anic vision of marriage. Because the acknowledgment of the many rights Muslim women enjoy today should not prevent us from rethinking the rest of their lost Qur'anic rights. For example, interpreting parts of the Qur'an as a text addressed to men, which I refer to in the introduction as "the male addressee fallacy," plays a significant role in our understanding of Q.4:34, which is commonly misunderstood as permitting domestic violence. The "so-called authoritative ascendancy of early religious scholars" allowed the dominance and revival of medieval male-centered view of women's rights. Also, many Muslim feminists and activists are still challenged by what I refer to as the "antagonistic approach toward Western-oriented Qur'anic studies." Finally, "exegetical contextomy," allowed many exegetes to abandon the strict conditions for polygyny that are clear in the Qur'an.

A NEW CONCEPT OF MARRIAGE

In the Qur'an, marriage is uniquely described as a "solemn pledge" (*mithāq*) (Q.4:21). This expression undoubtedly indicates a sincere relationship that is based on a serious commitment. To fully understand the term *mithāq*, it is sufficient to note that the Qur'an uses the same term to describe the covenant between God and prophets: "We took a solemn pledge from the prophets—from you, from Noah, from Abraham, from Moses, from Jesus, son of Mary—We took a solemn pledge from all of them" (Q.33:7). The mere use of this term rules out any connection between the instrumental way marriage was viewed in pre-Islamic Arabia and the new Qur'anic concept of marriage. That is, the Qur'anic concept of marriage does not present the marital relationship solely as a means to an end, or as a means to ensure sufficient male offspring or fulfill men's sexual desires.

This ideological revolution against the traditional purpose of marriage or the nature of the marital relationship is made clearer in the following verse: "Another of His signs is that He created spouses from among yourselves for you to live with in tranquility: He ordained love and kindness between you" (Q.30:21). This verse asserts that tranquility is the ultimate purpose of marriage. In addition to this Qur'anic elevation of the aim of the martial relationship, we also find that God grants each couple love and kindness, as a divine gift, to enable them to reach the ultimate goal of marriage, namely, tranquility.

Thus, we assert that the Qur'an presents a new concept of marriage, one that is based on a strong spiritual connection between two human beings. Spouses are described in the Qur'an as a "joy"[1] and as close protecting "garments"[2] to each other. Furthermore, marriage in the Qur'an is viewed not only as a natural state but also as one's ideal state. "Celibacy and monasticism, far from being recommended, are described in the Qur'an as a human invention which could not be properly maintained."[3] In addition, this strong connection should harmoniously bring together only those who believe in God, as we can see in this verse, "Today all good things have been made lawful for you. The food of the People of the Book is lawful for you as your food is lawful for them. So are chaste, believing women, as well as chaste women of the people who were given the Scripture before you" (Q.5:5). In the Qur'an, religious congruence is asserted as a condition for marriage, for its undeniable role in helping a couple reach the ultimate goal of tranquility.[4] Another confirmation of the spiritual foundation of the marital relationship is found in the Qur'anic assertion of the eternal nature of this relationship.[5] In the Qur'an, marriage is a "decreed"[6] relation that does not end with death or the decay of the body, since the souls of both believing men and women are described as being rejoined in the afterlife, as we read in "The people of Paradise today are happily occupied [55] they and their spouses seated on couches in the shade [56]"

(Q.36:55–56), and as in "They will enter perpetual Gardens, along with their righteous ancestors, spouses, and descendants" (Q.13:23).[7]

THE QUR'AN ON THE SUBJECT OF INTIMACY

According to the Qur'anic criteria, an intimate relationship that elevates the sexual relationship in marriage to the ultimate goal of tranquility involves several conditions: First, the Qur'an specifies that women be pure: "They ask you [Prophet] about menstruation. Say, "Menstruation is a painful condition, so keep away from women during it. Do not approach them until they are cleansed; when they are cleansed, you may approach them as God has directed you" (Q.2:222). Second, while the first criterion addresses women, another criterion addresses men, this time with the requirement that they develop some sensitivity with regard to intimacy. "Your wives are [like] your fields, so go into your fields whichever way you like, and send [something good] ahead for yourselves. Be mindful of God: remember that you will meet Him" (Q.2:223). While the first recommendation is to avoid intimacy during menstruation, the second addresses men with the commandment to "send [something good] ahead for yourselves"—this is a message related to sexual behavior, one that has been, unfortunately, widely ignored. Ibn Kathīr (1300–1373), among many other commentators, interpreted "sending something good ahead" as a command to "do righteous deeds."[8] I would suggest that inserting a general meaning, like a commandment to do righteous deeds, into the middle of a verse about intimacy between spouses does not fulfill the message of the verse. While it is true that the verse commands one to undertake righteous deeds, the question remains: what are these good deeds, particularly in this context? Muḥammad al-Bukhārī (810–870) understood the Qur'anic command as an instruction to mention the name of God before intimacy.[9] However, I follow Muṣṭafā Maḥmūd (1921–2009) in arguing for a restricted interpretation of the command in Q.2:223 that applies specifically to the intimate relationship and sexual conduct within marriage, as this is the main topic of the verse.[10]

According to the Qur'an's guidance on sexuality, a fulfilling intimate relationship speaks to the needs of both partners; it is a relationship that should be anticipated with preparation. The type, the suitability, and the intensity of the preparation is left general, in accordance with the cross-cultural nature of the Qur'anic message. What matters is that the preparation is directed specifically to men. This "preparation" may include, but is not limited to, flirtation, one's appearance, affection, giving gifts and so on. Why was such a command given exclusively to men and not to both husbands and wives? Of the many reasons we might suggest, what would seem clear is the reality that the "psychological mechanisms governing male sexuality are not the same as those guiding female sexuality."[11] Perhaps this verse relates to gender-based variations in human sexual arousal—a subject that has been discussed and argued extensively in a number of studies.

This consideration of women's more sensitive sexual nature is probably one of the reasons this Qur'anic verse is addressed solely to men; preparation is necessary for an intimate relationship to reach a level of tranquility, as this cannot be achieved without the sexual fulfillment of both parties. As al-'Aẓīm rightly explains, sexual fulfillment constitutes, "the necessary but not the sufficient condition of love."[12]

In terms of sexual stimulation, men and women are different. This premise is almost axiomatic. Many think men seem to be able to enjoy less emotionally demanding sex. That is, for men, sex is not necessarily the final coronation to already existing love and an emotionally fulfilling relationship. While many men view sex as an act that can boost love or at least can help improve the couples' emotional status, for women, sex is viewed more ideally as a final tangible affirmation of strong emotional ties. In order to experience a sexual relationship within marriage that can lead to tranquility, most women need to feel emotionally secure first; by contrast, most men use sex to build emotional security. This is one of the reasons why "men initiate sex often and refuse it rarely. Women initiate it much more rarely and refuse it much more often than men. Given an opportunity for sex, men leap at it, while women say no."[13]

Thus, this verse reminds husbands to affirm their love, as an essential aspect of sexual happiness within the marriage. Note that I am not arguing to affirm men's hyperactive sexuality—a myth that has long been used by Muslim traditionalists to support polygyny—rather, I am referring to nothing more than a minor incompatibility in the level of complexity between men and women on the topic of sexual stimulation.

THE QUR'ANIC VIEW OF MINOR MARRIAGE

The controversy regarding the permissibility of the marriage of minors in Islam—like so many other similar problematic issues—is not rooted in the Qur'an. Here, I argue that this misinterpretation—that the marriage of minors is permissible—was created by elements alien to the Qur'an. Many traditional, mainstream Muslim scholars still believe that Prophet Muhammad married his most beloved wife 'Ā'isha when she was six or seven years old and that the marriage was consummated when she was nine. This issue continues to ignite strong arguments among traditionalists who support the marriage of minors and argue that marriage is acceptable immediately after a girl reaches puberty. Moreover, some go so far to suggest that such a marriage is permissible even before puberty, with the consent of the girl's father. For example, in *al-Sharḥ al-kabīr*, Ibn Qudāma states, "The father has the right to give his young daughter even if she is less than nine years old for marriage if he places her with a deserving man."[14] The marriage of minors was also made lawful by some clerics, even if the marriage is against the will of the girl, "According to the consensus of all whom we follow among scholars, a father can give his young daughter in marriage as long as he gives her in marriage to a competent man; he has this right regardless of her refusal and distaste."[15]

While arguments in support of minor marriage have declined in the Arab world, mainly as a result of legal pressure from governments, the central remaining challenge has stemmed from the story of 'Ā'isha. This challenge motivated many scholars, like Islām al-Biḥayrī,[16] for example, to provide detailed arguments that miscalculations were made and this resulted in confusion between two dates that are essential to any approach to understanding the prophetic biography, namely, the date Muhammad received the first revelation and the date of the migration. Some scholars suggest that by recalculating the dates involved it can be proven that 'Ā'isha's real age when she married Muhammad was not less than eighteen years old. However, because my methodology in this book depends solely on the Qur'an, I do not deal with the many controversies that are based on hadith, and I still find strong Qur'anic evidence against marriage at such an early age.

First, the Qur'an distinguishes between puberty and adulthood. The distinction is made in Q.24:59, where it is stated that as soon as children reach puberty, they should ask permission before entering a room: "When your children reach puberty, they should [always] ask your permission to enter, like their elders do" (Q.24:59). This means that according to the Qur'anic criterion, puberty is not the same as maturity. According to the Qur'an, children who reach puberty are required to consider others' privacy, but they are still categorized as children, not as adults.

Second, and more importantly, the Qur'an even suggests an explicit criterion for the age that can be considered suitable for marriage. The criterion matches the Qur'an's general guidance that allows each community to define its own idea of maturity. For example, Q.4:6 concerns the best way to deal with orphans' money and the age at which they no longer require guardians, that is, the age of adulthood: "Test orphans until they reach marriageable age; then, if you find they have sound judgment, hand over their property to them" (Q.4:6). This verse explicitly defines the age of marriage as the age when one is able to make sound judgments. This is a clear indication that the appropriate age for marriage relates to sound judgment, not physical development (that is, puberty). The verse is clear in terms of distinguishing maturity from puberty; it also clearly states that the appropriate age of marriage is based on one's ability to make sound judgments.[17] The same assertion of maturity as a condition to give orphans their property is also asserted in Q.17:34: "Do not go near the orphan's property, except with the best [intentions], until he reaches the age of maturity." Together, these two verses state that the age of maturity is a condition for returning property to orphans and in Q.4:6 that age is clarified as the age of sound judgment, and more importantly, as the age of marriage.

Hadith sources which use the story of 'Ā'isha's marriage to justify minor marriage in Islam, the tendency I refer to as "the use of the hadith to invalidate the Qur'anic text," have kept this controversy alive. In contrast to what is asserted in hadiths concerning 'Ā'isha's marriage, the age of marriage can be determined from the Qur'an, that is, it is measured by one's ability to make sound judgments; this aligns with the Qur'anic concept of marriage, which is presented as a contract between two responsible human beings. Furthermore, the definition of the age of marriage as the age when one can make sound judgments is closer to the overall strategy of the Qur'an, which purposefully provides general guidance, but leaves certain cultural norms intact.

Another verse, namely Q.65:4, has been misinterpreted as promoting early marriage (even before menstruation). These misinterpretations overlook the real message conveyed by the verses and base this on the story of 'Ā'isha's early marriage, which is debatable. Therefore, in the following, I analyze verse Q.65:4 to assess what it really says about the marriage of minors. The verse in question is, "If you are in doubt, the period of waiting will be three months for those women who have ceased menstruation and for those who have not [yet] menstruated; the waiting period of those who are pregnant will be until they deliver their burden" (Q.65:4). The verse speaks about the *'idda* (the waiting time of a woman after divorce or after the death of her husband before she can remarry). According to many exegetes,[18] minor marriage was approved according to this verse because it includes a reference to a specific category of women who should wait (during the time of the *'idda*), namely, "for those who have not [yet] menstruated" (Q.65:4). This category was misunderstood to permit the marriage of "little girls"[19] who have not reached puberty; it is based on the understanding that the verse refers to "little girls."[20]

I argue that this misunderstanding is based on the idea that it refers to women who have never menstruated, instead of those women who have not menstruated "yet," after their divorce. Below I provide my reasons for rejecting the unanimous interpretation of this verse as a reference to young girls who have not reached puberty. First, if the verse refers to girls who have not reached the age of puberty, it would state "those who have never menstruated before" and not "those who have not [yet] menstruated." Second, the category referred to as "those who have not [yet] menstruated" (Q.65:4) in the verse is a subcategory of "your women" (Q.65:4), as the beginning of the verse clearly states. Thus, the verse clearly refers to women, while as we noted in Q.24:59, the Qur'an refers to those who have not yet reached puberty as children. This Qur'anic categorization should, by itself, exclude prepubescent girls who are categorized as children and have not reached puberty from being included in a subcategory of "women." Third, the verse cannot refer to girls who have never menstruated, because the context of the verse concerns the *'idda*, a period of time set aside to rule out the possibility of pregnancy, and this does not relate to a girl who is not biologically able to be pregnant in the first place.

I argue that Q.65:4 does not refer to prepubescent girls; therefore, it does not and cannot be used as an argument for the permissibility of minor marriage in Islam. But who, then, is included in the category of women mentioned in this verse? Some[21] interpret the verse as a reference to women, who are sexually active and fertile, but do not experience menstruation. I exclude this option because the linguistic specificity of the verse and the preposition used do not support such an interpretation. The expression, "and for those who have not [yet] menstruated" (Q.65:4) uses the word *lam* for the negation. If we consider divorce as our starting point (as indicated in Q.65:1), the negation of menstruation by using *lam* indicates the negation that takes place after divorce and not before it. That is, the verse does not say that those women never menstruate, because that would require using *lā* and not *lam* as the negation. If the verse refers to adult women who never experienced menstruation, due to an abnormality of some kind, then the verse would have used the negation *lā* instead of *lam* (as *lā* indicates a continuity of negation, that is, the period starting from before the divorce and extending and equally applying to the time after the divorce takes place), because women who never menstruate at all would not be expected to menstruate in the past or in the present. To further clarify, the verse is *wa-llatī lam yaḥiḍna* ("and for those who have not [yet] menstruated") not *wa-llatī lā yaḥiḍna* ("and for those who do not menstruate.")

To stay faithful to my Qur'anic methodology, I use only two examples (there are many other similar examples in the Qur'an) to support my argument for the two different meanings of negation that can be clarified by using *lam* and *lā*.

Qur'an Q.2:190 reads "Fight in God's cause against those who fight you, but do not overstep the limits: God does not (*lā*) love those who overstep the limits." Here the negation *lā* precedes the present tense verb and clearly asserts a present continuous negation, that is, God does not love (in an ongoing sense) those who insist on overstepping the limits. It does not make sense—theologically speaking—to think of God as a deity who can love aggressors as long as they can be described as aggressors, that is, if they do not repent. In this verse, the continuity of the action is asserted in three ways: First, by using the negation *lā* before the present tense. Second, by the use of the verb "love," which indicates, by its nature, a longer duration than verbs of a more temporary nature (like eat, drink, etc.). Finally, it is logically embodied in the nature of God, according to what we know about him from the rest of the Qur'an.

By contrast, *lam* is used differently in Q.4:164 before the present tense as we read, "—to other Messengers We have already mentioned to you, and also to some We (*lam*) have not. To Moses God spoke directly." In this verse, the negation by using *lam* (in *lam naqṣuṣhum*) and the contrast the verse draws between this negation of narrating the stories of some messengers and the affirmation of narrating other stories about other messengers (in *qad qaṣaṣnahum*), which has been completed in the past allow us to understand how can *yet* fit and better explain the meaning. The expression in the verse can be better understood then if translated as, We have not yet.

With regard to applying this point to Q.65:4, as in Q.4:164, using *lam* for the negation simply indicates that the Qur'an is referring to women who have not menstruated yet after the divorce, not women who do not menstruate at all. Those women did not experience mensuration during the first three-month waiting period after their divorce. The waiting period starts when divorce takes place (as mentioned in Q.65:1), and in general cases lasts three months (as mentioned in Q.2:228), according to, "Divorced women must wait for three monthly periods before remarrying." While Q.2:228 refers to the general waiting period of divorced women, Q.65:4 deals with special and more problematic cases. In the first special case, Q.65:4 refers to aged women who no longer menstruate. The second special case refers to women who did not menstruate during the first three months after they were divorced. The last special case is pregnant women. With regard to the second category, I suggest that negating a verb by using *lā* should be translated as "never" and negating a verb using *lam* should be translated as "yet." If we apply this understanding to Q.65:4, and consider divorce as our starting point (as asserted in Q.65:1), then the three-month general waiting period (as asserted in Q.2:228) means that using *lam* and not *lā* in Q.65:4 refers not to women who never menstruate but to women who have not yet menstruated after the divorce took place.

These linguistic observations lead me to propose that the subcategory of women that is referred to in "those who have not [yet] menstruated" (Q.65:4) is women in the process of menopause. I argue that the women included in the *'idda* in Q.65:4 are of three categories: first, aged women who do not expect to menstruate; second, women in the process of menopause (during which time they may menstruate, but irregularly), which is the category in question; and finally, pregnant women.

So, women in the process of menopause are the subject of the second category. This is supported by the following: First, women described in the second category are those who did not menstruate during the first three months after the divorce; this is confirmed by the use of the negation *lam*. Second, since the negation by using *lam* does not indicate a permanent status—which only the negation by using *la* can convey—it must refer to women who usually menstruate, which logically rules out women who never menstruated. Third, this is a category of women who menstruated in the past, since they are a subcategory of women (*al-nisā'*), as the verse itself indicates. This becomes clearer especially if we remember our previous discussion of the Qur'anic categorization that children who reach puberty are still children, not women or men. Fourth, because the main concern of Q.65:4 as we read "if you are in doubt, the period of waiting will be" is the calculation of the waiting period. Therefore, it is logical for the verse to proceed with different problematic categories of women who might find it difficult to determine their waiting period. Fifth, Q.65:4 should be understood as a continuity to the command in Q.65:1 to be accurate in terms of counting the *'idda* and not in isolation from it. In Q.65:1 we read "and calculate the period carefully." Sixth, this is a category of women who may still be able to become pregnant; this makes the waiting time of the *'idda* a realistic requirement; it is clearly not a realistic requirement for young girls who could not become pregnant in the first place. Seventh, the category described in Q.65:4 cannot be women who do not menstruate since the complete and permanent lack of menstrual cycles or what is medically referred to as primary amenorrhea is not a condition that common to be included as a separate subcategory in Q.65:4.

We might question why the Qur'an includes women in the process of menopause as a subcategory, and are these women exceptional cases or does this subcategory represent a reasonable number that should be considered significant enough to address? In fact, the verse seems to accurately address the medical reality that menopause takes place over an extended time. It is well known that menopause cannot be determined by one, two or even three missed cycles. Therefore, this verse solves a problem for women in this circumstance by directing them to wait no more than three months.[22]

We should make a final point: *'Idda* for divorced women is not only a necessary time for women to determine if they are pregnant, as now this can easily be detected and does not require time. Rather, the *'idda* is an important waiting period that addresses the psychological as well as the economic consequences of breaking the solemn contract of marriage. The *'idda* enables both husbands and wives to reconsider reconciliation before the decision to divorce is final. More importantly, it is a time for women to financially prepare themselves for a new life, before they lose their husbands' financial support. During the *'idda*, women have the right to remain in their homes[23] and receive financial marital compensation (*ajr*), which I discuss in detail in the last chapter. The Qur'anic explanation is meant to clarify the amount of time each woman needs before she must make this change in status from that of a married woman: the time frame is three months for (menstruating) women, for aged women, and for women in the process of menopause, and the delivery of the child for pregnant women, who, as we see, can continue to claim financial compensation up to two years while nursing, even after the divorce is finalized.

To sum up, I argue that the marriage of minors is not approved in the Qur'an. On the contrary, the Qur'an specifies that marriage is contingent on reaching maturity, or the age at which a young person can prove that he or she is able to make sound judgments. The decisive specification of that age was intentionally omitted, to allow each community to make a suitable determination. According to the Qur'anic criterion, children who reach puberty are still considered children, therefore, young girls who reach puberty cannot be merged into the category of women. Finally, the Qur'anic *'idda* does not refer to girls who have not reached puberty, as many exegetes have misinterpreted, rather the *'idda* includes, in addition to women in "normal" circumstances, aged women, pregnant women, and women going through menopause. *'Idda*, as we see, includes the financial right for divorced women that grants them shelter and continued marital compensation according to their needs for a period of time before they move on with their lives.

QUR'ANIC GUIDANCE ON MARITAL HAPPINESS (THE *MA'RŪF* RULE)

The Qur'an sets the foundation for the general rules that a marital relationship should follow in order to achieve tranquility, which is the purpose of marriage. The Qur'an refers to the *ma'rūf* rule, "Live with them in accordance with *ma'rūf* [what is fair and kind]; if you dislike them, it may well be that you dislike something in which God has put much good" (Q.4:19). For a happy marriage, husbands are commanded to treat their wives in accordance with what is *ma'rūf*. The term is derived from the root *'a-r-f*, which means, among its other meanings, "to know." As a general term, *ma'rūf* can be applied to any set of conventionally approved moral, ethical, and even legal behaviors; thus, its use emphasizes what is collectively and conventionally known to be appropriate, fair, and kind in each community. Once again, we see that the Qur'an's use of a general term is an effective way to make its message broad enough for all times and places, for all types of legislation and diverse cultures. In the previous verse, as in many other verses, the term *ma'rūf* is intentionally left open, to enable it to be equally applicable to the various human social constructions that may be adopted throughout history. For a happy marriage, a man's behavior should live up to the best standards approved of and adopted by his community. Thus, according to this rule, the Qur'an's moral and ethical humanitarian guidance can coexist in complete harmony with any number of actual or possible human laws, provided the core of these laws is in alignment with the general Qur'anic guidance.

In addition to the Qur'anic assertion of the *ma'rūf* rule as general, yet essential, guidance to marital happiness, another more serious assertion is made in Q.65:2, where *ma'rūf* is presented as a condition for the continuity of marriage in the first place; we read, "When they have completed their appointed term, either keep them honorably (*ma'rūf*), or part with them honorably (*ma'rūf*)." This verse indicates that husbands are given two choices: either to treat their wives according to *ma'rūf* or to divorce them. Thus, Q.65:2 asserts *ma'rūf* not only as a Qur'anic commandment to couples in marriage but as a necessity for the continuity of marriage. In addition, we can easily infer that women have the right to be treated according to *ma'rūf* and this is a continuous right that women do not lose, even in case of divorce. The right to be treated according to *ma'rūf* is required not only during marriage and after the marriage is over, but also during divorce related negotiations, according to "If, by mutual consent and consultation, the couple wish to wean [the child], they will not be blamed, nor will there be any blame if you wish to engage a wet nurse, provided you pay as agreed in a fair manner (*ma'rūf*)" (Q.2:233). In short, the Qur'an asserts *ma'rūf* as an irreplaceable rule that couples must observe while married, during divorce, and even after divorce takes place.

Finally, I compare the assertion of *ma'rūf* as the rule to deal with divorced wives (as in Q.65:2) and the replacement of the word *ma'rūf* with the word *iḥsan* in Q.2:229, as we read, "Divorce can happen twice, and [each time] wives either be kept on in acceptable manner (*ma'rūf*) or released in a good way (*iḥsan*)."[24] While Q.65:2 gives husbands a choice between continuing the marriage according to *ma'rūf* or initiating a divorce according to *ma'rūf*, Q.2:229 replaces the commandment to treat divorced wives according to *ma'rūf* with the commandment to treat divorced wives according to *iḥsan*. This comes in a clear reference to the special care and delicate attention that should be given to women divorced twice and not only once, as Q.2:229 indicates.[25] *Iḥsan*, along with justice and generosity toward relatives, is at the top of the tripartite Qur'anic summary of what God commands: "God commands justice, doing good (*iḥsan*), and generosity toward relatives" (Q.16:90). Thus, *iḥsan* represents the highest possible human moral perfection.

The commandment to *iḥsan* relates specifically to the tender treatment that women who are divorced twice are expected to have. Therefore, the insertion of "[each time]" in Abdel Haleem's translation of the verse does not address the rationale for the replacement of *ma'rūf* with *iḥsan* in this verse.

THE QUR'AN ON DOMESTIC VIOLENCE

Without doubt, Q.4:34 is the most controversial and "ambiguous"[26] verse in the Qur'an. Many scholars claim that it is incorrectly interpreted more commonly than any other. It is what some Muslims often interpret as evidence for the necessity of "men's guardianship and superiority over women."[27] Before I provide my own analysis of the verse, which applies not only to the way in which the verse can be interpreted but also to the way it should be translated, I begin by introducing the verse as it appears in the translation I use in this book,

> Righteous wives are devout and guard what God would have them guard in their husband's absence. If you fear high-handedness from your wives, remind them [of the teachings of God], then ignore them when you go to bed, then hit them. If they obey you, you have no right to act against them: God is most high and great. (Q.4:34)

This verse as commonly understood provides a justification for the abuse of women's rights in marriage, and is problematic, if not entirely irreconcilable, with any feminist approach to the Qur'an. Efforts were made to soften the tone of the verse and many insisted that additional conditions should be placed on the methods of "correction" suggested in Q.4:34. In their interpretations, some insist on a prioritization of the correctional steps, such that striking would only be allowed as a "bitter remedy"[28] for "extreme circumstances and when all other remedies fail,"[29] and when nothing else works. Thus, some allow hitting as a final solution, permitted only to avoid divorce. Others interpret the verse to suggest "light striking";[30] that is, an action that takes the shape of a punishment that can gradually and increasingly escalate from reproach to withholding sex to light striking. Some even suggest hitting with a feather, as a symbolic gesture of disapproval. Another attempt to deal with the verse limits the permissibility of striking to a narrow cultural context, whereby striking wives is only permissible in societies where such practices are normalized and wife beating is considered, "neither harmful nor insulting."[31] More importantly and more recently, some suggest a linguistic approach that offers alternative meanings for the word *ḍaraba* (to strike); that is, it may mean things other than striking. Scholars have sought all these approaches in order to avoid dealing with a Qur'anic verse that seems to command domestic violence. For example, as Ayesha S. Chaudhry argues, the verb *ḍaraba* in Arabic is like the English "to strike" which "can be used in the phrases "strike a pose," "strike a bargain," "strike a similitude," and so on, but never has these meanings in isolation."[32]

Sadiyya Shaikh took a more pragmatic approach to explore the ways in which Muslim women deal with the social consequences of the patriarchal understanding of this verse. She interviewed women struggling with domestic violence, and concluded by proposing what she calls *tafsīr* through praxis, as the coping mechanism which enables women to reject their husbands' violent behavior, without feeling forced to reject the ideological religious grounds of that behavior. She explains this *tafsīr* through praxis in the following: "It may be practiced by rejecting their husbands' violent behavior as contrary to real Islam, or by teaching their sons or daughters to become different kinds of Muslim men and women."[33]

Unfortunately, all these attempts—despite their prominence—have not brought about any noticeable change in the way the verse is still viewed and used, mainly because of the problematic nature of some of the suggested solutions. While I do not consider every suggested feminist interpretation of Q.4:34, I refer briefly to some of these suggestions before I propose my own alternative understanding of the verse. Generally speaking, I believe we have more reasons to reject the previous attempts to understand Q.4:34 than we have to accept them.

Instead of going into the details of each argument, I group these approaches into categories and then explain my objection to each category. First, some feminist approaches to Q.4:34 can be classified as culturally based arguments. Those who make this argument think of Q.4:34 as a verse that cannot and should not exceed the cultural needs and practices of the Arabian Peninsula at the time of revelation, when striking women was a social norm. Those who take this approach attempt to resolve the problem by arguing that the validity of Q.4:34 should not extend beyond the time of revelation. I find these arguments problematic because they ascribe a passive attitude to the Qur'an; that is, they suggest that the Qur'an did not do anything to end the domestic violence that was practiced at the time of revelation. While this argument might seem helpful to make Q.4:34 more acceptable today, the argument that this verse has no applicability to the modern day opens a larger problem: how can the Qur'anic message be understood as universal if parts of it cannot be applied to the present day? As noted, almost all schools of Islamic *tafsīr* believe in the universality of the Qur'anic text; this is well-established. Therefore, limiting the applicability of Q.4:34 to a narrow cultural manifestation is a violation of that belief. In addition, accepting Q.4:34 as "descriptive of the gender norms characterizing the context of revelation rather than . . . prescriptive [of] the Qur'anic verse on the nature of gender relations"[34] as some Islamic feminists advocate, and as Shaikh outlines, shows a lack of appreciation for the revolutionary and reformist nature of the Qur'anic message, a message that takes a proactive attitude toward other socially accepted norms at the time of revelation. Consider, for example, that female infanticide, drinking, gambling, and adultery were all socially acceptable in pre-Islamic culture, and the Qur'an is clear in criticizing and sharply attacking these norms and practices.

Second, I reject the Islamic feminist approaches to Q.4:34 that can be generally classified as linguistically based arguments, since, while these arguments might vary, they share the need to violate the text by assuming that the verse is missing something, like a preposition or an adjective that would specify more precisely the meaning or even the intensity of wife beating allowed. For example, the interpretation in favor of understanding Q.4:34 as a gradual method of discipline can be easily challenged by the fact that the verse never prioritizes the steps of these so-called methods; on the contrary, the previous verse uses the conjunction *wa* (and) and not *thumma* (then). In other words, the verse does not support the view that there is a prioritization or order to the three steps a man allegedly can take to address his wife's behavior.

The same objection applies to those who suggest replacing the word "beating" by "light striking," as with a light napkin or a feather. Again, the Qur'anic text does not indicate the type or the severity of striking and does not add any adjective to define what can be considered permissible striking.

As an example of this linguistic approach, Laleh Bakhtiar[35] famously argues that the verb *ḍaraba* does not mean the command to strike, but the command for men "to go away" from their wives.[36] This linguistic "solution" does not really work since the verb *ḍaraba* does not have that meaning unless it is followed by the preposition *'an*. Realizing the linguistic problem her solution suggests, she defends her argument by suggesting that the missing preposition that should have been added to *ḍaraba* would not be unusual for someone who was illiterate, like the Prophet Muḥammad.[37] While Bakhtiar likely has good intentions to address the challenge of this verse, I do not believe such an interpretation is useful given that it is based on the idea that there are linguistic mistakes in the Qur'an, a book believed to be revealed by an all-knowing God. In addition, portraying Muḥammad as someone who is too ignorant to check the accuracy of the revelation he receives, or as someone who made mistakes and even conveyed divine messages inaccurately is another argument entirely. Even more seriously, if this argument were accepted, then it could and should be extended to the rest of the Qur'an, and should not be limited to what might be offensive to feminists and our modern way of thinking about women's rights in marriage. In other words, if we solve a perceived problem by accepting the hypothesis that a preposition is missing, we open the door to adding other prepositions and "missing" words, and even whole phrases in other places in the Qur'an. Clearly, this kind of cherry picking "solution" is logically fallacious, too controversial to accept and causes more harm than good. If we go this far to explain one issue, then we quickly reach an entirely different argument against Qur'an as *lingua sacra*, namely, that the Qur'an is not a divinely revealed (perfect) scripture. Logically speaking, allowing one undesired case to be solved as based on a linguistic error is a route that once adopted should not be limited to chosen parts; which is what Bakhtiar did in her argument.

In addition, Chaudhry's previously mentioned linguistic argument that *ḍaraba* does not mean "to strike" when it appears in isolation is quite the opposite of what the verb means in Arabic. Her argument for other meanings of *ḍaraba* also fail, as she supports them by drawing analogies with English. In fact, the verb as it appears in the Qur'anic text comes in Arabic precisely conjugated, and like all conjugated forms in Arabic, it is quite clear and leaves no ambiguities. Unlike the analogy Chaudhry draws between *ḍaraba* and "strike," the Arabic verb *ḍaraba* is conjugated in verse Q.4:34 as *wa-iḍribuhun*. Which indicates—due to its conjugation—a command given to a male or gender mixed group to strike a group of women as the object. All these details are imbedded in the same phrase as follows: The verb is a command, and when the letter *waw* is attached to the verb, it indicates a male or a mixed group of addressees as the subject. Finally, the suffix indicates a group of women as the object. In sum, considering the verb in question in isolation from its precisely conjugated Qur'anic form as it appears in Q.4:34 to argue for a different meaning is a tortuous route that doesn't solve the problem. Because any interpretation or translation should not ignore the fact that what we have in Q.4:34 is the verb in its precisely conjugated form and not the verb in isolation or the root of the verb. The verb in its conjugated form in Q.4:34 is clearly suggesting a command addressed to a masculine group or a mixed group and a women group as an object. In addition, the verb itself *ḍaraba* is not followed by an appropriate preposition to allow arguments for other meanings.

Instead of these linguistic maneuvers, I believe an exegesis should aim to stay faithful to the original and literal text and convey the exact message of the text, regardless of what it may express, rather than advocating the message we want the text to reflect. Ultimately, objectivity and academic integrity are the keys to exegetical credibility. Therefore, in my approach to Q.4:34, which is a linguistic approach, I remain faithful to the text; I do not assume that something is missing from the text, and I do not argue for other meanings of *ḍaraba* or use lexical machinations to forcefully extract more modern meanings from the text.

THE REAL MEANING OF QUR'AN 4:34

Kecia Ali expressed her "frustration with pro-woman, pro-justice, or gender-egalitarian interpretations that fail to confront squarely the difficulties inherent in interpreting [some anti-women] verses."[38] This is certainly true for verses like Q.4:34. Although it might seem as if the only interpretation of Q.4:34 is in reference to marital discipline, a holistic approach that starts by reconnecting Q.4:34 to its logical context reveals another meaning altogether. As we see in this section, a holistic hermeneutical approach that reconnects individual verses with the general construction of the Qur'anic text proves more effective, in terms of rethinking these verses. This approach avoids a mistake I refer to as "the exegetical contextomy fallacy" and which is commonly seen in many Qur'anic interpretations. Ziauddin Sardar (b. 1951) accurately describes this mistake by saying, "Commentaries that provide verse-by-verse analysis atomise the Sacred Text. They encourage the tendency to take individual verses out of the context of the Holy Book as an integrated whole."[39]

In addition, I show that Q.4:34 is an example of what I refer to as the "male addressee fallacy." I argue that this verse does not, in fact, address men with recommendations concerning the way they should treat disobedient wives. Rather, the verse addresses the community with ways to punish women who violate laws; it is not related to the resolution of marriage conflicts. I support this claim with the reasons outlined below.

Let's consider Q.4:34[40]—as it appears in the majority of translations including the translation I use in this book—and the reasons I have for arguing for the verse as referring to women who violate laws and not wives:

> Husbands [*rijal*] should take good care [*qawammūn*] of their wives [*nisa'*] with [the bounties] God has given to some [*rijal*] more than others [*rijal*] and with what they spend out of their money[41]. Righteous [*salihat*] wives [*nisa'*] are devout [*qanitat*] and guard what God would have them guard in their husband's absence [when unseen]. If you fear high-handedness [*nushūz*] from your wives [*nisa'*], remind them [of the teachings of God], then ignore them [in *madaj'*] when you go to bed, then hit them. If they obey you, you have no right to act against them: God is most high and great.

(1) First, translating *rijal* in Q.4:34 as "husbands" is basedū on an interpretive linguistic choice. Literally *rijal* means "men."
(2) Similar to the first concern, translating *nisa'* as "wives" is based on an interpretive meaning and should be replaced by the literal meaning which is "women."
(3) Q.4:34 unlike its mainstream interpretation does not address marital conflict. The term *nushūz* wrongly understood here as exclusively referring to marital conflict—as I prove here and in the coming discussion—is a general Qur'anic term that can refer to any high-handedness in marriage or outside marriage. A simple comparison between Q.4:34 and Q.4:128 may compel us to rethink the real context of Q.4:34. First, compare Q.4:34 to Q.4:128.

> If a wife fears high-handedness (*nushūz*) or alienation (*i'rāḍ*) from her husband, neither of them will be blamed if they come to a peaceful settlement,

> for peace is best. Although human souls are prone to selfishness, if you do good and are mindful of God, He is well aware of all that you do. (Q.4:128)

In contrast to Q.4:34, Q.4:128 confirms and verbally asserts that the people addressed in the verse are wives facing hardships caused by their husbands. By contrast, the subject pronoun for the masculine plural "you" in Q.4:34 can be used to address husbands (this is how the overwhelming majority of exegetes misinterpret verse Q.4:34), or it can be equally soundly used to address the community of believers. Why would we prefer one interpretation to the other? That is, why would we assume that Q.4:34 should be interpreted as addressing husbands, when the verse does not clearly assert such a meaning?

As I explain below, we have evidence to support the belief that Q.4:34 is addressed to the community of believers, both men and women, and not only to men or husbands. In the verse, we find the plural masculine "you," which can be used (in a grammatically correct way) to address a group of men or a group of men and women, as in the community of believers. In addition, Q.4:34 unlike Q.4:128 doesn't provide any single linguistic reference to marriage or marital related conflicts[42].

I argue that Q.4:128 should be explained by Q.4:34, not the opposite. The use of the same term *nushūz* in Q.4:34, does not and should not guarantee by itself the continuity of the reference to marital conflict. *Nushūz* is a general Qur'anic term for high-handedness in behavior that only in Q.4:128 appears as specific to marital conflict. *Nushūz* in Q.4:128 can be proven to precisely refer to marital conflict because of the explicit and clear context that refers to marital conflict or to be more precise to the husband's behavior. Verse Q.4:34 unlike Q.4:128 does not explicitly make any reference to key words like husbands, wives, marriage, and so on and replaces that by general terms like men, women, and so on.

(4) Interpreting Q.4:34 to suggest withholding sex as a punishment that husbands can use to solve marital problems or to correct their wives' behavior contradicts the strict prohibition made in Q.58:1–4, which forbids even announcing such an intention:

> God has heard the words of the woman who disputed with you [Prophet] about her husband and complained to God: God has heard what you both had to say, He is all hearing, all seeing. [1] Even if any of you say to their wives, "You are to me like my mother's back," they are not their mothers; their only mothers are those who gave birth to them. What they say is certainly blameworthy and false, but God is pardoning and forgiving. [2] Those of you who say such a thing to their wives, then go back on what they have said, must free a slave before the couple

> may touch one another again—this is what you are commanded to do, and God is fully aware of what you do—[3] but anyone who does not have the means should fast continuously for two months before they touch each other, and anyone unable to do this should feed sixty needy people. This is so that you may [truly] have faith in God and His Messenger. (Q.58:1–4)

We can clearly see that these verses end the practice of *ẓihar*—a pre-Islamic practice of psychological abuse of women in marriage. *Ẓihar* permitted the husband to punish his wife by announcing his intention to withhold sex, by telling his wife that she is like a mother to him. This strict prohibition and the expiation required for uttering this type of curse reveals how far the Qur'an went to remove pre-Islamic, misogynist social and domestic practices that wronged women. I suggest that the contradiction between the way this topic is treated in Q.58:1–4 and the leniency with which Q.4:34 was interpreted as asserting withholding of sex as a commanded punishment in marriage calls into question the reliability of the mainstream interpretation of Q.4:34. If a husband is not even allowed to announce his intention to withhold sex, how could he be instructed to withhold sex if he believes that his wife is disobeying him? Some might claim that there is a consistency between prohibiting *ẓihar* and allowing the withholding of sex as a corrective method by pointing to a difference between *ẓihar* as a long-term or even permanent punishment and withholding sex in Q.4:34 as a temporary solution. We can see that Q.58:1–4 only comments on the statement that men used to say to their wives: "You are to me like my mother's back," regardless of the duration of this punishment and how long it lasts.

I suggest that Q.58:1–4 is designed to end a specific type of verbal abuse of wives—an abuse that uses intimacy as a way to humiliate women in marriage. The Qur'an categorically ends the mere announcement of the intention to withhold sex as a punishment of wives, regardless of the duration of the punishment. Therefore, I argue that from a purely Qur'anic perspective, Q.4:34 cannot be understood as permitting, much less commanding what is decisively prohibited in Q.58:1–4. The logical inconsistency and contradictions between the two commands is too profound to be ignored or reconciled in favor of allowing the mainstream traditional understanding of Q.4:34.

(5) My interpretation of Q.4:34 is supported by a lexicographical investigation of the meaning of *nushūz*. *Nushūz*, translated here as high-handedness, comes from the root *n-sh-z*, which means to go beyond the norm or break a rule. As a Qur'anic expression and in isolation from its later fixed judicial implementation, *nushūz* does not necessarily and essentially refer to marital disobedience, as is commonly thought. Rather, it can refer to any type of abnormal, unexpected, or

bizarre behavior, sound, or appearance, within or outside marriage. While I am aware of the difficulty created by the fact that the term is currently understood in a judicial sense as referring to a spouse's disobedience, initially, and in principle, the root of the word simply suggests inconsiderate behavior that shows no regard for the rights, concerns, or feelings of others. This matches my conclusion that the verse indeed explains ways of dealing with women who violate laws or socially accepted norms.

I utilize the methodology of interpreting the Qur'an from the Qur'an in order to overcome the difficulties inherent in the later judicial and lexicographical definition of the term *nushūz*, that is, the narrow interpretation of this term in relation to marriage only. As I argue, one manifestation of the inimitability of the Qur'anic language is the way this language embodies, within the Qur'an, all the keys necessary to decode itself. This is what I refer to as the "semantic completeness of the Qur'anic language." Therefore, exploring the way the word *nushūz* is used elsewhere in the Qur'an helps to resolve the disconnection between the term itself and its restricted usage in the context of marriage. For example, the following verse includes another form of this verb.

> You who believe, if you are told to make room for one another in your assemblies, then do so, and God will make room for you, and if you are told to rise up (*inshizū*) do so (*inshizū*): God will raise up, by many degrees, those of you who believe and those who have been given knowledge: He is fully aware of what you do. (Q.58:11)

In the previous verse, the term by itself is not related to marital disobedience, rather it relates to a behavior that can best be described as different. In this verse, the command to rise up—even when the rest remain seated—is analogous to behavior that stands out when compared to norms, traditions, or customs. I argue that the true meaning of Q.4:34 is this more general meaning. Exegetes who borrowed the specific meaning and application of the term *nushūz* from Q.2:128, which is specific to marital conflict as I explained before, and applied it to Q.4:34 committed a logical fallacy by equivocally using the same term in both verses with no textual support. Simply, because it is the context in Q.2:128 which assures the applicability of the specific meaning and not the term as many might think. While the later conventional usage of the term *nushūz* has totally excluded the plausibility of other lexical choices, starting from the Qur'anic text in reinvestigating the etymology of the word can bring about outcomes other than what we can get from considering the term in its later exegetical and juristic development.

(6) I argue that the community of believers is the real addressee of the verse, as it is explicitly mentioned in the Qur'an. The uninterrupted dialogue begins at Q.4:29, with the addressee as "You who believe," and continues in Q.4:34.

(7) The verse following Q.4:34, namely Q.4:35, offers another assurance that the community of believers is the real addressee. This verse recommends ways for the community of believers to help a couple in cases of marital problems. In Q.4:35 it is clear that "you" in the verse does not refer to husbands alone, rather, it refers to the community of believers: "If you [believers] fear that a couple may break up, appoint one arbiter from his family and one from hers. Then, if the couple want to put things right, God will bring about a reconciliation between them: He is all knowing, all aware" (Q.4:35). If we exclude the idea that the Qur'an switches addressees without reason (as this is not a Qur'anic style), then, logically speaking, the addressee in Q.4:34 should be the same as the addressee in the preceding and following verses, that is, the community of believers.

(8) Interpreting Q.4:34 as addressed to the community, not husbands, is more consistent with the Qur'anic message of gender equality, which is asserted throughout the Qur'an.

(9) Interpreting Q.4:34 as addressed to the community, not husbands, is more consistent with the previously discussed Qur'anic *ma'rūf* rule mentioned in Q.4:19.

(10) The interpretation I propose here is more consistent with the reported behavior of the Prophet, who did not use, in relation to his wives, any of the three methods mentioned in Q.4:34! Despite the difficulty of using hadith sources (as noted, I do not use hadith as a source for this book) I make an exception here for three reasons: First, there are no Qur'anic references to the Prophet's adoption of any of these three steps; this at least indirectly supports my argument that these methods of disciplining a wife are not fundamentally Qur'anic. Second, the Qur'an identifies the Prophet as "an excellent model" (Q.33:21), a point that should lead us to question the validity of a behavior that cannot be ascribed to the Prophet himself. Third, I appeal to the common sense of those who insist on the validity of using the Qur'an and hadith as equally reliable sources. According to all narrations, the Prophet never applied any of these three methods of correction with any of his wives. Therefore, the apparent contradiction between the Prophet's behavior and the criterion that traditional exegetes extrapolate from Q.4:34 constitutes another reason to question the traditional understanding of this verse.

(11) According to my interpretation, Q.4:34 specifies the appropriate legal punishments for women who violate the law. The logical analysis of the kind of punishments suggested in Q.4:34 reveals an undeniable nexus with what we can—very broadly—call, a Qur'anic strategy

to publicly discipline women who violate the law. To fully appreciate this, we can outline the commands made in Q.4:34 as suggesting admonition, house arrest (*maḍajʿ*, "ignore them" loosely translated as "beds," a point I address below), and the physical punishment of beating. In fact, if we examine other punishments suggested in the Qur'an, we find an unmistakable consistency that supports my interpretation of Q.4:34. We can begin with house arrest. At the time, it was the norm to imprison wrongdoers inside their homes. We know this from early Islamic history and from the Qur'an itself. For example, the punishment for publicly witnessed lesbianism includes not only house arrest but house arrest for life if the women violators insist on their behavior: "If any of your women commit a lewd act, call four witnesses from among you, then, if they testify to their guilt, keep the women at home until death comes to them or until God shows them another way" (Q.4:15). Therefore, the house arrest of women is not an exceptional or unprecedented Qur'anic punishment.

The same argument applies to beating; this punishment is also consistent with the system of Qur'anic punishments. For example, the Qur'an approves of beating as an act of punishment for publicly witnessed adultery: "Strike the adulteress and the adulterer one hundred times" (Q.24:2). In sum, Q.4:34 suggests to the community three different kinds of admonishment; these can be translated according to modern legal language as a warning, house arrest, and physical punishment. All these methods of punishment are consistent with the Qur'an's overall strategy for addressing legal violations.

(12) The argument for a gender-based legal punishment as we see in my interpretation of Q.4:34 might sound awkward to us now, as it calls for the special treatment of female criminals (with the exception of specific crimes). I agree that the rationale behind this gender-specific legislation runs counter to modern legal systems that derive their sense of gender equality from commitments to gender neutrality. I believe that the current understanding of justice attains its merit from gender indifference and treats any other approach as biased and sexist. The Qur'anic approach to gender equality and justice undoubtedly differs from our modern approach; it seems to derive its sense of justice from acknowledging that if they are merged with men in one legal category, women and other minorities may be more vulnerable to discrimination in a world that "has always belonged to males."[43] In the Qur'an, women are treated as a delicate social category, a group that has certain vulnerabilities and therefore requires protections that cannot be ensured if they are grouped with men. This argument matches the reality, that throughout history, women have been and are still vulnerable to mistreatment, abuse, and sexual exploitation.

In addition to women, the Qur'an identifies and prioritizes needs of other less fortunate subgroups in society: the people in need, the elderly,[44] the homeless, and orphans and instructs people to protect these groups. While space does not allow a discussion of the nature of the Qur'an's justice-based social message, I would assert that the special attention it pays to the oppressed, which includes but is not limited to women, is evidence of this message.

(13) The scrupulous linguistic analysis of the terms used in Q.4:34 supports my interpretation. First, the Qur'an specifies that women who have committed these crimes should be locked in a place, which it refers to as *maḍaji'*. This word has been commonly interpreted to refer to a husband's withholding of sex, since the word *maḍaji'* can mean "bed" in Arabic. However, the word *maḍaja'* itself does not mean, precisely, "bed" when it is used in the Qur'an, rather, it refers, as al-Ṭabarī argues[45], to a place where a bed may be, that is, a bedroom. Reconsidering this linguistic peculiarity in light of Qur'anic Arabic, which is the key to decoding the Qur'an's semantic perfection, changes our understanding of Q.4:34. *Maḍaja'* means bedroom, not simply "bed"; furthermore, *maḍaja'* is not a metaphorical reference to an intimate relationship, as commonly understood, but should be understood by its literal meaning. The form of the word "*maḍaja'*" (derived from the root ḍ-j-') refers to the place where a certain activity takes place, that is, it is a "place-noun" (*ism al-makan*). The verse Q.2:144 provides another Qur'anic example of a similar use of a place-noun. The term *masjid*, which refers to "mosque," is similarly derived from the root "s-j-d" which means "to prostrate"; it refers to the place where people make prostrations: the mosque. In the Qur'an, the word *maḍaja'* refers to the place where the verb *ḍaja'* ("to lie down on the ground")[46] takes place, that is, a bedroom, not a "bed." The exegetes, except for al-Ṭabarī, understood the word as "bed" and interpreted it figuratively, as a reference to a sexual relationship. In fact, the term can be understood as a literal reference to the place where women criminals should be detained or locked in, namely, their bedrooms. I see no reason to ignore the literal meaning (bedroom) and give the word a figurative meaning (bed) and then extrapolate from that.

Some may ask why the verse did not use the word *bayt*, which means "home," instead of *maḍaja'*, which means a place where one can lie down. In fact, the clarification of the precise usage of *maḍaja'* supports my interpretation. In another verse, the Prophet's wives are advised to stay in their homes and avoid excessive socializing. In this instance, the word "bayt" is used to mean "stay at home" (Q.33:33).

So, while Q.33:33 advises the Prophet's wives to stay in their homes (*bayt*, pl. *buyūt*), in Q.4:34, women criminals were commanded to stay in a *maḍaja'*. That is, women criminals were meant to be detained in their bedrooms (not their homes, as this would not have truly isolated them or served as a punishment).[47]

(14) My interpretation of Q.4:34 as a verse that is unrelated to marital conflict is more consistent with the generality of the verse. If the Qur'an is in fact a gender egalitarian book, as I argue it is, then how would it be correct to give one gender the right to discipline the other? And why would wife-beating be treated in such a simple manner in the Qur'an? As we see, Q.4:34 does not make any reference to the type of beating, the number of times one could be struck, the intensity, the order of the three correction steps, and so forth. This is quite problematic if in fact the right to beat a woman is loosely given to men in relation to their wives. According to my interpretation, the generality of the verse is perfectly understandable because the legal and judicial guidance of the Qur'an is always purposefully and intentionally general, so that it can be applied to ongoing independent legislation. If Q.4:34 is the community's suggested legal punishment for female criminals, then it is up to the courts, judges, and approved authorities to decide the amount, the order, and intensity of the proposed sentence. As noted, admonition can serve as a warning, which is what legal systems usually begin with, house arrest can be understood as today's prisons (again, the court determines how long imprisonment should last or how many times it should be repeated), and physical punishment is what the Qur'an refers to in Q.4:34 and in other places as a possible legal punishment, although modern legislatures have abandoned this option as a correctional method.[48,49]

The fact that Q.4:34 uses the conjunction "and" and does not use "then" to connect the three methods of correction is another proof that Q.4:34 must be addressing legal and not domestic issues. Generality, as we have seen in this book, is a well-established Qur'anic style adopted in a variety of places, but particularly with regard to legal regulations. I argue, for example, that the Qur'an leaves it to communities to decide what type of government they should have; it only requires justice, as in Q.4:58. The Qur'an leaves it for people to decide the ideal age for marriage and only requires that those marrying have "sound judgment," as in Q.4:6. The traditional interpretation of Q.4:34 does not indicate that this is a legal regulation; therefore, the open generality in a topic as serious as the (alleged) permissibility of domestic violence should be reevaluated. The open-ended legal context that many Qur'anic verses adopt is very different from personal evaluations, which can vary because they do not have a common standard of evaluation or shared justification. Certainly, the collective judicial assessment of communities and congregations can be more objective in seeking justice than individual husbands, much less angry husbands.

(15) My interpretation of Q.4:34 is more consistent with basic psychological and physical understandings of masculine sexuality. According to the traditional interpretation of the verse, men can withhold sex as a way to punish their disobedient wives. However, withholding sex seems a more likely method of punishment that women, who are generally less sexually demanding and more "eager for love and commitment"[50] would effectively use. The interpretation of the verse as withholding sex to pressure women does not speak to the most basic facts we know about human sexual arousal, since—very generally speaking—withholding sex is likely to be more harmful to men than to women.

(16) Q.4:34 describes righteous women as *salehat*. This is an expression that is commonly but wrongly interpreted as essentially limited to "righteous wives." However, the adjective itself as it is used in the Qur'an in other places does not indicate any necessary connection to marital status. To appreciate this let us consider some other places where the same adjective is used to describe righteous people as we read in "'My righteous servants will inherit the earth'" (Q.21:105) and even to describe righteous *jin* as we read in "Some of us are righteous and others less so" (Q.72:11).

(17) In Q.4:34 righteous women are specifically described as *qanitat* which is wrongly and commonly interpreted as essentially connected to marital obedience. Investigating the way the same expression is used in Q.33:31 can assure my argument for a more general meaning of obedience. In Q.33:31 the command to the wives of the Prophet to obey God and his Prophet is driven from the shared root *q-n-t*. "Wives of the Prophet, if any of you does something clearly outrageous, she will be doubly punished—that is easy for God—but if any of you is obedient to God and His Messenger and does good deeds, know that We shall give her a double reward and have prepared a generous provision for her" (Q.33:30–31). The verse clearly uses the expression to refer to obedience to God and His Messenger. Also, referring to Muhammed here in a dialogue addressed to his wives as the Messenger and not as a "husband" or as "your husband" is a clear indication of the command to obey him as the Messenger and not as a husband, at least in this verse. Even more clearly the command from the root *q-n-t* addresses Mary in (Q.3:43) in a nonmarital context as we read, "Mary, be devout to your Lord, prostrate yourself in worship, bow down with those who pray."

(18) Q.4:34 makes a reference to righteous women before the three correction methods are introduced. This reference is introduced to draw a contrast between righteous women who are described as those who guard what God asked to be guarded even when not seen by anyone and those violators who act differently. This careful reference to fearing God even when unseen, which comes immediately before describing ways of dealing with women who behave differently is another assurance that the verse is addressing how to deal with women who violate God's laws. Translating this part of the verse as "Righteous wives are devout and guard what God would have them guard in their husbands' absence"[51] is not faithful to the verse as it switches from the general meaning of "absence," which is what is mentioned in the verse, to a special interpretive meaning, specific to the "absence of husbands." I reject this interpretation, first because it has no textual support. And second, because this interpretation asserts one more time male moral and ethical superiority as a Qur'anic argument—the argument that I have previously refuted and dismissed as alien to the Qur'an.

(19) The specific literal command of guarding what God himself asked to be guarded in *bima hafiz Allah* in Q.3:34 is another affirmation of my argument for a more general meaning of obedience here, which is not restricted to husbands' obedience. The verse doesn't command women to guard what husbands ask to be guarded or to follow husbands' preferences; rather, the verse literally clarifies the criterion by ascribing it to God himself. This is a clear assertion that what needs to be observed here is God's commands and not husbands' orders.[52]

(20) While Q.4:34 starts by referring to *nisa'* which means "women" and not "wives," using a conjunction letter *(fa)* before *salihat* which means "righteous women" assures the continuity of the reference. In other words, there is no reason in the verse to assume any change in reference from "women" to "wives."

At this point, I would suggest a new translation of Q.4:34, along with this new interpretation,

> Men are financial guardians of women, those men whom God has favored some of them to others, and those who spend from their money. Righteous women are devout, they guard what God asked to be guarded, even when [they are] unseen. Those women among you [believers] whom you fear high-handedness, admonish them, and place them in house arrest, and strike them. If they obey you seek no more correction. God is most high and great. (Q.4:34)[53]

THE LOST EMPOWERING MESSAGE OF Q.4:128

In this section, I elaborate on a verse that offers women empowering advice in the event of marital conflict. We read,

> If a wife fears high-handedness [*nushūz*] or alienation [*i'rāḍ*] from her husband, neither of them will be blamed if they come to a peaceful settlement, for peace is best. Although human souls are prone to selfishness, if you do good and are mindful of God, He is well aware of all that you do. (Q.4:128)

This verse speaks to women's psychology by acknowledging not only *nushūz* ("high-handedness") but also *i'rāḍ* ("alienation," or "negligence")[54] as types of domestic abuse. This verse acknowledges that women can be harmed not only by what their husbands do, but also by what their husbands do not do, or by their neglect. Unfortunately, the word *i'rāḍ* is usually treated as a synonym for *nushūz* ("high-handedness"), when in fact it has the meaning of negligence[55].

Unfortunately, in this verse, the meaning was interpreted as a justification to deprive women of some of their rights in marriage. Traditional interpretations of this verse understand it as granting men the right to no longer provide for their wives, or sleep with them, as they become older. Based on this unjust misogynist interpretation, clerics have (traditionally) advised women to give up their rights and accept ill-treatment, in order to retain the social status of being "someone's wife," and thereby avoid what they consider a social stigma.

For example, traditional exegetes have taken this verse and argued, as al-Qurṭubī (1214–1273) does, that this verse rebuts "those ignorant [people] who believe that a man cannot replace his old wife by a young one as she ages."[56] Al-Ṭabarī (839–923) interprets this verse as referring to a woman whose husband dislikes her "ugliness"[57] or is distressed that she has "become old";[58] therefore, if she does not want to leave him, she should offer him some of her dowry, or give up some of her days or her right to intimacy with him, in order to remain married. Al-Ṭabarī understands that this is the meaning of the verse, and adds that "reaching an agreement by way of giving up some rights is better than divorce."[59] This particular understanding of Q.4:128 has been applied in the following *fatwa* of 'Abd al-'Aziz b. 'Abdallāh b. Baz (1910–1999), who addresses men in similar situations,

> A man must be just if he has two or more wives. If he dislikes one of his wives, he should say, "I do not want you anymore." He should say: "If you wish you can stay as a wife to me, I can come only when I want to come, otherwise, I will divorce you." By saying this, a man sets himself free from the sin [of rejecting

> his wife]. If his wife accepts his conditions, he will not be considered guilty or sinful; if she does not accept, he can divorce her.[60]

Al-Rāzī[61] (1149–1209) interprets the verse in relation to the story of one of the Prophet's wives, Sawdah, who, some say the Prophet intended to divorce because she had aged. She allegedly asked him to keep her as one of his wives if she gave her right to intimacy with him to his young wife 'Ā'isha. According to Muḥammad Mutwalī l-Sha'rāwī's (1911–1998) interpretation, in some cases, women should give up their rights because,

> the wife might become old or sick while her husband is still strong. Or it might be the case that he becomes attracted to another woman, or he might wish to marry another woman for any reason. In this case, a woman should be wise and handle the issue by giving up her right to her husband. The wife might be unattractive, therefore, she should allow her husband to marry another woman, or she should give back some of her dowry; what matters most is that they reach an agreement—this is a man's responsibility as much as it is a woman's responsibility.[62]

Even the mention of selfishness in the verse, which should be applied equally to men and women, was interpreted as uniquely and exclusively required by women, who might be hesitant to give up some of their rights or who might insist that their husbands remain with them.

These examples of traditional interpretations are sufficient to identify the nature of the misogyny they entail; there is no need to quote more similar opinions. In sum, a woman who has devoted her life to her husband, and who has (if she has followed the advice of traditionalists) not pursued her own career or secured a separate income, should accept that, having experienced pregnancy, childbirth, nursing, and the associated signs of aging that likely changed her shape or body and may leave her less sexually attractive, should allow her husband to seek a new life with another woman. And not only should she allow this but she should make it easy for him by withdrawing any demands on his time, intimacy, companionship, or spending. In fact, this interpretation clearly indicates that, in addition to accepting polygyny that at least requires the fair treatment of multiple wives, wives should accept an inferior type of polygyny, in which they give up some rights, such as their right to intimacy, provision, or even their dowry—all in order to avoid divorce!

I argue that this scenario, which has been carefully interpreted by traditionalists in a way that masculinizes the Qur'an, should be rejected, not only because the verse does not support these interpretations but also for the reasons I outline below.

(1) The traditional understanding of Q.4:128 contradicts the mainstream Islamic arguments of polygyny, which is conditional, based on fairness and equality among wives.[63] According to the traditional understanding of Q.4:128, men are provided a guilt-free exemption from their marital responsibilities and the commitments they already made to their (presumably) aged wives. In other words, this interpretation of the verse would seem to endorse a new version of polygyny that is unlike the so-called Islamic polygyny (that I discuss in detail below) in that it does not even require any equal treatment between wives.
(2) By asking women to surrender their dowry or even a portion of it, the traditional understanding of Q.4:128 contradicts the clear prohibition made in Q.4:20–21. Although Q.4:20 refers to divorce, the verse prohibits men from reclaiming the dowry, as the dowry is a fundamental aspect of a legal marriage, and a man cannot take it back, even in cases of divorce.

> If you wish to replace one wife with another, do not take any of her bride-gifts back, even if you have given her a great amount of gold. [20] How could you take it when this is unjust and a blatant sin? How could you take it when you have lain with each other and they have taken a solemn pledge from you? (Q.4:20–21)

This verse strongly condemns any attempt to take back the dowry in the case of divorce, and leads us to ask, if a man is condemned for taking back the dowry when he divorces his wife, how can he claim any of it while he remains married to her?

(3) According to traditional interpretations of Q.4:128, wives would seem to be punished for reasons that have nothing to do with their behavior or conduct. They are simply forsaken for becoming older, or less attractive;[64] this contradicts the Qur'anic principle that should guide marital conduct, namely, "Live with them in accordance with what is fair and kind (*ma'rūf*)" (Q.4:19).
(4) The traditional interpretation of Q.4:128 contradicts Qur'anic guidance for husbands who find themselves in situations like those the exegetes seem to be addressing, that is, cases in which a man loses interest in, or attraction for, his wife, either temporarily or for a longer period. Interestingly, the Qur'anic advice in verse Q.4:19 is exactly the opposite to the exegetical interpretations of Q.4:128. The Qur'an in Q.4:19 addresses men who have lost interest in their wives: "Live with them in accordance with what is fair and kind (*ma'rūf*); if you dislike them, it may well be that you dislike something in which God has put much good" (Q.4:19). So, even in the event that a man dislikes his wife, the Qur'anic guidance reminds men

> that those wives, whom they stopped loving for some reason, might still be best for them. Thus, the literal meaning of verse Q.4:19 contradicts the traditional and figurative interpretation of Q.4:128.
>
> In contrast to the traditional understanding of Q.4:128, I argue that the verse empowers women in a number of ways: First, it speaks to women's emotional needs in marriage. As Q.4:128 asserts, women can be harmed not only by their husbands' abusive acts, but also by their husbands' neglect. This acknowledgment of women's sensitivity sends an empowering message that speaks to women's psychology. The second peculiarity we can observe here is the absence of a criterion of high-handedness, or negligence (these words can be interpreted in a variety of ways according to time and cultural contexts). This verse perfectly fits the overall framework of the universal Qur'anic guidance. The third point we must note is the sharp transition from a woman's concerns to the use of the dual pronoun, which unites wives and husbands in resolving problems. The immediate change from the pronoun "she" to "neither of them" (with "them" in the dual pronoun) in "If a wife fears high-handedness or alienation from her husband, neither of them will be blamed if they come to a peaceful settlement" (Q.4:128) suggests that an open dialogue between the spouses should be the first step toward resolution—before the problem escalates to the point that external intervention is needed. And even more importantly, the verse fully acknowledges that opening a fruitful dialogue between a couple to solve their problems is not easy, and so it reminds both husbands and wives to put aside selfishness. Thus, the verse stresses that making peace requires both parties to be patient, courageous, and willing to admit their own mistakes, and this will help them restore tranquility. The verse refers to *iḥsān*—a commandment that implies going beyond one's duty, and *taqwa*—which is to be God-fearing.

Finally, in addition to the advice provided in Q.4:128 another advice is provided in Q.4:35. This time the advice addresses a situation when efforts to resolve marital conflict described in Q.4:128 fail; the Qur'an in such a situation encourages the couple to seek what we recognize today as marriage counseling. In cases in which the conflict escalates beyond the point that reminding husbands and wives to maintain a healthy dialogue, fear God, and strive to the best of their ability, the Qur'an goes a further step and advises couples to seek outside help. The verse addresses the believing community this time with a plan that includes the active involvement of representatives from the families of the husband and the wife. "If you [believers] fear that a couple may break up, appoint one arbiter from his family and one from hers. Then, if the couple want to put things right, God will bring about a reconciliation between them: He is all knowing, all aware" (Q.4:35).

QUR'ANIC POLYGYNY VERSUS ISLAMIC POLYGYNY

What Is Quranic Polygyny?

Thus far, the majority of attempts made to rethink Islamic polygyny fall under the general umbrella of reforming pre-Islamic polygyny, by praising the limitations of polygyny to four wives (from an unlimited number of wives as in pre-Islamic Arabia).[65] Other arguments aim to reform Islamic polygyny by restricting it to necessity, or insisting that multiple wives be treated justly and fairly. Nevertheless, some scholars oppose the concept of polygyny itself. In his evaluation of the problematic nature of polygamous families, Muḥammad Rashīd Riḍā (1856–1935) argues, "Polygyny is a deviation from the original status of marriage, since a man should have one wife."[66] 'Alī Sharīa'tī (1933–1977) referred to the same point when he stated that "the practice of polygyny totally contradicts sharia' law."[67] Likewise, Hadī al-'Alawi (1933–1998) criticized the sexist way sexual desire has been understood between genders, and noted that Muslims "think of men's sexual desire as more intense than [that of] women, therefore they allowed men more sexual opportunities by permitting four wives and an unlimited number of concubines."[68] Malak Hifni Nasif (1886–1918) addressed polygyny more straightforwardly when she wrote, "Polygyny is a corruption for men, a corruption of money, a corruption of morality and a corruption for women's hearts."[69]

Of all the misinterpretations we find in the way the teachings of the Qur'an have been interpreted and practiced, nothing exceeds the topic of polygyny and the way in which it has been wrongly understood and adopted by Muslim jurists. Islamic polygyny, which I distinguish from Qur'anic polygyny, appears in Islamic judicial practice as a mere slightly reformed version of pre-Islamic polygyny. In addition, the majority of Muslim jurists base their discussions of polygyny not on modern issues related to it, but by comparing it to pre-Islamic polygyny; I refer to this approach as "the fallacy of relative reform." Also, misunderstanding Qur'anic polygyny is also problematically connected—as I explain in this section—to what I refer to as "the exegetical contextomy fallacy," "the authoritative ascendancy of early religious scholars," "the use of the hadith to invalidate the Qur'anic text," and "the fallacy of exegetical semantic satiation."

First, it is necessary to distinguish between the two terms "Islamic" and "Qur'anic," because we might be tempted to think that since the Qur'an is the sacred scripture of Islam, all terms derived from it should be treated as both "Qur'anic" and "Islamic." By "Qur'anic polygyny," I refer to polygyny as a theological term, as it appears in the Qur'anic text—that is, as conditional, gender egalitarian, and precisely codified. By contrast, "Islamic polygyny" refers to polygyny as it was adopted legally by Muslim jurists throughout the history of Islamic jurisprudence; this is loosely defined, seldom soundly justified, and "continues to protect the interests of the elite class and ignores the rights and interests of disadvantaged women despite mounting evidence and changing circumstances that support flexibility in interpretation."[70] Even if we consider the difficulty of referring to my proposed understanding of polygyny as "Qur'anic polygyny," we cannot ignore the evidence that supports the existence of a deep cleavage between the meaning of "Qur'anic polygyny" and its practical exegetical, judicial, and legal application.

In order to fully explain the distinction I make between "Qur'anic polygyny" and "Islamic polygyny," I begin by defining pre-Islamic polygyny. In the pre-Islamic period in Arabia, women had culturally assigned roles; they were essentially tools for sexual pleasure and reproduction. At the time, life was harsh and people had no choice but to side with their tribes in ongoing fights for scarce resources. Enmity, as a law of life, affected social and legal systems and even reshaped moral beliefs. Each tribe sought to increase its chances for survival; whatever means were necessary were deemed acceptable and even ethical. Unlimited polygyny emerged as one option that helped increase the number of male offspring in the tribe; therefore, it was tolerated and socially endorsed, along with other practices that shared the same goal, such as marriage to those captured in skirmishes. Pre-Islamic polygyny, despite being misogynist and unfair to women, can best be understood as a pragmatic necessity that was closely related to the best interests of the tribe. In other words, the practice of pre-Islamic polygyny was a misogynist, yet a strategic choice that allowed women, as well as men, the best chances of survival, by enabling the whole tribe to survive.

The advent of Islam brought new teachings that replaced pre-Islamic tribalism and competitive enmity with religious brotherhood. Antagonism was no longer the norm; the need to survive was increasingly viewed as a collaborative task that should be secured by encouraging religious altruism. As a consequence of these social changes, pre-Islamic polygyny lost its sociopolitical function, and thus we might expect it to vanish like other outdated pre-Islamic social institutions. Interestingly, it did not vanish, I believe, because a slightly reformed type of polygyny was advocated—this is what was later called "Islamic polygyny." Muslim advocates of polygyny seemed to have manipulated the Qur'an's radical reformation of the concept of polygyny and used it to justify a new system of polygyny that was similar to the obsolete pre-Islamic polygyny in every respect, except the number of wives permitted, and a superficial requirement to treat all wives equally. It would seem that the majority of those who argued in favor of "Islamic polygyny" were all trapped in the same ideology, when they treated "Islamic polygyny" as a revision of pre-Islamic polygyny.

I argue that "Qur'anic polygyny," as opposed to "Islamic polygyny," is a completely new practice that has nothing in common with pre-Islamic polygyny other than the name. In fact, "Qur'anic polygyny" can best be understood as the opposite of "Islamic polygyny" (or what is still practiced and defended by Muslim jurists today).

We are left to define "Qur'anic polygyny'." The Qur'an seems to support a conditional polygyny that fits the new role of women in the Muslim community. The Qur'an permits polygyny as a unique pro-woman, pro-family solution that is acceptable, but only as a last choice, as necessary to deal with exceptional social catastrophes. "And if you fear that you will not deal justly with the orphans (*yatamā*), then marry those that please you of women, two or three or four. But if you fear that you will not be just, then marry only one" (Q.4:3).[71] First, the verse is addressing the community, as it is clear in Q.4:1, with a solution, that such a permission is allowed if the community accepts its legality and in cases of emergency. The plural masculine "you" in Q.4:3 refers to a community of "people" as Q.4:1 clearly asserts, and is not addressed to husbands,[72] who cannot individually and separately judge what is considered a social emergency; rather the verse is addressed to the judicial authorities of the community. I argue that assuming that Q.4:3 is addressed to husbands is another example of what I refer to as the "male addressee fallacy." This misunderstanding of the identity of addressees (an issue that plays an essential role in the interpretation of any verse) fundamentally changes our understanding of the Qur'anic message.

In addition, the sentence uses a doubly conditional phrase: first, it allows polygyny only in cases in which the community fears that it might not deal justly with orphans[73] (this is the first condition), and second, it allows polygyny only when justice between wives is sought and achieved, the condition which—according to the criterion of the Qur'an—should be prioritized over the first condition and should motivate men to refrain from polygyny, even if the community allows polygyny because it faces a catastrophe.

The Qur'an requires three conditions for polygyny to be permissible then: First, the community must approve of it, because Q.4:3 addresses the community (as we see at the beginning of the dialogue in Q.4:1). Second, there must exist a current fear that orphans cannot be dealt with justly, and this should be collectively assessed by the community, not by husbands or wives. This condition is clear in Q.4:3 and Q.4:2, which initiate the subject of dealing justly with orphans.[74] Third, the condition is included in Q.4:3, namely, that a man must be fair with his wives; the verse asserts that if this condition cannot be fulfilled, the permissibility is canceled. I argue that this condition includes a set of rights and obligations that include, but are not limited to, the wife's permission. In the following, I explain the details of the three Qur'anic conditions.

First, the Qur'an's conditional permissibility of polygyny is addressed to the community (in Q.4:1). It clearly indicates that allowing men to marry the mothers of orphans is an acceptable emergency plan to care for fatherless children only when the community permits it. This, as noted, makes polygyny conditional on the community's approval and must precede any individual assessment or consideration.

In addition, we can easily see that the Qur'anic dialogue that starts at Q.4:1 addresses not the community of believers, as we might expect and as we often see in the Qur'an (as in Q.2:104, Q.2:153, Q.3:200, Q.9:34, Q.9:119, Q.24:21, and other places); rather it addresses the entire human community, that is, "people" (Q.4:1). This particular Qur'anic reference to the human community (and not just the believing community) for a sensitive topic like polygyny is important and should not be overlooked. While some Muslims in the West and in countries that ban polygyny believe that it is illegal but Islamic, I argue that nothing can be both illegal and religiously permissible. The argument that nothing legally banned can or should be considered religiously permissible—both for Muslims who live in Islamic countries or those who are minorities in countries governed by non-Muslims—can be inferred from many Qur'anic verses, including but not limited to the following:

> "God commands you [people] to return things entrusted to you to their rightful owners"; (Q.4:58)
> "those who fulfill the agreements they make in God's name and do not break their pledges"; (Q.13:20)
> "You who believe, fulfill your obligations." (Q.5:1)

Thus, being a citizen of a country (even one ruled by non-Muslims), involves pledging an oath of loyalty and an oath to obey the laws of that country. These verses emphasize the importance of remaining faithful to (all) pledges. The specificity of using "people" in Q.4:1 (instead of "believers") indicates that the matter is dependent on the authority of the community, that is, any community in which Muslims live, as an essential condition for the permissibility of polygyny. This means that the actions of some polygynous Muslims who live in the West are not only illegal but are in violation of Qur'anic standards.[75][76]

Second, the condition for the Qur'anic permissibility of polygyny is that it be intended to provide guardianship for the woman's fatherless children. For a better understanding of what "Qur'anic polygyny" means, note that it was only made permissible in relation to the guardianship of orphans. The Qur'an does not propose polygyny (that is, marrying the mothers of orphans) as the necessary and only step to care for orphans, even in cases of emergencies and catastrophes. The Qur'an does not simply say, "If you have neglected orphans in your community then marry [their mothers] those who please you." Rather, the Qur'an allows the community to evaluate the situation; it says, "If you fear..." This means that for communities that have a social structure to care for orphans, polygyny is not even a necessary option. We must reconsider the complexity and the generality of the permissibility of polygyny (in Q.4:3) to understand it. This verse, like many other verses that address the legal issues of a community, uses general language to enable communities to choose what will work best for them; it does not impose answers and rigid regulations. On the contrary, the Qur'an leaves it to the community to allow polygyny only in cases in which they fear that fatherless children (i.e., "orphans" in an Islamic sense) will not be treated justly. This fear would not even exist if other social nets for the guardianship of orphans had been adopted and effectively implemented. That is, polygyny is a last choice, and not even an option when the community provides other means of support for orphans.

The question of whether polygyny should be considered a last option, or an option at all, to care for neglected orphans does not require justification; rather it requires citation and acknowledgment of what is mentioned (literally) in Q.4:3. Polygyny, in the context of taking care of orphans, is stated in Q.4:3. The verse starts as a conditional sentence and the permissibility of polygyny is clearly conditioned on (among other elements) the community's fear of neglecting orphans. Muḥammad Shaḥrūr accurately notes that "it is very harmful to the society today to disconnect the permissibility of polygyny from the divine commandment of taking care of orphans . . . as some clerics do today, by inventing reasons to justify polygyny, weak, ridiculous and unjust."[77]

Third, fairness to wives as the third condition of "Qur'anic polygyny." Fairness to wives can include almost all aspects of life, but here, I start by the permission of the first wife as a requirement for the soundness of the second marriage. I argue for the permission of the first wife as a subcategory of fairness for the following reasons: First, as long as polygyny is considered a type of marriage, "Qur'anic polygyny" cannot be understood as separate from the previous discussions of marriage and the status of women in marriage. A woman does not lose her right to be treated according to the principle of *ma'rūf*—previously discussed—because her husband marries another woman or wishes to marry another woman. On the contrary, I believe the permission of the first wife is an essential condition to a second marriage, as this is part of the principle of *ma'rūf*. A man who seeks a second marriage without the full approval and blessing from his first wife violates the principle of *ma'rūf*. Second, a condition for polygyny is fairness, or justice, and it cannot be considered fair or just to marry a second wife without regard to the desires of the first wife. As noted, the Qur'an presents marriage as an eternal relationship, the ultimate goal of which is tranquility. Clearly, tranquility is not possible if one's wife is not involved in a major decision like that which is taken in the case of polygyny. "Qur'anic polygyny" (that is, marrying widows with fatherless children) that is sought with the intention of helping society is a decision that a man and his wife should take jointly, and one that cannot be fair if the wife's opinion is not considered.

The strict conditions of "Qur'anic polygyny" might seem strange to Muslims today, because the version of polygyny they have learned about, that have been approved by Muslim jurists, accepted and practiced as "Islamic polygyny," are not the true "Qur'anic polygyny." Later exegetes who usually start quoting Q.4:3 from the command "marry" and not from the conditional "if" where the verse really starts, separated the issue of the guardianship of orphans and polygyny; which is an example of "exegetical contextomy."

By remaining faithful to my methodology and by using an argument based purely on the Qur'an, I rebut the practice of polygyny. My goal is religious reform, not legal reform; legal reforms have been undertaken in many Arabic and Islamic countries, though these are largely secular reforms. In this book, I argue in favor of the advancement of women's status in the context of religious reform, by identifying the gender-egalitarian message in the Qur'an. With regard to polygyny, I mainly assert the "authoritative ascendancy of early religious scholars" as what prevented and still prevents many scholars from challenging the current polygyny that is known as "Islamic polygyny." My stance against polygyny is based on the Qur'an. I do not argue against polygyny because it can be easily proven to be harmful to women, children, and society today—these arguments are usually refuted by the assertion that polygyny is mentioned in the Qur'an and therefore it should be made permissible at least for religiously commented people—Rather, I argue against "Islamic polygyny" from within the Qur'an; the Qur'an cites conditions in which polygyny can be practiced—conditions that are difficult if not impossible to fulfill in the modern world as we know it. The observation of these strict Qur'anic conditions of polygyny should motivate us to reconsider the loose interpretation of polygyny that many advocate (that is, what we know as "Islamic polygyny").

Another verse closely related to the dissection is Q.4:129 which suggests the impossibility of achieving justice in a polygamous marriage. In fact, this verse led some to believe that it was a negation of Q.4:3. The verse Q.4:129, "You will never be able to treat your wives with equal fairness, however much you may desire to do so" supports my interpretation of Q.4:3. I do not believe that Qur'anic verses contradict, cancel, or abrogate each other, as I noted in the introduction. But how can Q.4:3 require fairness and Q.4:129 state that fairness between wives cannot be possible? Asking for something impossible is illogical and contradicts the Qur'an, as we see in Q.22:78 and in other verses that confirm that Islam is an accessible religion. I argue that the impossibility of fairness in Q.4:129 is because of an essential inequality in the status of the two women in the case of polygyny. While both women should be treated equally, the first woman is permanently better because she accepted what the majority of women would not accept. Second, the reference to fairness should be seen as a serious warning to those who might think it is possible to be fair with more than one wife. As I noted, the fear of wronging the first wife (as in Q.4:3) is a condition serious enough to cancel the permissibility of polygyny, even when the first two conditions are fulfilled. That is, this condition—if not fulfilled—can cancel the permissibility of the act, even if it is based on the successful fulfillment of the previous two conditions (in Q.4:3); therefore, it was highlighted again, individually and separately, as we see in Q.4:129.

How Was the Real Meaning of Quranic Polygyny Lost in Interpretation?

The traditional interpretation of polygyny started by interpreting the word "orphans" in verse Q.4:3 as a reference not to orphans (commonly understood as children without parents), but to orphan girls or women. This way restricting the permissibility to a specific group of mothers of fatherless children was eliminated. My objection to this interpretation comes not only from the previous discussion of "Qur'anic polygyny" but also from the semantics of Q.4:3 itself. I reject the interpretation of *yatamā* in Q.4:3 as referring to orphan girls after they reach the age of marriage for the following reasons:

(1) The verse Q.4:3 uses the masculine plural *yatamā*, which includes fatherless children—both boys and girls. That is, the verse does not use the feminine plural *yatimāt*, which refers to orphan girls. This misunderstanding is the result of devaluing the textual accuracy of the Qur'an, or a result of male bias, or a mixture of both.

(2) The expression *yatamā* in Q.4:3 cannot include orphan girls after they reach the age of marriage, because when the Qur'an refers to orphan girls after they reach the age of marriage, as we find in Q.4:127, it explicitly refers to them as a special category called *yatamā al-nisā'* as below,

> They ask you [Prophet] for a ruling about women. Say, 'God Himself gives you a ruling about them. You already have what has been recited to you in the Scripture about orphan girls (*yatamā al-nisā'*) from whom you withhold the prescribed shares [of their inheritance] and whom you wish to marry, and also about helpless children—God instructs you to treat orphans fairly: He is well aware of whatever good you do.' (Q.4:127)

In the previous verse, orphan women (girls after they reach the age of marriage) are referred to explicitly and clearly with the term *yatamā al-nisā'* (lit., "orphans [who are] women"). This Qur'anic expression is mentioned in Q.4:127 to refer to a category that we can loosely translate as "orphan women." A detailed explanation of this term is useful, as it will help, not only to avoid the confusion of who is meant in Q.4:127 and Q.4:3 but also to highlight the literal usage of this expression in Q.4:127. As we have seen, many of the original meanings of Qur'anic terms and expressions have been lost because they are incorrectly grouped with other categories. To remain faithful to my Qur'anic semantic methodology and avoid the use of lexical commentaries, we should consider three verses in order to determine the meaning of *yatamā al-nisā'*. These verses are Q.4:127, Q.4:3, and the previously discussed Q.24:59. In the Qur'an, children and women are two separate categories, as we understood from Q.24:59, where we read, "When your children reach puberty," this means that *yatamā al-nisā'* in Q.4:124 refers not to orphan girls but to orphan girls who lost their parental support after they reached the age of marriage; this enabled the Qur'an to refer to them as women (*nisā'*). In the Qur'an, these girls are treated as a vulnerable group (as we see in Q.4:127) because adult women without parental support might be more vulnerable to being abused in marriage (because they do not have a father to take their side in the event of marital troubles), or even being cheated out of their inheritance or dowry by their future husbands (again, because they do not have male family members to defend them).

(3) In Q.4:127 the command to seek justice includes three categories, namely, *yatamā al-nisā'* (orphan girls who have reached the age of marriage), the oppressed among children, and finally orphans, as in fatherless children (*yatamā*). This means that, according to Qur'anic usage, *yatamā* (orphans/fatherless children) and *yatamā al-nisā'* (orphan girls who have reached the age of marriage) are two different categories. Treating these two terms interchangeably renders the reference in Q.4:127 redundant and meaningless and is due to what I refer to as "the fallacy of exegetical semantic satiation."

(4) This convoluted understanding of Q.4:3, and confusing it with Q.4:127, is very problematic, since its validity depends on a flaw that I have already identified in this book and referred to as "the use of the hadith to invalidate the Qur'anic text." Based on the Qur'an, I have proved that *yatamā al-nisā'* and *yatamā* are two different groups that cannot and should not be mixed, as they are in a hadith in *Ṣaḥīḥ al-Bukhārī*,[78] in which 'Ā'isha explains *yatamā* in Q.4:30 as referring to orphan girls at the age of marriage, or what we refer to as *yatamā al-nisā*.'

What I find to be particularly problematic though is the fact that overlooking the Qur'anic permissibility of polygyny as a conditional permissibility as Q.4:3 clearly indicates goes beyond the specific linguistic difficulty created by mixing the two terms of *yatamā* and *yatamā al-nisā'*, because "Islamic polygyny" as commonly understood and practiced is restricted neither to *yatamā* nor to *yatamā al-nisā'*; rather it is unconditionally allowed to all women and not only to mothers of fatherless children or orphan girls after they reach the age of marriage. This open permissibility that overlooks both terms is an indication of a deliberate misunderstanding promoted by the upper-class misogynist elite and the "male chauvinist studies of medieval exegetes and Hadith scholars [which reflected] the influences of the social conditions of their times,"[79] This convoluted understanding of polygyny in the Qur'an arose then from the traditional interpretations of the patriarchal elite.

What Is Islamic Polygyny?

With this explanation of "Qur'anic polygyny," we move on to the second question, what is "Islamic polygyny"? First, "Islamic polygyny" deviates from "Qur'anic polygyny" in a number of ways, most notably, by claiming that it is an option at any time, not just a conditionally allowed practice in specific circumstances. In an extremely strict *fatwā*, Ibn Baz argues that "anyone who hates polygyny or argues that monogamy is better, is an apostate."[80] Some scholars endorse polygyny as a way to solve demographic problems, for example, in countries with a surplus of women,[81] while others argue for polygyny as a solution to men's hypersexuality, which (allegedly) cannot be fulfilled by one wife, especially given that women experience times (such as childbirth and menstruation) during which they cannot engage in a regular sexual life.[82]. Note that the Qur'an does not justify polygyny in relation to fulfilling men's' sexual desires (and claim that these desires cannot be satisfied by just one woman). Asma Barlas rightly observes this point by saying, "The Qur'an itself does not refer to the sexual nature or needs of women or men in dealing with polygyny."[83]

"Islamic polygyny" is problematic in numerous ways. Among the issues that arise, we can point to female objectification, which is clearly counter to the Qur'an and is implied by the "fungibility"[84] of replacing one wife with another, the dehumanization and humiliation[85] that results from this line of discussion, and the repulsive treatment of women as little more than sexual instruments, as implied by certain justifications of polygyny (especially those that see women's sole use as sexual).

In addition, another problematic, yet commonly used strategy to justify "Islamic polygyny" involves using an unjust analogy between polygyny and monogamy, which allegedly essentially leads to adultery. Those who support polygyny claim that husbands in monogamous relationships eventually engage in secret affairs, and this leaves mistresses without dignity or a way to acknowledge the offspring of such adulterous unions. Therefore, according to them, women have a choice between two scenarios: accepting polygyny or tolerating adultery. This either–or logically fallacious comparison is presented as if men have only two choices: to be polygamists or adulterers. This argument asserts men's uncontrollable sexuality as a fact, and presents women as tools for sexual pleasure. The analogy is particularly disgraceful because it is disrespectful of the humanity of both men and women; it assumes that men are sexual predators who are fundamentally disloyal and then it offers women nothing more than a choice between accepting polygyny or tolerating infidelity. Unfortunately, this line of argument is still popular among those who defend "Islamic polygyny." In her defense of polygyny, 'Aysha 'Abd al-Rahman (1913–1998) provides an example of a similar deplorable strategy:

> It might look like Islamic polygyny was a kind of women's subjection and an assertion of womens' so-called slavery. Or it might appear as if it was legislated to satisfy men. On the contrary, polygyny assigns a heavy responsibility to men and rescues Arabic women from a system that is uglier than polygyny [namely], modern slavery that grants only one woman the right to marriage and leaves the rest of the women whom the husband sleeps with, nothing more than humiliation, loss, and shame.[86]

Perhaps, most importantly, all these commonly used defenses of "Islamic polygyny" regardless of their merit share one commonality: the lack of any Qura'nic textual support. The issue of whether or not these reasons make a good case for polygyny can be debated endlessly, yet cannot be resolved according to the Qur'an. While Nina Nurmila concludes her anthropological study of the problem of polygyny in Indonesia by rejecting polygyny as an Islamic practice and asserting that "rejecting polygyny is not equivalent to rejecting Islam, but involves a view of polygyny which is different from the mainstream interpretation,"[87] I similarly conclude by rejecting polygyny, as it is commonly known and practiced. But, furthermore, I argue that this rejection is not only a new understanding that differs from the mainstream view and practice but an interpretation that is truly Qur'anic.

In sum, it is imperative to distinguish "Islamic polygyny" from "Qur'anic polygyny"; "Islamic polygyny" is profoundly defective and has no Qur'anic support of any kind. The concept itself is incompatible with Qur'anic teachings about women and marriage, and the cultural justifications cited in support of "Islamic polygyny" bear no resemblance to the Qur'an's carefully codified polygyny.

As noted, "Islamic polygyny" is closer to pre-Islamic polygyny than it is to "Qur'anic polygyny," both in nature and functionality. The so-called justifications of "Islamic polygyny" that I outline here all fail to appreciate the difference between pre-Islamic polygyny and "Qur'anic polygyny." First, the two concepts differ in terms of their functionality, since the pre-Islamic practices were no longer "necessary" once the believing community was transformed from competitive tribal enmity to coexistence through brotherhood and harmony. Second, the two concepts differ in their very nature; the Qur'an revolutionized the way women were valued. It condemns the long tradition of thinking of women as tools for breeding and sexual pleasure. Regardless of the commonly cited justifications for "Islamic polygyny" (saving women without support, balancing the population in the event that the number of unmarried women exceeds the number of available men, and so forth), the fact remains that in a majority of cases, men who seek second (or third or fourth) wives, go after younger and more attractive women, not less attractive spinsters, or poor widows. Moreover, men usually only consider polygyny when they accumulate enough wealth to make their proposal acceptable to the new wife, who would not accept an offer from an older poor man. 'Alī Ḥarb refers to women's responsibility to end polygyny; he rightly observes that polygyny is, first and foremost, practiced by women against women: "Women who denounce polygyny should convince other women to abstain from marrying a married man, the same way men refuse to marry a married woman [and have long ensured that it is not legal for a woman to marry more than one man]. Only then can women prove their equality to men and make polygyny impossible."[88]

In conclusion, I argue that there is a serious disconnect between the text of the Qur'an and the interpretation of traditional exegetes. In this chapter I distinguish between 'Qur'anic polygyny' and the way it has been practiced throughout history. The distinction I make between "Islamic polygyny" (as it is practiced) and polygyny as it appears in the Qur'an resolves the problem faced by committed Muslims who want to reject the practice of polygyny, yet believe they cannot because it is permitted according to the Qur'an. In fact, truly understanding the meaning of polygyny as it is allowed in the Qur'an—in extremely limited or even imposs circumstances—will provide these Muslims solid ground on which to reject what I have identified as "Islamic polygyny."

NOTES

1. Q.25:74.
2. Q.2:187.
3. 'Abdel Haleem, *Understanding the Qur'an*, 136.
4. This particular verse expands the options to include believing women in the broader sense, including chaste believers of the previous scriptures. This is a clear validation of the inclusiveness of the monotheistic Islamic tradition.
5. While I try to avoid discussing details of the unseen which, epistemologically speaking, can overwhelm human comprehension, I believe Q.55:56 refers to the eternal union of righteous believers with their righteous worldly spouses in heaven. I believe that we do not have enough textual evidence to conclude otherwise. The Qur'an states in Q.55:56 "their spouses" and makes it even more clear in Q.13:23 by referring to "righteous spouses"; therefore, we cannot assume otherwise or insert what does not appear in the Qur'an, simply from a desire to create a complete epistemological theory to answer our questions about the hereafter.
6. 'Abd al-Wahhāb Bouhdiba, *al-Islam wa-l-jins* (Beirut: Riyāḍ al-Rayyes, 2001), 63.
7. See similar confirmations in Q.43:70 and Q.40:8. Also, interestingly enough, Q.4:57, Q.3:15, and Q.2:25 reassert the same idea and add "pure" as a description of the status of spouses in heaven. I take this affirmation of a purified status of couples as a reference to our granted perfection in heaven. These verses might be asserting our reunion with our prefect selves in the hereafter, this reunion that we helplessly try to achieve in the worldly life. The blessed in the hereafter will suffer no more from any imperfections, no one will need to work on improving themselves, learn, lose weight, struggle against bad habits, and so on. The blessed in the hereafter—and I mean by them those who have successfully passed the earthy test—will live as the perfect version of themselves, as they will be purified from all flaws and imperfections. Therefore, spouses reunited in heaven are reunited with the perfect version of each other, not with the earthly version they know.
8. Ibn Kathīr, *Tafsīr*, 599.
9. Muḥammad al-Bukhārī, *Saḥīḥ al-Bukhārī* (Damascus and Beirut: Dār Ibn Kathīr, 2002), 49, hadith 141.
10. Muṣṭafā Maḥmūd (December 14, 2013), online: www.youtube.com/watch?v=SMuNU5ocA48.
11. Neil Malamuth, "Sexually Explicit Media, Gender Differences and Evolutionary Theory," *Journal of Communication* 46, no. 3 (1996), 13.
12. Ṣādiq Jalāl al-'Aẓīm, *Fī l-ḥubb wa-l-ḥubb al-'uthrī* (Baghdad: Dār al-Mada, 2002), 11.
13. al-'Aẓīm, *Fī l-ḥubb wa-l-ḥubb al-'uthrī*, 225.
14. 'Abd al-Raḥman Ibn Qudāma, *al-Sharḥ al-kabīr* (Aleppo: Dār al-Kitāb al-'Arabī), 7:386.
15. Ibn Qudāma, *al-Sharḥ al-kabīr*.
16. Islām al-Biḥayrī, *Zawāj al-nabī min 'Ā'isha* (Giza: al-Yawm al-Sābi', 2008)
17. For many, this is the age between eighteen and nineteen.

18. Like al-Ṭabarī, Ibn Kathīr, al-Qurṭubī, al-'Alūsī, and al-Ṭanṭāwī.

19. Muḥammad b. Aḥmad al-Qurṭubī, *al-Jāmi' li-aḥkām al-Qur'ān* (Beirut: al-Risāla, 2006), 21:51.

20. Ṣaqr 'Aṭiyya, *Fatāwa wa-aḥkām li-l-mar'a al-muslima* (Cairo: Wahba, 2006), 182.

21. Suhila Zayn al-'Abidīn Ḥamād, "Zawāj al-qāṣarāt wa-āyā wa-llaytī lam yaḥḍna," *al-Medina*, February 5, 2016.

22. Some exegetes suggested solving the issue of missed menstrual cycles by having a woman in this situation wait, after divorce, for "one year, five years, or even seven years" (al-Qurṭubī, *al-Jāmi' li-aḥkām*, 21:50). I would note that this is a particularly unreasonable interpretation, especially in light of the verse: "When you divorce women and they have reached their set time, then either keep or release them in a fair manner. Do not hold on to them with intent to harm them and commit aggression" (Q.2:231).

23. In a meaningful way, Q.56:1 asserts women's ownership of their homes by using the feminine possessive ending in "do not make them leave their homes."

24. I am using Abdel Haleem's translation here, although I ultimately reject his insertion of "[each time]."

25. Qur'an Q.2:229 asserts that divorce is allowed a maximum of three times.

26. Asma Barlas, *Believing Women in Islam* (Austin: University of Texas Press, 2002), 189.

27. Barazangi, *Woman's Identity*, 52.

28. Rashīd Riḍā, *Ḥuqūq al-nisā' fī l-Islām* (Beirut and Damascus: al-Maktab al-Islāmī, 1984), 55.

29. Ali, *The Position of Women*, 55.

30. 'Abdallāh Ibn 'Abbās, *Tanwīr al-miqbās min tafsīr Ibn 'Abbās* (Beirut: Dār al-Kutub al-'Ilmiyya, 1992), 91.

31. Ibn 'Āshūr, *al-Taḥrīr*, 5:44.

32. Chaudhry, *Domestic Violence*, 14.

33. Daniel C. Maguire and Sadiyya Shaikh, *Violence Against Women in Contemporary World Religions* (Cleveland, OH: Pilgrim Press, 2007), 89.

34. Maguire and Shaikh, *Violence Against Women in Contemporary World Religions*, 74.

35. Laleh Bakhtiar, "On the Misinterpretation of 4:34 in the Quran," January 16, 2011; available online: https://www.youtube.com/watch?v=833pm2pOhgw, accessed April 9, 2018.

36. Laleh Bakhtiar, *The Sublime Qur'an* (Chicago: Kazi Publishers, 2007), 4:34.

37. I do not address the issue of illiteracy of Muḥammad, as it is unrelated to the present discussion.

38. Kecia Ali, "On Critique and Careful Reading," *Journal of Feminist Studies in Religion* 32, no. 2 (2006), 122.

39. Ziauddin Sardar, *Reading the Qur'an: The Contemporary Relevance of the Sacred Text of Islam* (Oxford and New York: Oxford University Press, 2011), 60.

40. As mentioned before, I will end my discussion by proposing a new translation for 4:34.

41. I have already introduced a new translation for this part as "Men are the financial guardians of women, [men] whom God has favored some of them to others,

and those who spend from their money". But for consistency here I am using 'Abdel Haleem same translation. Eventually, I will end the discussion by providing my final translation of all parts of Q.4:34.

42. As I argue here and in other places *nushūz*—as a Qur'anic term—is only wrongly believed to be exclusive to marital high-handedness.

43. Simone de Beauvoir, *The Second Sex* (New York: Vintage Books, 2010), 96.

44. Note that in the Qur'an, the second worst sin (second only to apostasy) is mistreating elderly parents; this should motivate us to rethink the way the Qur'an prioritizes the rights of vulnerable subgroups in a social construction. See Qur'an Q.17:23.

45. al-Ṭabarī, *Jāmi' al-bayān*, 2:452.

46. *al-Wasīṭ* (Cairo: al-Shurūq al-Dawaliyya, 2004).

47. In Q. 4:15, the word, *bayt* refers to a punishment that can be best described as lifelong exile from the community and not imprisonment in one room.

48. While the Qur'an provides gender neutral punishments for specific crimes, like stealing and publicly witnessed adultery, the broader juristic guidance here addresses other violations committed by women.

49. Rethinking physical punishments as valid legal correction methods and even abandoning them doesn't violate the general Qur'anic guidance that leaves it to public authorities to decide what works best for each community as long as these local legislations are guided by the general Qur'anic guidance we find in Q.4:58 which stresses justice as the only condition—as I referred to previously.

50. Russell Clark and Elaine Hatfield, "Gender Differences in Receptivity to Sexual Offers," *Journal of Psychology and Human Sexuality* 2, no. 1 (1989), 51.

51. 'Abdel Haleem's translation.

52. I am not arguing here for marital disobedience. To the opposite, marital obedience can be considered one way of applying God's commands. All what I am arguing for here is to dismiss limiting obedience in Q.4:34 to marital obedience, because this limits the general meaning in the verse to one specific meaning with no textual support.

53. Translated by Abla Hasan.

54. Muḥammad Shaḥrūr, *Nahw awsūl jadīda lī-l-fikr al-Islāmī* (Damascus: al-Ahali, 2000), 350.

55. As we read in Q.12:29.

56. al-Qurṭubī, *al-Jāmi' li-aḥkām*, 7:162.

57. al-Ṭabarī, *Jāmi' al-bayān*, 2:571.

58. Ibid.

59. al-Ṭabarī, *Jāmi' al-bayān*, 2:572.

60. Ibn Baz, *Nūr 'alā l-darb* (Riyadh: al-Riyāsa al-'Āma li-l-Buḥūth al-'Ilmiyya wa-l-Iftā', 2011), 21:347.

61. al-Rāzī, *al-Tafsīr*, 11:66.

62. Muḥammad Mutwalī l-Sha'rāwī, *Tafsīr al-Sha'rāwī* (N.p.: Akhbār al-Yawm, 1991), 2684.

63. Below, I discuss the issue that "Islamic" polygyny differs from "Qur'anic" polygyny.

64. Traditional exegetes did not discuss the idea that husbands may also become less attractive as they age!

65. B. O. Yusuf, "Feminism in the Shade of the Qur'an," *Journal of Nigerian Association of Arabic and Islamic Studies* 15, no. 1 (2000), 78.

66. Rashīd Riḍā, *Tafsīr al-manār* (Egypt: Dār al-Manār, 1947), 4:350.

67. 'Alī Sharīa'tī, *Mas'ūliyyāt al-mar'a* (Beirut: al-Amīr, 2007), 69.

68. al-'Alawī, *Fuṣūl 'an al-mar'ā*, 77.

69. May Ziāda, *Bahithat al-badiyya* (Beirut: Mu'assasat Nawfil, 1983), 28.

70. Ahmed E. Souaiaia, *Contesting Justice: Women, Islam, Law, and Society* (Albany: State University of New York Press, 2008), 56.

71. Translated by Abla Hasan. I translate *yatamā* as orphans, not as "orphan girls."

72. As it is commonly misunderstood.

73. The word *yatamā* is generally translated as "orphan," though in Arabic it refers specifically to a child who has lost his or her father. That is, in the Islamic context, an "orphan" is a child who has no means of financial support (as this is the responsibility of the father, not necessarily the mother).

74. It is understood that dealing justly with orphans relates to polygyny, as the intent is for men who take second wives to marry widows with "orphans" (i.e., fatherless children) who need financial support.

75. While everything illegal should be considered irreligious, the opposite does not apply. Some things may be legal but not religiously permitted (e.g., drinking alcohol, for Muslims).

76. I am not dealing here with complicated cases of minorities living in authoritarian or oppressive secular countries that choose to treat everything religious as illegal. However, I can still assert my argument even in those extreme cases. Because according to the Qur'anic guidance we find in Q.4:97, it is an obligation to leave such countries where no freedom of belief or expression is allowed. In extreme cases where leaving is not even an option the complete absence of the right to practice religion due to compulsion can turn the irreligious act religious for the lack of autonomy required for any religious act to count as religious. This is asserted in Q.2:286. No one can be held accountable for what he/she is forced to do or forced to leave.

77. Muḥammad Shaḥrūr, *Fiqh al-mar'a* (N.p.: al-Ahali, 2000), 304.

78. al-Bukhārī, *Ṣaḥīḥ al-Bukhārī*, 1724, hadith number 6965.

79. Muḥammad Shaḥrur and Andreas Christmann, *The Qur'an, Morality and Critical Reason: The Essential Muhammad Shahrur* (Leiden and Boston: Brill, 2009), 303.

80. Ibn Baz, *Nūr 'alā l-darb*, 21:337.

81. Anwar al-Jundī, *al-Mar'a al-muslima fī wajh al-tahddiyyat* (Cairo: Dār al-I'tisām, 1979), 43; Nūr al-Dīn 'Atr, *Mādha 'an al-mar'a?* (Damascus and Beirut: al-Yamama, 2003), 184.

82. Ibn Baz, *Nūr 'alā l-darb*, 21:337.

83. Barlas, *Believing Women*, 191.

84. Martha Nussbaum, "Objectification," *Philosophy and Public Affairs* 24, no. 4 (1995), 257.

85. Fatima Mernissi, *Ma wara' al-ḥijāb* (Casablanca: al-Fanak, 2005), 39.

86. 'Ā'isha 'Abd al-Raḥmān, *Nisā' al-nabī* (Beirut: Dār al-Kitāb al-'Arabī, 1979), 24.

87. Nina Nurmila, *Women, Islam and Everyday Life: Renegotiating Polygyny in Indonesia* (New York: Routledge, 2009), 174.

88. Ḥarb, *al-Ḥub wa-l-fanā'*, 55.

Chapter 4

Female Body-Ownership

In this chapter, I begin by analyzing one of the most notable aspects of Muslim women's appearance in public, namely, *ḥijāb*. I introduce the Islamic feminist philosophy that lies behind it and clarify the confusion created by the various controversial scholarly views on *ḥijāb*. The fundamental question generally underlying these controversies relates to whether or not the Qur'an mandates *ḥijāb*. In this chapter, I consider modesty as a way of dressing and as a way of life, that is, I address its role with regard to appearance and as an expression of behavior or mentality.

MODESTY IN THE QUR'AN

Modesty as an obligation is mentioned in two verses in the Qur'an, in Q.24:30–31 and in Q.33:59. I begin with Q.24:30–31,

> Tell believing men to lower their glances and guard their private parts: that is purer for them. God is well aware of everything they do. [30] And tell believing women that they should lower their glances, guard their private parts, and not display their charms beyond what [it is acceptable] to reveal; they should let their headscarves fall to cover their necklines and not reveal their charms except to their husbands, their fathers, their husbands' fathers, their sons, their husbands' sons, their brothers, their brothers' sons, their sisters' sons, their womenfolk, their slaves, such men as attend them who have no desire, or children who are not yet aware of women's nakedness; they should not stamp their feet so as to draw attention to any hidden charms. Believers, all of you, turn to God so that you may prosper. (Q.24:30–31)

> Second, we read in Q.33:59, "Prophet, tell your wives, your daughters, and women believers to make their outer garments hang low over them so as to be recognized and not insulted." (Q.33:59)

First, the command of modesty focuses on modest behavior through modest dressing. This means that dressing appropriately is only one step among other steps Muslim men and women should implement in order to live a righteous lifestyle. It is clear from these verses that the command for believers—both men and women—to lower their gaze precedes the other commands; this clearly indicates a behavioral discipline that includes both appearance and conduct. Second, despite the common idea that the requirement for modesty is centered on women, the verse addresses both men and women equally. Interestingly, the verse starts by addressing men and then addresses women with the commandment to consider the way they dress in public. This simple observation stands in contrast to the later patriarchal developments in which the concept of modesty was gradually reconstructed along cultural norms to justify gender-based segregation, opposition to women's work and education, and even to prohibit women's full and unconditional participation in legal, political, and economic affairs. As we see, these sexist attitudes were adopted to fulfill this twisted understanding of women's duty to guard their modesty, and as part of a total denial that men have the same duty to guard their modesty as well, though the commandment to men has never been interpreted the same way.

Third, the generality and the flexibility of the Qur'anic description of *ziinā*, translated here as "charms," shows tolerance; the verse can be interpreted broadly to meet the changing spatiotemporal, cultural, and ethnic needs. Fourth, as in the previous verse, women are advised to hide their desirable characteristics and reveal only what it is acceptable to reveal. Again, the question of what is considered acceptable is also left open, for the same reason. Here, it is necessary to reflect on the Arabic verse, to explain what acceptable refers to. In Arabic, the command for women "not to display their charms beyond what [it is acceptable] to reveal" shifts from "believing women" as the subject of the command to "charms" as the subject in referring to what can be shown, though both verbs are directly connected by the conjunction *wa* (and), which normally appears between similar linguistic constructions. The verse says that women should not intentionally reveal their charms, except for what might accidentally appear by itself (*wa-lā yubdīna zinatahunna illā mā ẓahara minha*). That is, the adornment that is acceptable to be revealed is what is revealed by itself, without intention; this is the adornment that appears accidentally, as a woman moves throughout her day or while performing her job. Therefore, I believe the best way to translate the verse is to refer to the absence of intentionality; this is accomplished by adding a parenthetical expression like, "[accidentally shown] adornment."

Fifth, the preposition *min* which means "some of," in "tell believing men to lower their glances" (Q.24:30) indicates, as Muḥammad Shaḥrūr makes clear,[1] that the commandment to men and women is to lower their gaze somewhat, not entirely, when they meet someone from the opposite gender. For Shaḥrūr, this command was left general so that it could be interpreted according to different cultural and spatiotemporal norms. In addition, the verse might refer to different types of glances—as not all glances are equally permissible. Clearly, glancing at someone is not the same as staring at him or her lustfully. As Yusuf Sidani aptly observes, this verse does not mean that men cannot look at women at all or women cannot look at men at all. If the verse had been meant in this way, it would exclude women from public life, and the political sphere (and this would necessitate parallel gender-segregated public institutions), not instruct men and women to lower their gazes.

> It is impossible to envisage two parallel political structures, one for men and the other for women. Thus, while women can operate within their own female-only business institutions, they cannot have their own separate political ones. As a result, under this understanding, women have to be mostly secluded from political participation.[2]

Sixth, from reading "they should let their headscarves fall to cover their necklines" (Q.24:30), we can easily see how the verse asserts that the command extends the cover usually understood as the head cover to include covering the bosom. Here, it is necessary to mention that despite the sound consensus of the mainstream understanding of the Qur'anic *ḥijāb*[3] as the requirement to cover the body except for the face and the hands, this part of the verse remains controversial for many. The controversy regards whether the verse commands women to cover their bosom solely, or does it mean that women should cover all of their bodies including the bosom. For example, Marnia Lazreg (b. 1941) concludes the following from the mention of "private parts" and "necklines" in the previously mentioned reading of Q.24:30, "To be crude about it, since the text mentions bosoms and pudenda, dressing in a way that does not reveal these would satisfy any requirements of appropriate dress for women."[4]

In fact, the question of the extent of *ḥijāb*, whether it is exclusively meant to cover the bosom and the private parts, or more, seems first to ignore a fundamental aspect of Islam as a religion. Islam was not revealed as a new religion; rather, Islam, as the Qur'an repeatedly confirms, came as a revival and renewal of the ongoing Abrahamic tradition.[5] Islam came to revive monotheism and purify it from man-made impurities.[6] In this particular case, by recalling the Abrahamic roots[7] of the Qur'anic commandment to dress and behave modestly, we see a paradigm of what modesty should mean, which is not an exclusive command to cover the bosom and the private parts. The same can be equally applied to the various commands toward moral behavior and devotion that, despite significant variation, undeniably share a foundation of morality and rationality. Second, the reduction of what needs to be covered to "private parts" and "necklines" ignores the linguistic observation that the real command in (Q.24: 30) is not simply to "cover" the "private parts" but to "guard" the "private parts" as we read, " Tell believing men to lower their glances and guard their private parts: that is purer for them. God is well aware of everything they do" (Q.24:30). This command which uses a metaphoric language to command the avoidance of anything leading to sexual misconduct clearly goes beyond the simplicity suggested by the mere covering of one's "private parts." Third, this narrow interpretation leaves behind the command for women not to display "their charms" in (Q.24:31) which refers to more than the "bosoms" and the "private parts," unless a woman's beauty is restricted to her bosoms and private parts! In short, limiting what needs to be covered to ones' "bosoms" and "private parts" is not really supported by what a comprehensible reading of the text can easily support.

Seventh, in addition to the question whether *ḥijāb* can be understood as the command to cover the body including the bosom or should it be restricted to covering the bosom—the opinion that I have already dismissed—another question deals with whether the *ḥijāb* commandment was equally addressed to free women and slave girls. For example, Shahrur argues that the idea of *ḥijāb*, as a way to prevent women from seducing men, has no legal nor religious basis; instead, he argues that *ḥijāb* was made obligatory in response to an "exceptional case"[8] in the newly formed community of Medina, where it was approved as a tool of social demarcation, to make it easier to distinguish free women from slave girls. He argues that this distinction was necessary, since free women were supposed to be treated with dignity and respect, while concubines, who were free to reveal their attractiveness, were considered and treated as sexual commodities in the market. Likewise, Fatima Mernissi argues that *ḥijāb* was a necessary social tool used by free women to protect themselves from the harassment of the "hypocrites of Medina,"[9] who used the difficulties of distinguishing free women from slave women as an excuse for harassing women. For Mernissi, *ḥijāb* was and still is a critical issue in the Islamic community because women's bodies are viewed as "symbolic representation of the community"[10] that needs to be protected by shutting it out of the world.

This understanding of *ḥijāb* as an obsolete cultural practice or as a mechanism of cultural resistance depends on a special interpretation of the expression "to be recognized" in Q.33:59 (which I discuss in detail later): "Prophet, tell your wives, your daughters, and women believers to make their outer garments hang low over them so as to be recognized and not insulted" (Q.33:59). This verse has been used extensively by opponents of *ḥijāb* to argue that it is a tool to divide society racially and socially; that it enables people to distinguish slaves from free women, even from a distance.

I reject this argument for *ḥijāb* as a mere cultural practice and as a social tool that can be used by free women to be recognized since it has no Qur'anic support. The Qur'an addresses the believing community as one community. There is no Qur'anic support to assert that the verses related to *ḥijāb* are addressed only to free women and not to the whole community. The problem of slavery already existed when the Qur'an was revealed; the Qur'an addresses it clearly, in other places. Therefore, Qur'anic verses that do not mention slaves literally and clearly should not be interpreted as being related to the issue of slavery.[11] More importantly, this interpretation of the verse changes the Qur'anic text into a discriminatory dialogue and implies that the Qur'an gives men permission to harass slave women; as if men only needed to be able to distinguish them from free women in order to know who to harass. Finally, in addition to missing any Qur'anic support since the verse does not mention any free/slave distinction but uses the expressions "believing men" and "believing women" as its addresses, and in addition to violating the Qur'anic repeated confirmations of people's equality regardless of their social status,[12] this interpretation is clearly incompatible with the passage commanding men to guard their gaze, that is, with regard to all women (not just free women).

Eighth, at the other end of the spectrum, and contrary to the argument that *ḥijāb* is not a Qur'anic obligation and should be restricted to slave women, another interpretation takes an extreme view of defining the required modesty referred to in the Qur'an. This argument not only acknowledges *ḥijāb* as a requirement that includes head covering but uses this obligation to justify restrictive criteria that transformed modesty from a prerequisite for women's participation in the public realm into a justification to ban women from participation in society, or even from being seen in public. According to this conservative approach, *ḥijāb*, which was commanded as a way to enable women to engage in social and economic affairs, by minimizing a sexually-charged public atmosphere, was used to justify the total exclusion of women from public life. For example, despite his sexist reading of the Qur'an, 'Abbās Maḥmūd al-'Aqqād (1889–1964) recognized that *ḥijāb* offered women better options in public. He says, "What can be understood about *ḥijāb* is clear and does not require interpretation, it does not mean that women should be hidden or imprisoned in their homes, because the command to guard the gaze is not consistent with hiding women in their homes."[13]

Many conservative interpretations of *ḥijāb* went beyond the Qur'anic message and further restricted what Qur'anic modesty represents. For example, many scholars claim that it is necessary to cover the face, as part of the obligation of modesty mentioned in the Qur'an. Another narrow understanding limits what is revealed accidentally to a woman's family and blood relatives (*maḥrām*) named in the Qur'an. A similar restriction goes far beyond the prohibition of lustful staring—as we have seen in the Qur'anic text—to include every kind of gaze between men and women. In his book, 'Abd al-Qādir al-Sanadī argues in favor of this view, which was adopted by many scholars, including Ibn Taymiyya (1263–1328).[14] Al-Sanadī says, "Many scholars believe that women should not look at men with lust or without lust."[15]

THE MEANING OF *ADHA* IN Q.33:59: WHY DO MUSLIM WOMEN WEAR *ḤIJĀB*?

As noted, Q.33:59 has been used extensively by opponents of *ḥijāb* to argue that it is a tool to divide society racially and socially; that it enables people to distinguish slaves from free women, even from a distance. "Prophet, tell your wives, your daughters, and women believers to make their outer garments hang low over them so as to be recognized and not insulted" (Q.33:59). This interpretation of the verse changes the Qur'anic text into a discriminatory dialogue, which I have argued against before. But, what does the phrase "so as to be recognized and not insulted (*yu'adhīna*)"[16] mean? We must pay special attention to this part of the verse, since this is what caused many scholars to believe that the commandment was addressed to free women who wanted to be recognizable. The verse states that women should consider *ḥijāb* as a way to avoid *adha*. In the Qur'an *adha* stands for "minor harm" as we see in the reading "they will not do you much harm [except for *adha*]: even if they come out to fight you, they will soon turn tail; they will get no help" (Q.3:111).[17] This reference is particularly important in terms of modern feminist arguments against misogynous attempts to normalize rape, or what is known as victim-blaming arguments (referred to as rape-culture theory). Regardless of these arguments, which were first coined by Western feminists, the tools and ideologies used in arguments that implicitly or explicitly blame or demonize victims of rape are relevant to many misleading pro-*ḥijāb* arguments. Some of these arguments claim that *ḥijāb* is a tool to protect women from men's "uncontrollable" sexuality. In fact, as the previous verse clarifies, it is incorrect to think of *ḥijāb* as a defensive tool, because the Qur'anic term *adha* (minor harm or annoyance)[18] does not refer to sexual assault or a serious attack like rape. The semantic argument in Q.33:59 refers to minor harm that may occur as a result of violating the commandment.

Minor harm may refer to miscommunication that could annoy women or cause misunderstandings in public. This expression does not refer to serious physical or psychological harm; rather, it is a sort of minor annoyance that is not criminal in intention or action. It is can be understood as awkward social situations that are ideally avoided. *Ḥijāb* is an Islamic command addressed to a community of believing women and believing men, who are expected not to act as rapists and sexual predators. While minor harmful social miscommunication between men and women varies from community to community and from culture to culture, in our time, it may include being asked out by men whose intentions are not serious. Muslim women might wear *ḥijāb*, among other reasons, to indicate that they are serious believers interested only in marriage and in serious relations leading to marriage. According to the Qur'anic criterion we find in Q.4:25, "so marry them with their people's consent and their proper bride-gifts, [making them] married women, not adulteresses or lovers" Muslim women should only be interested in serious offers with the goal of marriage[19]. When correctly understood, *ḥijāb* assures men and women that they are serious and interested in marriage. Yet this should not be understood as an indication that women who do not wear *ḥijāb* are less serious, because verbal and behavioral communication also has an important role; indeed it can either replace or complement the visual social communication of *ḥijāb*.

Thus, *Ḥijāb* is a simple social message sent by women to facilitate healthy communication in daily life. In principle, *ḥijāb* indicates a woman's seriousness and religious devotion. By dressing modestly, women can use *ḥijāb* to avoid unintentional annoyance caused, mainly, by misunderstandings and innocent ignorance. More importantly, they can avoid getting too emotionally involved in less serious relations. *Ḥijāb* is better understood as an unspoken social gesture indicating a woman's disinterest in casual sex or pointless dating. Women dressed in *ḥijāb* make a public statement by distinguishing themselves from other women in the community, who might view these options differently.

This explanation of *ḥijāb* is not meant to imply that unveiled women are less virtuous, serious, and devout than veiled women. Rather, my argument emphasizes that *ḥijāb* is one option among many other options a woman can utilize when in public; it is a visual method to publicly communicate her attitude (particularly if her *ḥijāb* is accompanied by equally modest behavior). *Ḥijāb* is one way to help facilitate women's full and equal public engagement and enable women to avoid annoyance, miscommunication, and wasted time. In sum, *ḥijāb* is neither a way to recognize free women from slaves nor a protective tool that can help avoid rape and sexual harassment; it is rather a demarcation and an unspoken social gesture of a woman's high expectations and seriousness.

LIBERATED BY *ḤIJĀB*

Ḥijāb has multiple functions, one of which is a symbolic social gesture that indicates high expectations of men. Second, in the Western world, where, "the popular media situates the veiled Muslim woman as a symbol of both gender inequality in Islam and of the perceived incapacity of Islam to exist in the liberal West,"[20] *ḥijāb* is in fact a symbol of resistance to a culture that continues to insist on media stereotypes of Muslim women. *Ḥijāb* is largely misunderstood even by Western feminists who "want to apply their own perspective about women's rights because according to them it is the norm."[21]Third, the Qur'anic concept of modesty reflects a deeply consolidated social system[22] that views happiness, including but not limited to marital happiness, as a project that can be fulfilled if it is sought collectively. As we have seen, Islam replaced pre-Islamic tribal enmity with brotherhood in religion and replaced the competition for survival with humanitarian and religious altruism[23] as a way to secure individual life through a collective social selflessness. In an ideal Islamic society, where women are modest in appearance and behavior, and where men avoid lustful staring (and certainly pornography, which is a modern extreme of this), every woman can be (not just metaphorically but literally) the only woman[24] in her husband's life. In this sense, marital happiness from an Islamic perspective goes beyond the boundaries of the individual husband and wife pair and becomes societal. An ideal Qur'anic community helps men and women preserve their decency. This is completely the opposite of what we find in society today, where every kind of social mixing involves sexual pressure of all types. Of course, marital fidelity is the responsibility of each couple, it is a result of their commitment, but realistically speaking, if marital fidelity is socially difficult, couples will face more unfortunate outcomes. Roy F. Baumeister provides a realistic approach; he highlights the difficulty of resisting temptation, instead of ignoring its existence:

> Certainly anyone who watches the news knows that many men, even highly respectable, prominent, successful men, have done sexual things of which they were ashamed. We have seen presidents and presidential candidates admit to sexual misdeeds that compromised their careers. We have seen senators and congressmen admit to doing things in public restrooms or in their offices that have made them laughingstocks. Are these men somehow atypical? More likely these incidents are the tip of the iceberg. These men were caught because they were such public figures that when they do what many other men do, the media are eager to report on them. There are many things men could mean when they say they have been ashamed by something sexual they once did. It is not just having sex with the wrong person or wrong type of person. It may include making inappropriate advances. It may include misleading a woman such as by pretending to be in love with her in order to convince her to have sex. It may have been trying again after she said no once.

> Before we condemn men as hopeless sinners, however—and I suspect many men regard themselves as such, at least when they reflect on their attempts to come to terms with the inner sexual beast—we might feel a moment of sympathy for their unrewarded successes. How many times on the dance floor, possibly head swimming with too many drinks, did he want to reach out and touch some woman's derriere, and yet he resisted? How many times did he stop as soon as the woman with whom he was necking said to stop? (Research has suggested that most women have said "no" when they meant "yes" at least occasionally, which introduces a further element of confusion to even the most well-intentioned young man.) He doesn't get any credit for all the times he stifles his desires, despite all the struggle and sacrifice that they cost him.[25]

Fourth, *ḥijāb* should be an option, given that women's sexual objectification is an ongoing reality. *Ḥijāb*, as viewed by Muslim women, is an active response that goes beyond the denial of patriarchy. *Ḥijāb* is an authentic act designed to enable women to reclaim gender equality. It is a way of completely transcending the societal values in which women are obliged to show more of their bodies to gain social approval or professional opportunities. *Ḥijāb* is better viewed as a recusant feminist attempt to stop the social objectification of women, which, as Diana Russell states, is "not confirmed to pornography. It is also a staple of mainstream movies, ads, record covers, songs, magazines, television, art, cartoons, literature, pin-ups, and so on, as well as being a way of conceptualizing how many men learn to see women."[26] But more importantly, *ḥijāb* seems to be needed today, probably more than any time before. The ways women are routinely portrayed in media today are a clear indication that a modern metamorphosis has taken place, changing historical patriarchy into a new and carefully disguised form. While the sad reality of the exploitation of women's body images remains a fact, modern male–centered evaluative criteria seem to have successfully replaced the overt exploitation of women in new and more carefully masked ways. Fatima Mernissi brings our attention to the seriousness of the less visible ways Western men use to control women as she makes a distinction between the Orient's "space harem" and the Occident's "time harem." She explains the difference as she says,

> These Western attitudes, I thought, are even more dangerous and cunning that the Muslim ones because the weapon used against women is time. Time is less visible, more fluid than space. The Western man uses images and spotlights to freeze female beauty within an idealized childhood, and forces women to perceive aging—that normal unfolding of the years—as a shameful devaluation. . . . The violence embodied in the Western harem is less visible than in the Eastern harem because aging is not attacked directly, but rather masked as an aesthetic choice.[27]

The concept of *ḥijāb* transforms women's physical appearance into a specific feminine attitude of the world. This is in fact a sophisticated, yet outwardly simple, way of communicating socially; it is a social habit that sends an instantaneous public message. Elena-Larisa Stanciu and Bjørn Christensen highlight the strength of visual messages when both the visual and ontological aspects are considered simultaneously: "This practice of constructing and defining social groups and individuals at an ontological level starting from mere visual traits of their corporeality is necessarily imbued with elements of social 'habit,' which relies primarily on a visual register."[28]

Specifically, the social message that *ḥijāb* helps a woman to communicate is a revolutionary feminist position against emotional exploitation in the modern culture in which casual sexual encounters have proven to be more emotionally harmful to women than men. To avoid trivializing this problem, and to appreciate how casual sexuality affects women negatively, it is useful to reflect on these numbers,

> A recent study of the hook-up culture at Princeton University reveals that before the hook-up, girls expect emotional involvement almost twice as often as guys, and 34 percent hope "a relationship might evolve." Guys, more than girls, are in part motivated by hopes of improving their social reputation, or of bragging about their exploits to friends the next day. After the hook-up, 91 percent of girls admit to having feelings of regret, at least occasionally. Guilt and "feeling used" is commonly cited, and overall, 80 percent of girls wish the hookup hadn't happened. Other studies have shown that 84 percent of women said that after having sex a few times, even with someone they didn't want to be emotionally involved with, they begin to feel vulnerable and would at least like to know if the other person cares about them.[29]

For veiled Muslim women, values related to some media-made modern standards (e.g., being a "hot chick," "arm candy," or a "sex kitten") are offensive and unacceptable in public and beyond the strict boundaries of the private realm. These values, driven by the media, compel women to "view themselves as objects,"[30] and have been repeatedly proven to be damaging, as "the exposure to the televised sexual objectification of women cultivates a particular view of the self, a view that emphasizes the importance of physical appearance."[31] A study targeting body image among British Muslim women suggests that "participants who wore the hijab generally had more positive body image, were less reliant on media messages about beauty ideals, and placed less importance on appearance than participants who did not wear the hijab."[32]

Today, men have proven themselves the more stable and more reasonable gender by the way they address the needs of life and the practical demands of the work place. Unfortunately, many women still lag behind. Simple observations reveal this: men do not seek social validation by showing more skin, they do not walk in uncomfortable and unhealthy high heels, they do not blindly respond to whatever the fashion industry demands, and the majority do not feel an uncontrollable urge to maximize their sex appeal, especially in inappropriate situations (for example, in work environments). Paradoxically, men continue to prove themselves capable of resisting this collective media-created sexual hypnotism. They manage to distance themselves from this physical competition to be the sexiest man. For example, in a professional meeting, in political analyses on TV, or in a morning show, while men are dressed casually or formally in suits or jeans that cover their bodies, women appear in miniskirts, suits with cleavage, or revealing short dresses. The fact that our male-centered media and fashion industry have normalized this practice (of scantily dressed women and modestly and comfortably dressed men) should cause us to reconsider what lies behind a collective mentality that makes nudity an appealing choice for women and an implausible option for men. The rational choice that some Muslim women have made to dress and behave modestly should not be criticized by the Western media, which adopts a double standard in viewing men's modesty as normal and women's modesty as a dissonant unfashionable choice that they assume must have been taken under duress.

In the modern world, which is totally dominated by Western male-centric norms, men are secure enough that they do not feel the need to highlight their physical masculinity unless this is part of their profession. Yet, many women seem to have lost their way; they insist that they are free from male-centric norms, but they are not. For men, with the exception of specific jobs (circuses, stripteases, wrestling programs, etc.) that require physical exploitation as part of the profession, they do not seem to feel the need to wear inappropriately sexy clothing to demonstrate their physical masculinity and sexual attractiveness, explicitly nor implicitly, not even to show that they are free from social norms and expectations. Unfortunately, many, if not a majority of women, still insist on seeking men's approval, even when they pretend to be doing the opposite. I am not arguing that men should be as sexualized the way women are; on the contrary, I am observing that when women choose modesty, it is perceived as such an implausible choice that the automatic assumption is that she must have been coerced or brainwashed. The fact that this assumption is normal should offend free women if, in fact, they are just as free to conform as they are to reject societal norms. Modesty should be treated as an acceptable norm for women, the same way it is treated as an acceptable norm for men.

In a world that is still dominated by women's sexualization, commercialization, and objectification of the female body, Muslim women should be able to choose to make a statement by committing themselves to modesty. This understanding of *ḥijāb* is particularly relevant to women's struggle for gender equality, because every outward action and attitude has a meaning. A woman chooses casual versus formal, decent versus revealing, modern versus classical, ethnic versus universal, and so on. Lila Abu-Lughod (b. 1952) rightly comments on this point by saying, "If we think that U.S. women live in a world of choice regarding clothing, we might also remind ourselves of the expression, 'the tyranny of fashion.'"[33] This being said, it will take time and effort for women who are constantly bombarded by ads, pictures, and male-centered agendas to advocate a sexual role that overpowers all other roles, to stand up to this systematic misogynous brainwashing, and any temptation to participate in a valuation system that is based on any criteria other than women's talent, merit, and ability. Islamic feminism undoubtedly shares a great deal with Western feminism; most notably, they share the belief that "until the day women's bodies are not used to sell cars, cosmetics are not a necessity to the success of a woman's image, and we are not humiliated and tortured for male pleasure, women will have no rights."[34]

However, *ḥijāb* is not the only way to be modest or for women to liberate themselves from male-centered norms. Women can respond to these challenges by asserting their full dignity and equality in a number of ways. My argument does not negate the fact that many women are able to free themselves from this game, even without divine guidance. Many women are modest in their own way; they know when and how to set boundaries about the way they appear or behave in public. Modesty comes in all shapes and forms. Islamic modesty is one way of being modest, perhaps the preferable choice for Muslim women, but this does not mean that women cannot practice modesty in any number of ways. The Qur'anic guidance on modesty is one choice among many; for Muslim women it is an informative decision they can take rationally, to adopt a true sense of women's liberation through their clothing.

Fifth, *hijāb* is an Islamic commitment. Any argument for *ḥijāb* in isolation from it as a religious obligation that is literally and specifically mentioned in the Qur'an does not address the core of it. It does not make sense to argue that non-Muslim women should consider *ḥijāb* or think of it the way Muslim women do. I am only inviting non-Muslims to try to understand the reasons Muslim women cover themselves. It is a specific religious obligation that, in addition to its rationality, speaks to a specific religious commitment and devotion. Like any other religious commitment, the commitment to *ḥijāb* is essentially conditioned by a devout religious attitude which, logically speaking, includes accepting God as a deity, Muhammad as a messenger, and the Qur'an as literal divine guidance. To elaborate more, accepting any given law, social norm, or even religious obligation comes, in addition to accepting its rationale, as part of a holistic attitude of recognition, trust, and even submission. To give a simple example, when someone drives and he/she reads a sign indicating a speed limit of 40 km/h, then a speed limit of 25 km/h, and then a speed limit of 60 km/h, he/she does not fully analyze the reason and rationale for the change in these speed limit signs, rather, he/she does his/her best to trust and then follow them. Likewise, the strict adoption of the Islamic code of dressing known as *ḥijāb* is an argument specific to committed Muslim women. As I asserted in the introduction, this book is an academic yet Islamically oriented book; therefore, my argument for *ḥijāb* is only intended to explain what *ḥijāb* means for Muslim women.

HIJĀB AS A FREE CHOICE

The concept of *ḥijāb* as a free choice is still not well understood. *Ḥijāb* is not an issue of wearing a forced scarf on one's head; it is a lifetime commitment, one that loses all meaning if it is not based on free choice. *Ḥijāb*, as conceptualized in the Qur'an, "needs to be a personal decision made in good faith according to a woman's own understanding of God's commands."[35] Circumspect autonomy is the essential concomitant to transform *ḥijāb* from a way of dressing to a liberal philosophy. Unfortunately, *ḥijāb* as a free feminist choice is seldom understood and much less appreciated. Ironically, *ḥijāb* as a free choice is misunderstood equally by Western media and Muslim traditionalists. In the West, as Sylvia Chan-Malik rightly observes, "when Muslim women are visible, they are largely portrayed as 'over there,' the objects of Western feminist pity living under oppressive regimes in the Middle East."[36] From a Western point of view, those who choose *ḥijāb* "don't know any better, and one day, with guidance and continued freedom, they will be enlightened and stop veiling."[37] Muslim traditionalists on the other hand who hold extreme views about the obligatory nature of *ḥijāb* do not give women the right to accept or reject it; for them, the idea of *ḥijāb* as a free choice is still quite threatening. This attitude about *ḥijāb* may be social initially, but it also has political implications. In the Middle East, *ḥijāb* as a free choice was often not an option. Regimes and governments, uprisings and revolutions, totalitarian powers and their opposition, all involve women's bodies in their political games and maneuvers. Mohja Kahf (b. 1967) reminds us that "forced unveiling"[38] was used systematically as part of government policy in Turkey, Tunisia, Iraq, and Syria; it brought humiliation to countless women. Ironically, when this humiliation to women's free will and autonomy ended in some parts of the Arab world, the ban on veiling was replaced by a ban on unveiling, as in the radical Islamic movements that have swept through the Arab world more recently.

Ḥijāb as a Qur'anic commandment can't be fulfilled if not viewed and adopted as a free choice for three reasons. First because freedom constitutes a condition to validate *ḥijāb* as a moral choice. In fact, "no deed of any moral value can be done that is not done by autonomous, voluntary choice,"[39] as Omar Edward Moad asserts. It is this freedom that allows for the "liberalism of Islam,"[40] which Moad explains by saying,

> Freedom, in the proper sense, is, therefore, a necessary condition of any human moral value. Simply put, people cannot be forced to be good, or manipulated into being good, or brainwashed into being good. Of course, they can be forced, manipulated, brainwashed, or otherwise coerced into doing that which would have real moral value if they were to do so freely. But doing so under coercion would be morally worthless.[41]

Second, autonomy does not only constitute a condition for an act or commitment to be moral but to be rightly considered religious. We read "there is no compulsion in religion: true guidance has become distinct from error" (Q.2:256). Third, the specific declaration we find in Q.33:59 that women can be "recognized" and distinguished as a virtuous woman because they wear *ḥijāb* is a clear assurance that *ḥijāb* is a free choice and a decision for committed Muslim women. A woman's choice to distinguish herself from others by dressing in a certain way clearly indicates that not every woman is dressed the same way and, therefore, we can affirm that the Qur'an vision of women is one in which they have complete free will to dress as they choose. In other words, the verse clearly refers to *ḥijāb* as a free choice that some believing women can consider when surrounded by others, who might prefer to dress otherwise.[42]

VERSE Q.24:31: ENDING WOMEN'S INTERNALIZED OBJECTIFICATION

A single sentence in the Qur'an revolutionized the way women thought of themselves and of their role in public life. It is important to discuss this sentence, as it is closely related to my previous analysis of how women can stop drawing attention to themselves as "desirable women" and begin focusing on gender-neutral humanity instead. In the verse about the requirement to wear *ḥijāb*, we read: "They should not stamp their feet so as to draw attention to any hidden charms" (Q.24:31). This verse is interesting because of the way it mentions a specific physical movement, while in many instances the Qur'an relies on generalities. Why would the Qur'an pay attention to what might seem like a minor issue or even a trivial deviation from the broader issue of modest conduct?

In fact, this pre-Islamic practice of stamping one's feet to gain men's attention is mentioned not only to end that particular practice but also to end what lies behind it. I argue that this part of the verse is intended to change the way women think of themselves. Women who live in a society that values nothing in them but their sexual attractiveness need to revolt not only against pressure from outside but also against their own dependence on that type of social validation to gain self-esteem because "seduction means begging for attention and admiration. It is a declaration of one's need for the [attention from the] other."[43]

The Qur'anic liberation of women suggests that women give up their traditional ways of dressing and instead free themselves, both psychologically and behaviorally, externally and internally, from this degrading mentality in which a woman's sexual appeal is her most important attribute. The verse clearly asks women to rethink the way men view them and the way they view themselves—because the way women think of themselves must change from within, in order to have the power to become a social phenomenon and change others and society at large. The first step in women's emancipation from a culture that is heavily and deeply influenced by all types of female exploitation requires that women stop viewing themselves as sexual objects.

This powerful message fits the overall structure of the universality of the Qur'anic text that, as noted, starts from a specific context, then expands into other dimensions. The command for women to free themselves from being satisfied with their role as desirable women, rather than being fulfilled as human beings, is relevant to all women in all times. Women who continue to desire public attention for reasons unrelated to their professional merit and humanity will never win any battle for gender equality. Women can only stand up for their equality when they start believing in themselves, and when they separate themselves from the need to conform to criteria set by the media. The symbolic implication of the specific physical movement described in Q.24:31 transcends the superficial simplicity of the act itself. This statement is an invitation for women to think of themselves as separate from the mentality of a desirable woman. More importantly, in this part of the verse, the requirement to wear *ḥijāb* moves beyond an obligation related to physical appearance and turns to a behavioral commitment because a woman's attitude is key to modesty; attitude and behavior change modest clothing into a genuine feminist commitment.

In this chapter, I show that *ḥijāb* and modesty as a way of dressing and as a way of life are based on Qur'anic verses. In addition, in this chapter I reveal Islamic feminism as a liberal philosophy, by which we can reconsider the social message a woman or a man communicates by dressing in a certain way or another. In contrast to many problematic approaches, *ḥijāb* speaks to the real needs of women in public life, to their full and dynamic participation in society, politics, and economy. While some may think of *ḥijāb* as a symbol of male subjection of women, in fact it is the visual representation of an honest, authentic feminist rejection of male-centered criteria, based exclusively on physical appearance and sexual attractiveness. Real Islamic feminism argues that female empowerment does not seek self-esteem or social validation from appealing to explicit or disguised male-centered sexual desires. As asserted in Q.24:30, Qur'anic modesty, which requires a head covering, is general; it does not dictate the specifics of color and design; furthermore, it does not exclude women from any activity or profession in the name of guarding their modesty. The view of women as seductresses only came later, along with misogynistic interpretations. The main purpose of making *ḥijāb* an obligation relates to providing women with equal economic opportunities and social participation and facilitating their vibrant participation in their communities.

NOTES

1. Shaḥrūr, *Nahw awsūl jadīda*, 361.
2. Yusuf Sidani, *Muslim Women at Work: Religious Discourses in Arab Society* (Beirut: Palgrave Macmillan, 2017), 35.
3. I use this term, not *niqāb*, which refers to covering the face; I do not address the issue of *niqāb*, as it is not mentioned in the Qur'an.
4. Marnia Lazreg, *Questioning the Veil: Open Letters to Muslim Women* (Princeton: Princeton University Press, 2009), 38.
5. Like in 22:78 for example.
6. Like in 7:157 for example.
7. The argument for head covering in Judaism and Christianity is, of course, deeper and more convoluted that this quick reference; see 1 Corinthians 11 and Numbers 5:18.
8. Shaḥrūr, *Nahw awsūl jadīda*, 356.
9. Mernissi, *al-Harīm al-siyāsī*, 223.
10. Fatima Mernissi, *The Veil and the Male Elite*, trans. Mary Jo Lakeland (New York: Basic Books, 1991), 99.
11. Although the issue of slavery in Islam is beyond the purview of this work, it is worth noting that the Qur'an only temporarily tolerated slavery as it already existed; the Qur'an never initiated or legislated slavery. Unfortunately, the Qur'an's gradual plan to end slavery remained an unfulfilled potentiality, because that plan was not strictly followed by the Muslim community after the death of the Prophet. What matters here though is the understanding of the Qur'an as a book that essentially addressed the community of believers as one community. The suggestion that the Qur'an makes a distinction between free members of the community and enslaved members is not Qur'anic.
12. Like in 49:13, 17:70, 4:1
13. ʿAbbās Maḥmūd al-ʿAqqād, *al-Mar'a fī l-Qur'ān* (Cairo: Nahḍat Miṣr, 1980), 60.

14. Abū Muḥammad 'Abd al-Qādir al-Sanadī, *Raf' al-janna amam jilbāb al-mar'a al-muslima fī l-kitāb wa-l-sunna* (Riyadh: Dār al-Kitāb wa-Sunna, 1996), 55.

15. al-Sanadī, *Raf' al-janna amam jilbāb al-mar'a al-muslima fī l-kitāb wa-l-sunna*, 35.

16. Ibid.

17. The same meaning can also be found in other places. Examples are 2:262, 2:263, and 2:222.

18. As for example, in Qur'an 3:111.

19. While I argue for this interpretation as a modern applicability of the verse—I mean *hijāb* as a way to facilitate a healthy male-female social communication—I am not excluding a similar applicability even during the time of revelation. As we know from pre-Islamic love poetry, gender segregation was not an Arabian practice. Men and women used to regularly meet, talk, and even date. *Hijāb* is better to be understood as a social way that was supposed to regulate and sanctify those practices and not to abolish them as some might think.

20. Christina Ho and Dreher Tanja, *Beyond the Hijab Debates: New Conversations on Gender, Race, and Religion* (Newcastle upon Tyne, UK: Cambridge Scholars Publishing, 2009), 30.

21. al-Sarrani and Alghamdi, "Through Third World Women's Eyes," 5.

22. Like in 49:10.

23. Like in 5:54.

24. In the romantic and sexual sense, as a desired woman.

25. Roy Baumeister, *Is There Anything Good About Men? How Cultures Flourish by Exploiting Men* (Oxford: Oxford University Press, 2010), 228.

26. Diana Russell, *Making Violence Sexy* (New York: Teachers College Press, 1993), 6.

27. Fatema Mernissi, *Scheherazade Goes West* (New York: Washington Square Press, 2001), 214.

28. Elena-Larisa Stanciu and Bjørn Christensen, "Controlling Women's Bodies: The Black and Veiled Female Body in Western Visual Culture: A Comparative View," *Analize* (2014); online: http://www.analize-journal.ro/library/files/stanciu.pdf, accessed April 9, 2018.

29. Suzanne Venker and Phyllis Schlafly, *The Flipside of Feminism: What Conservative Women Know and Men Can't Say* (New York: WND Books, 2011), 187.

30. Shelly Grabe and Janet Shibley Hyde, "Body Objectification, MTV, and Psychological Outcomes among Female Adolescents," *Journal of Applied Social Psychology* 39, no. 12 (2009), 2852.

31. Grabe and Hyde, "Body Objectification, MTV, and Psychological Outcomes among Female Adolescents."

32. Viren Swami, Jusnara Miah, Nazerine Noorani, and Donna Taylor, "Is the Hijab Protective? An Investigation of Body Image and Related Constructs among British Muslim Women," *British Journal of Psychology* 12, no. 105 (2014), 359.

33. Lila Abu-Lughod, *Do Muslim Women Need Saving?* (Cambridge, MA: Harvard University Press, 2013), 37.

34. Catharine Mackinon, *Feminism Unmodified* (Cambridge, MA: Harvard University Press, 1987), 28.

35. Kecia Ali, "Rethinking Women's Issues in Muslim Communities," in *Taking Back Islam: American Muslims Reclaim Their Faith*, ed. Michael Wolfe (Emmaus, PA: Rodale Press, 2002), 93.

36. Sylvia Chan-Malik, "A Space for the Spiritual," *Amerasia Journal* 40, no. 1 (2014), 17.

37. Kahf, "From Her Royal Body," 38.

38. Chan-Malik, "A Space for the Spiritual," 35.

39. Omar Edward Moad, "Honored Since Adam: Islam and the Value of Human Freedom," *Yaqeen* (23 October 2017), online: yaqeeninstitute.org.

40. Moad, "Honored Since Adam."

41. Ibid.

42. More importantly, this command, as in the case of many other commands in the Qur'an, clearly shows that Islamic values do not align with the idea of a compulsory state religion. In the Qur'an, *ḥijāb* is presented as a way for believing women to distinguish themselves from others, it is not compulsory.

43. Amāl Qaramī, *al-Ikhtilāf fi l-thaqafa al-'arabiyya al-islāmiyya* (Beirut: Dār al-Madar al-Islāmī, 2007), 374.

Chapter 5

Woman's Agency in the Qur'an

In this chapter, I argue that the Qur'an asserts women's full religious, political, and economic agency. I use elements from two Qur'anic stories, that of Mary and the story of the Queen of Sheba, to prove women's right to be prophets and women's right to public authority, respectively. In addition, I demonstrate women's economic agency and independence by carefully deconstructing two entangled meanings in the Qur'an, namely, the concept of *ajr*, which refers to a continuous marital financial obligation and the concept of *sidaq* (often translated as "dowry"), which refers to a one-time marriage gift. In this chapter, I prove that *ajr*, as a continuous financial compensation for women, was lost from Qur'anic interpretations, despite repeated references in the Qur'an to the two terms as different terms that cannot and should not be treated interchangeably.

In the following arguments, what I refer to as 'the so-called authoritative ascendancy of early religious scholars' plays a significant role in explaining the deficiency that caused, in part, the loss of the gender egalitarian message of the Qur'an. This religious ascendancy of the past explains the gap between the religious text and its application. This gap has caused and continues to cause Muslim women to wait for rights that were given to them in the Qur'an more than fourteen centuries ago, like the right to vote, the right to ongoing marital compensation, the right to work, the right to hold positions of public authority, and the right to be recognized as prophets.

WOMAN'S RELIGIOUS AGENCY

Women and men were created from one soul (*nafs*), "neither feminine, nor masculine."[1] The Qur'an acknowledges the full equality of women "as an ontological fact."[2] As I show in this chapter, this equality includes but cannot be limited to religious, political, and economic independence.

In the Qur'an , nothing explains the full religious equality of women like the story of Mary. According to modern as well as mainstream medieval schools of exegeses, Islamic jurisprudence, and even according to modern religious rulings (*fatwās*), women are considered too inferior, too weak, or just not pure enough to meet the requirements or handle the challenges associated with prophethood. However, rethinking the Qur'anic text, in isolation from narrow medieval gender-biased preferences, proves that this view is incorrect. In this section,[3] I provide a unique linguistic analysis of the Qur'anic story of Mary or *Maryam*, the mother of Jesus and the only woman mentioned by name in the Qur'an. I argue that the Qur'an acknowledges *Maryam* as a female prophet, chosen like how all other male prophets were chosen.

The Qur'anic Linguistic Evidence of *Maryam's* Prophethood

In the Qur'an we read about *Maryam* as a chosen, purified woman. The Qur'an confirms that *Maryam* was chosen in many ways: first, she was from a chosen family, "God chose Adam, Noah, Abraham's family, and the family of Imran, over all other people" (Q.3:33). In addition, *Maryam* seems to have been personally chosen, not once, but twice: "The angels said to Mary: 'Mary, God has chosen you and made you pure and chosen you above all women" (Q.3:42).[4] The issue of being chosen should be discussed because of the repeated mention of the expression "has chosen you." However, before we address the unexplained repetition in the verse, another linguistic peculiarity in this verse must be noted because, as al-Sha'rāwī accurately notes, in the same verse the preposition *'alā*, which means "above," only follows the second time "has chosen you" appears. Al-Sha'rāwī interprets this verse and explains the absence of this preposition in the first mention of "has chosen you," as follows:

> When interpreting: "God has chosen you and purified you and chosen you above the women of the worlds," we find ourselves faced with two kinds of preference. The first was mentioned not followed by the word *'alā* [above] but the second is followed by *'alā*. The first preference is meant to inform *Maryam* that she has been made special because of her faith and good manners, but since this preference did not use *'alā*, this means that she is not the only one preferred in this way. . . . The second type, which says "and chosen you above the women of the world," indicates the exclusion of men from this type of preference, because the preference is not related to masculinity. She is the only woman of all the women of the world who will exclusively give birth to a baby without a male; no other woman shares this ability.[5]

However, while it is clear that this opinion accurately explains the repeated mention of "has chosen you," which clarifies that *Maryam's* high rank is shared with others in one respect and is exclusive in the other, al-Sha'rāwī does not take his discussion to its logical conclusion. If we agree that *Maryam* shares a special rank with other anointed human beings, the next logical question to ask is, who are these other anointed human beings? Who can they be other than prophets? If unnecessary repetition is not a stylistic semantic tool in the Qur'an, as it is here, then the repetition must refer to two ways in which *Maryam* was chosen. *Maryam* was first chosen the way prophets are chosen. She was placed in a rank clearly equal to the rank of prophets. The next type, which comes after a purification process, is exclusive to women. This means that *Maryam* was chosen in a way that is equal to all male prophets. She is neither superior to nor inferior to any of them. Then she was chosen above a specific category, that is, above all the women of the worlds. This means that *Maryam* was chosen like how all male prophets were chosen, but she still holds a unique rank as the best of all women in all worlds. What matters most is the gender-egalitarian reference in the first step that leaves no room for any sexist thinking that *Maryam*—because of her gender—is less than any chosen male prophet.

Furthermore, the special process of purification that is not explained in the verse comes after the first mention of "has chosen you." This is extremely important, as it asserts the full right of women to become prophets, like men, with no purification needed. We must bear in mind that the purification that was needed for *Maryam* to miraculously conceive without a male was not purification in order to be able to become a prophet; this is indicated from the order in the verse. That is, as the verse asserts, there is nothing in *Maryam's* nature as a woman that prevents her from being chosen like men. The special purification she needed was not to enable her to be chosen like men were chosen, but to make her unique as a woman, and superior to all women in all worlds.

Unfortunately, this clear gender-egalitarian message in Q.3:42 was not appreciated by mainstream Muslim exegetes, due to what I have previously referred to as "the fallacy of exegetical semantic satiation." The majority of available Qur'anic interpretations ignore this revolutionary way of viewing women. Reading through many Qur'anic interpretations, we find that this is overlooked and no effort is made to explain the repetition. At the same time, sexist readings of the verse completely falsify its rich content, and jump to conclusions that do not explain the text. To illustrate this, I consider some interpretations of the verse.

Al-Ṭabarī (839–923) seems to restrict *Maryam's* superiority to women of her time. He says, "The meaning of 'has chosen you above the women of the worlds' means choosing you above the women of your time due to your obedience."[6] In *tafsīr* al-Ṭabarsī (1073–1153), the story of choosing *Maryam* appears to lack any intrinsic gender-egalitarian content; in addition, the interpreter takes a step back, by limiting *Maryam's* superiority to women of her time, and not to all women of all worlds, as the verse seems to clearly assert. Alternatively, his interpretation nominates another woman to this high rank, namely, Fāṭima, the daughter of Prophet Muḥammad. Al-Ṭabarsī says, "'Has chosen you above the women of the worlds' means the women of your time, because Fāṭima the daughter of the Prophet is the [best] woman of all the worlds' women."[7]

Even exegetes who recognized that there must be a reason for this repetition of the expression "has chosen you," suggest explanations that are completely unrelated to the gender-egalitarian message of the verse in question. For example, al-Rāzī (1149–1209) says,

> Since declaring a repetition in the Qur'an is not appropriate, it is necessary to say that the first type refers to all the good things and events that took place in her early life and that the second type refers to what took place later in her life.[8]

But if the verse merely indicates events that happen later in time, or a chronological order of events, or a periodization, then the Qur'an would have used a specific linguistic tool to show that, like "then." The verse might have been something like: "God has chosen you and purified you, then has chosen you above the women of the worlds," instead of, "God has chosen you and purified you and has chosen you above the women of the worlds" (Q.3:42). In his *tafsīr*, al-Māwardī (974–1058) recognizes the distinction between the two steps or types of choosing *Maryam* but makes no reference to gender egalitarianism. For him, the second mention of "has chosen you" was just an affirmation of the first one, or it can be understood as exclusively related to giving birth to Jesus.[9]

In any case, the interpretation I provide logically concludes that we must reconsider *Maryam* as a prophet. This conclusion is clearly suggested by an objective analytical reading of the verse, though it is only supported by some scholars and it contradicts the mainstream consensus.

This leaves us to resolve what some see as a conflict with another verse in the Qur'an, which is wrongly interpreted as negating women's prophethood. This verse states, "All the messengers We sent before you were simply men" (Q.16:43). It is not difficult to resolve this conflict because we can immediately note the clear distinction between the case of *Maryam* and the generalization in Q.16:43, which distinguishes between the concept of prophethood and the concept of messengerhood. A prophet may or may not be a messenger. A messenger is a prophet with a mission, who brings a message (usually a book) to be conveyed to others. For example, Muhammad is a prophet and a messenger. Mary was not a messenger, yet she was a prophet.

Very few theologians, among them Ibn Ḥazm (994–1064) and al-Qurṭubī (1214–73), argued for *Maryam's* prophethood. The majority either refused this view or were suspicious of the concept of women prophets. Even those who supported *Maryam's* prophethood referred to reasons other than the clear-cut linguistic evidence I use for my argument. In his interpretation of Q.3:42, al-Qurṭubī says, "*Maryam* is a prophet, this is the sound opinion. Because God sent revelation to her by using an angel as a medium, the same way he did to the rest of prophets."[10] More famously, Ibn Ḥazm defended the same opinion by saying,

> As for the mothers of Jesus, Moses, and *Isḥāq*, the Qur'an made a reference to them receiving a revelation. Some were given news about what will take place before it happened; which is the exact same meaning of prophethood, there is no prophethood beyond that. Therefore, their prophethood is sound according to the Qur'anic text.[11]

It is also relevant to mention that in his study of women in the Qur'an, Rāshid al-Ghanūshī (b. 1941),[12] the modern Islamic scholar, reached the same conclusion concerning *Maryam's* prophethood. Unfortunately, the dominant view, as Barbara Stowasser makes clear, is still the denial of this conclusion: "Consensus-based Sunni theology rejected this doctrine and labeled it 'heretical innovation.'"[13]

Finally, another verse that is related to the assertion that Mary was a prophet describes Mary as *ṣiddiqa*: "The Messiah, son of Mary, was only a messenger; other messengers had come and gone before him; his mother was a virtuous woman (*ṣiddiqa)*; both ate food [like other mortals]" (Q.5:75). This verse suggests that we consider this description of Mary as *ṣiddiqa* and ask whether this supports or contradicts her role as a prophet. In fact, comparing this verse to the way other prophets were described in the Qur'an, as *ṣiddiqīn*, confirms the link between this description and prophethood. Describing prophets as *ṣiddiqīn* appears in the readings, "Truthful (*ṣiddiq*) Joseph! Tell us the meaning of seven fat cows being eaten by seven lean ones" (Q.12:46), "Mention too, in the Scripture, the story of Abraham. He was a man of truth (*ṣiddiq*), a prophet" (Q.19:41), and, "Mention too, in the Scripture, the story of *Idris*. He was a man of truth (*ṣiddiqīn*), a prophet" (Q.19:59).

The Qur'anic Logical Evidence of *Maryam's* Prophethood

Prophethood undoubtedly includes many elements, which might include receiving revelations, experiencing or even performing miracles, and possessing the ability to interact with supernatural beings or powers. In this section, I investigate what the Qur'anic story confirms about *Maryam's* prophethood.

The Qur'an tells us the story of *Maryam's* birth: her mother vowed that her unborn baby would be devoted to God. Later, the story informs us that she was surprised to find that her child is a girl. *Maryam* was accepted by God, with no reference to any difficulty in accepting a female servant of the temple, contrary to the traditions. This acceptance clearly indicates that the gender of the baby might have been an issue for her mother and for her people but was never an issue for God. "Her Lord graciously accepted her" (Q.3:37).

The Qur'anic story of *Maryam* mentions some interesting facts about her early life. First, as I mentioned before, she was accepted by God, contrary to customs, in which serving in the temple was assigned exclusively to men. Second, she was raised, "and [God] made her grow in goodness" (Q.3:37) and was placed by God under the care of Zachariah. The Qur'an notes an important, extraordinary fact about the way she lived, "Whenever Zachariah went in to see her in her sanctuary, he found her supplied with provisions. He said, "Mary, how is it you have these provisions? And she said, 'they are from God: God provides limitlessly for whoever He will'" (Q.3:37).

What type of provision was given to *Maryam* that puzzled her guardian Zachariah? According to al-Qurṭubī, "Zachariah used to find winter fruit during summer and summer fruit during winter in her sanctuary."[14] From the way Zachariah asks about the provisions, we expect an extraordinary or even miraculous explanation. In his inquiry, Zachariah uses the interrogative *annā*, which is informative; in the Qur'an, *annā* is commonly used for questions in which a supernatural or strange fact is expected in the explanation. For example, in Q.2:259 we read, "Or take the one who passed by a ruined town. He said, 'How (*annā*) will God give this life when it has died?'" (Q.2:259). Interestingly, the question the man asked by using the same interrogative *annā* similarly anticipated a strange or a supernatural answer. In the same chapter, Zachariah used *annā* to show his surprise that something unusual might happen to him. He said, "My Lord, how can I have a son when I am so old and my wife is barren" (Q.3:40). In other words, Zachariah expected something unusual when he asked *Maryam* about the source of her provision. Note that after hearing *Maryam's* answer, Zachariah immediately turned to God to ask for another miracle the way righteous people turn to God after witnessing a miracle; "they are from God" (Q.3:37), she said. There and then Zachariah prayed to his Lord, saying, "Lord, from Your grace grant me virtuous offspring" (Q.3:38). It is as if the occurrence of the miracle of *Maryam's* provision gave him hope of the occurrence of another miracle. We read in the Qur'an that Zachariah asked God to be granted a son, in spite of his age, and his wife's barren state. The story continues and Zachariah was blessed with a baby boy named *Yaḥyā*. For my discussion, I note the unmistakable psychological relevance: Zachariah witnessed a miracle—a powerful message from God—and then asked God to perform another one. Regardless of the authenticity of the interpretations, which diverge concerning the nature of *Maryam's* provision of food, in the story, there is an implicit confirmation that she is provided with provisions in an extraordinary way. Perhaps *Maryam* needed a different kind of nutrition, or a unique type of physical and biological preparation to conceive without a male partner.

We see another confirmation of *Maryam's* supernatural upbringing in the way *Maryam* was given provisions. *Maryam* did not have to do anything to earn her food. She did not have to leave her sanctuary to look for food; this by itself is another miracle that goes beyond earthly norms, as even Adam and Eve had to seek food. *Maryam* did not have to do anything, her food was provided while she was devoted to worship. Her miraculous upbringing even continued and included the effortless way this food was given to her. Interestingly, this unique provision for *Maryam* seems to have lasted at least during the period in which *Maryam* was being prepared for the upcoming event, namely, the virgin birth of Jesus. As we see later, the moment Jesus was born, *Maryam* was directed to return to a more normal lifestyle, a lifestyle that required her to earn her food and take care of herself, instead of being divinely cared for by God. As we read in the Qur'an, *Maryam* was asked to do something to provide for herself while she was in labor. Although she was only asked to shake the trunk of a palm tree next to her, to bring down some dates, the order to do something to get food is a clear reference that a change must have taken place the moment Jesus was born. This change was a shift from being extraordinarily provided for to being a more ordinary human life, "If you shake the trunk of the palm tree toward you, it will deliver fresh ripe dates for you" (Q.19:25). What we do not know, what remains a mystery, is the reason for this shift. Al-Qurṭubī suggests an explanation for this switch:

> According to our scholars, when her heart was devoted only to God she did not have to be concerned with providing for herself. But when she gave birth to Jesus and her heart was attached to what he was saying [al-Qurṭubī interprets this verse by noting that Jesus was able to communicate with his mother from the moment he was born], then God made her return to the norms of life [working for her provisions].[15]

Many exegetes describe the palm tree as dead; it was miraculously brought back to life as *Maryam* shook it to bring the dates down. However, there is not sufficient evidence from the Qur'an to support the insertion of an extraordinary element into this scene. On the contrary, from what I can see, receiving the order to grab the tree trunk and shake it to bring down the dates indicates the absence of any extraordinary provision for *Maryam*; that is, normalcy was reasserted from the moment Jesus was born. The question regards the timing of this shift from extraordinary to ordinary; if *Maryam* was provided for, from God's merciful nature, then her enduring labor alone, as the Qur'anic scene explains, would seem to be the best time for God's continuing mercy. Could it be that *Maryam's* miraculous pregnancy required a special miraculous nutrition that was no longer needed once Jesus was born?

The mysterious way in which *Maryam* conceived Jesus is mentioned in the Qur'an in four scenes. First, the scene from chapter 3 reads: "The angels said, 'Mary, God gives you news of a Word from Him, whose name will be the Messiah, Jesus, son of Mary, who will be held in honor in this world and the next, who will be one of those brought near to God" (Q.3:45). Second, I quote the scene in chapter 19, which is commonly misunderstood as a repetition of Q.3:45; this is not the case, as I clarify below.

> Mention in the Scripture the story of Mary. She withdrew from her family to a place to the east [16] and secluded herself away; We sent her Our Spirit to appear before her in the form of a perfected man. [17] She said, "I seek the Lord of Mercy's protection against you: if you have any fear of Him [do not approach]." [18] But he said, "I am but a messenger from your Lord, [come] to announce to you the gift of a pure son." [19] She said, "How can I have a son when no man has touched me? I have not been unchaste." (Q.19:16–19)

The third scene immediately follows the praise of the family of Imran: "Remember the one who guarded her chastity. We breathed into her from Our Spirit and made her and her son a sign for all people" (Q.21:91). Finally, the fourth scene includes a more specific description of the conception process. "And Mary, daughter of Imran. She guarded her chastity, so We breathed into her from Our spirit" (Q.66:12).

By reflecting on the hermeneutics of these four scenes, particularly on the differences between the first two scenes, we can discover some interesting facts. The first scene starts with a dialogue between the angels and *Maryam*, not just one angel, as we find in chapter 19. This suggests that there are two scenes in the Qur'an and not one scene described in two places. In Q.3:45, the scene describes a group of angels, and not just one angel. These angels told *Maryam* the good news of the Word of God. The angels then provided the name of this child. In Q.19:16–19, however, one angel, Gabriel, addresses *Maryam* in what might seem to be a repetition of Q.3:45; however, this time *Maryam* seems more frightened. She not only expresses surprise at the possibility of conceiving a child while having remained chaste but also seeks refuge in God from this stranger who tells her that he is there to give her a pure boy. The second scene is the only one that is immediately followed by "she conceived him" (Q.19:22).

If we assume that the Qur'an does not include unnecessary repetition, which in fact is an implausible possibility in terms of Qur'anic style, then, we must consider that there is a reason for including the two scenes. According to the *tafsīr* of al-Sha'rāwī (1911–98),[16] when the angels told *Maryam* that her son will be called the son of *Maryam* (in Q.3:45), she knew that the child would be born without a father, since it was not the custom for children to be named after their mothers. In chapter 19, as the *tafsīr* of al-Shanqīṭī (1907–73) notes, *Maryam* expresses wonder not only because no man has ever touched her but also because she has never been unchaste. In this verse, she is much more concerned with "how"[17] she will be given the promised son.

If we rearrange the story, we can better understand it. First, in Q.3:45, *Maryam* was told by the angels that she will be given a child. Although she was surprised by the news, she was not frightened or worried. But in chapter 19, when *Maryam* suddenly sees a man standing before her, telling her that he is a messenger sent by God to continue the mission, she is surprised and concerned not because of the news she already knew but because of the way this child would be given to her. Perhaps, as a virtuous woman in an isolated place, when she was suddenly addressed by a man-like figure, her central concern was the way she will be granted the son.

The way *Maryam* conceived Jesus is also mentioned in two places, namely, Q.21:91 and Q.66:12. Both verses refer to God breathing the soul into her. Interestingly, the same mechanism is mentioned elsewhere in the Qur'an, as the way Adam was created, that is, "breathed My spirit into him" (Q.15:29). This clear similarity in the way both Jesus and Adam were conceived is reaffirmed in another verse that draws an analogy between the two cases; this leaves no room to suspect that Jesus is divine, "In God's eyes Jesus is just like Adam. He created him from dust, said to him, 'Be, and he was" (Q.3:59).

The story of *Maryam* presents an undeniably strong message; she was a unique woman whose high status is a recognition of gender equality and an assertion of women's prophethood. In this section, I explain, based on the Qur'anic text, that *Maryam* was a prophet. And I prove this, logically, by the miraculous way in which God gave her provisions, and in her multiple interactions with angels, and her supernatural conception and pregnancy.

WOMAN'S POLITICAL AGENCY

The Right to Vote

In the Qur'an, the following verse is an undeniable confirmation of women's right to declare their allegiance to a state; this right was guaranteed by their "allegiance, since the time of the Prophet."[18] The Qur'an shows that this political right was guaranteed to the women of the Arabian Peninsula centuries before the suffragist movement in the United States, which finally granted women that right in the 1920s.

> Prophet, when believing women come and pledge to you that they will not ascribe any partner to God, nor steal, nor commit adultery, nor kill their children, nor lie about who has fathered their children, nor disobey you in any righteous thing, then you should accept their pledge of allegiance and pray to God to forgive them: God is most forgiving and merciful. (Q.60:12)

The community of Medina was the first Islamic state to be established. The Prophet, as the head of the state—as the previous verse asserts—was commanded to accept the pledge of allegiance made by the women of Medina. Unfortunately—due to what I refer to as the authoritarian approach to the Qur'an and the so-called authoritative ascendancy of early religious scholars—unlike the women of Medina, Muslim women around the world have had to fight to reclaim this right. For example, the right to vote was given to women in Pakistan in 1947, in Oman in 1997, in Qatar in 1999, and in Saudi Arabia in 2015.

The Right to Hold Positions of Public Authority

The Qur'anic story of the Queen of Sheba is "the most manifest example of women's leadership in Islamic society."[19] This story of an impressive quee who is praised in the Qur'an and acknowledged as a distinguished leader, constitutes an example that directly challenges the traditional Islamic arguments against Muslim women holding positions of public leadership. Unfortunately, the clear gender-egalitarian message in the Qur'anic story has been ignored by the majority of classical and even modern exegetes who did not and have not given this story much attention. In the following,[20] I provide an analytical and linguistic reevaluation of the story from an Islamic feminist point of view. I argue, contrary to mainstream Muslim interpretations, that women have a full and unconditional right to hold public leadership positions.

Like other Qur'anic stories, the story of the Queen of Sheba consists of different scenes and does not offer much detail. The story starts with the hoopoe bringing Solomon exciting news about people governed by a woman. To the hoopoe's surprise, those people worshiped the sun instead of God. After Solomon orders the hoopoe to take a letter to them, and wait for their response, the scene moves to the Queen of Sheba, who seems to have finished reading the letter, and is consulting her counselors about the letter she describes as "gracious" (Q.27:29), and as written, "In the name of God" (Q.27:30). After consulting her counselors, the Queen of Sheba decided to send a gift to Solomon. She eventually accepted an invitation to visit his palace. Solomon challenged her by moving her throne miraculously to his palace, and tricked her, by building a crystal that looked like water, such that she uncovered her legs to wade through it. Eventually, she realized that the supernatural power Solomon demonstrated could only be accessible with the help of a mighty being. The story ends with the Queen of Sheba acknowledging her mistake for worshiping a being other than God, and with her full submission to God, the Lord of all worlds.

For my purposes, it is necessary to undertake a detailed linguistic analysis of the story, to uncover the meaning of the Qur'anic presentation of this female leader. First, we consider the way the hoopoe described her to Solomon; he said, "I found a woman ruling over the people" (Q.27:23). The Arabic expression *tamlikuhum*, which describes her status, comes from the root m-l-k, which means to own something. This expression reflects her powerful authority over her people; it also describes her as a woman that "has been given a share of everything" (Q.27:23), suggesting an undoubtedly prestigious rank. This expression is not only important for its content but also because it is the same expression used in the Qur'anic text to describe Solomon himself. Solomon describes himself and his family as, "we have been given a share of everything" (Q.27:16). The fact that the Queen of Sheba is described as one, "who has been given a share of everything" (Q.27:23) the same way a mighty prophet like Solomon was described, is a clearly gender-egalitarian message that has been neglected for centuries.

Moreover, the Qur'anic text provides other important details from the story. First, a meaningful reference is made to the strategy she adopted to deal with Solomon's letter. She turned to her counselors for advice, "Give me your counsel" (Q.27:32); this scene undoubtedly portrays her as a wise democratic leader who consulted her counselors in the process of making decisions. Second, her counselors responded to her request by indicating their full trust in her and their submission to her ability to make decisions, "You are in command" (Q.27:33). Third, and most importantly, even after she was reminded of their military ability, she did not resort to force; instead, she as an experienced leader considered the way mighty kings like Solomon react when they take over a town, "Whenever kings go into a city, they ruin it and humiliate its leaders—that is what they do" (Q.27:34). Fourth, after refusing to react with a typically male show of force, she offered a diplomatic introduction as she developed a plan to determine Solomon's intentions and examine whether he would react like a king or more like a faithful messenger. Was he interested in occupying her kingdom or in calling them to his new religion, as his letter claimed? It seems that the way Solomon began his letter, in the name of God, caused her to consider her decision carefully. So, in a clever attempt to test Solomon's real intentions, she sent him a gift.[21] The Queen of Sheba was truly, as Nevin Reda describes, "ahead of her time in dealing with her people, her actions reflecting present-day aspirations. Perhaps even her choice of a diplomatic solution can be considered an expression of contemporary notions of a ruler's priorities, as it spares her people the humiliations of war."[22]

> The strategies adopted by the Queen of Sheba include consulting her court, resorting to traditional wisdom, contemplating her options before resorting to power, considering all possible responses, and exploring and learning more about her enemy before taking a decision; these all reflect her intelligence and

> her unique leadership style. In addition, her submission to God after losing the challenge from Solomon indicates that the Queen of Sheba must have been an intelligent woman, one who was difficult to trick. Solomon's strategy worked because it appealed to her point of strength, that is, her ability to make wise decisions. But more importantly, the story teaches us a singular fact about the Queen of Sheba; she proved herself and the soundness of her opinion in the midst of her male counselors, even when she refused to resort to power.

Unfortunately, in spite of this Qur'anic image of the Queen of Sheba, the majority of interpretations of the story fail to note the liberal gender-egalitarian content. The fact that Solomon and the Queen of Sheba are described with the same expression is commonly overlooked, despite the clear egalitarian message suggested in this expression. Even more puzzling is the fact that exegetes interpret the same expression differently; they perceive it one way when it is applied to Solomon and another when it is applied to the Queen of Sheba. This causes us to suspect that the verses in question were not allowed to speak for themselves, rather they were used to project cultural presumptions about the so-called God-given gender roles. In the following examples, we see that while the Qur'anic text praises the Queen of Sheba, and shows her exceptional abilities as a leader, traditional interpretations convey a different message, one that identifies doubts about a woman's ability to lead.

For example, the expression "has been given a share of everything" is interpreted differently when ascribed to Solomon than it is when it is ascribed to the Queen of Sheba. Al-Qurṭubī (1214–73) interprets that "she has been given a share of everything," "as everything the kingdom needs"[23] or as, "has been given [an abundance] of all things that kings might require, like machines and instruments."[24] Similarly, al-Ṭabarī (838–923) interprets the expression to mean that she was provided with "everything needed in worldly life like weapons and machines."[25] Generally speaking, these interpretations seem to understand the expression to refer to her ownership of what a king might need to rule a kingdom. Yet, when the same expression is used in a description of Solomon, there seems to be a consensus among interpreters that it means Solomon's possession of the leadership qualities required to be a successful leader, including perspicacity and wisdom. This inconsistency even appears in the same interpretations. For example, the *tafsīr* of al-Ṭabāṭabā'ī (1903–81) interprets "everything" ascribed to Solomon as, "All the blessing anyone can have, like prophethood, knowledge, authority, a kingdom, and all material as well as moral virtues."[26] However, when the same expression is ascribed to the Queen of Sheba, he interprets it as, "Everything a great kingdom requires, like power, a wide kingdom, fighters, and obedient people."[27]

In addition to these discrepancies, as we reflect more on the story, we can easily see misogynous tendencies to reject the message about a woman's leadership, a message that this story clearly supports. Many mainstream interpretations belittle the role of the Queen of Sheba. In his comment on the verse, al-Alūsī (1802–54) states that it does not indicate the permissibility of assigning public authority to a woman because "those people were nonbelievers."[28] However, the overwhelming objection to any feminist interpretation of the story is based on what I refer to as "the use of hadith to invalidate the Qur'anic text." In this particular case, exegetes usually refer to the hadith, "No people will prosper as long as they assign their leadership to a woman."[29] In some interpretations, the language is more aggressively sexist, as in the following explanation about the Queen of Sheba's hesitation to resort to power after she consulted her court. Al-Māwardī says this hesitation was "because they assigned their leadership to *elja*,[30] whose bosoms shake."[31] In addition, many books of *tafsīr* insert unconfirmed details into their interpretations. However, this "excessive exegetical narrativization of the Qur'an" only serves to distract the reader from the legal applicability of the story. The story is controlled by unverified and distracting details such as the Queen of Sheba's marriage to Solomon, her ancestry from jinn, and even her hairy legs. All the while, the gender-egalitarian applicability of the story and the possibility of rethinking allegedly God-given gender roles have been completely ignored. In her explanation, Barbara Stowasser suggests that this "may have to do with the fact that her qur'anic story deals with events prior to her acceptance of Islam."[32]

In any event, beyond the systematic devaluation of the story of the Queen of Sheba among exegetes, it represents a Qur'anic counter-narrative to the traditionalists' disapproval of women's public leadership. As I argue in this section, the easily distinguishable references in the Qur'anic text indicate a transparent acknowledgment of her leadership skills. More importantly, as Syed Mohammed Ali rightly observes, "Nowhere in these verses is there an indication that the Qur'an disapproves of her rule as head of state."[33] The Qur'anic text does not question her right to public authority; and if the Qur'an had sought prohibit women from taking leadership positions, this story would have been the perfect place to do so.

WOMAN'S ECONOMIC AGENCY

Women's Economic Independence in Public Life

As we have seen, often the convoluted understanding of *ḥijāb* has had a disproportionate role in gender segregation policies, which are used as an excuse to prohibit women from work (with the exception of work strictly out of economic necessity); yet, the argument has no Qur'anic support of any kind. As a result, a new ideology of sexual objectification, similar to the one pre-Islamic Arabs held, seems to have found its way back into the Islamic community, along with the revival of old concepts that diminished the status of Muslim women to that of male-owned property. In the name of protecting their honor, Muslim women were increasingly dismissed from public life, and gradually, a growing sense of shame (*'wra*) has become associated, in the collective consciousness, with the mere mention of women's names, working with them, talking to them or even hearing their voices. In many cases, the previously abandoned androcentric pre-Islamic concepts have made their way back, but this time disguised as religious commandments, even when the Qur'an clearly advocates the opposite view.

In the late nineteenth and early twentieth centuries, a more liberal view of women's work was prioritized among Muslim reformers and enlightened scholars. Qasim Amin (1856–1908), the first Arab feminist, considered the status of women to be inseparably tied to the status of their nations.[34] In her book *al-Untha hiya al-aṣl* (The female is the origin), the Egyptian feminist Nawāl al-Sa'dawī (b. 1931) drew attention to the misogynous attitude of women's work by saying,

> The ultimate fear of the patriarchal society is [evident] when women prove their excellence in education, in scientific and in academic work environments. The reason for their [men's] panic is the belief that when women taste the happiness of mental fulfilment and its forbidden pleasure, they might become carried away in that direction. Then men will not find anyone to serve them in homes, to cook for them, and wash the children's clothing.[35]

Likewise, Muṣṭafā Maḥmūd criticized the insistence on leaving Arab women in the kitchen. He stated, "This would lead to a gap between men's and women's ways of thinking and living in the Arab world, . . . [a gap that, he anticipated, would need] 'one hundred years'[36] to bridge." In addition, in his pioneering work, Rāshid al-Ghanūshī argued for the necessity of work for Muslim women in order for Islamic communities to set themselves free from "the spirit of overprotection, which curbed Islamic society for so long."[37] He argues that this would require the society to provide all possible assistance to enable women to reconcile their many responsibilities. Jamāl al-Bannā (1920–2013) argued for the reconsideration of current Islamic attitudes toward women's work and authority and the prioritization of bringing women into positions of public authority, especially in cases in which a woman has a unique talent or merit.[38] According to al-Bannā, women's work is necessary for two reasons,

> It provides women with economic independence, which prevents women from becoming a burden on their families. Work rescues women from dependent

> servile status. Work is a way of polishing the personality and developing talent, and constitutes an introduction to the way things are done, which women should know, lest they become victims of superstition and nonsense.[39]

On the other hand, Islamic traditionalists insisted and continue to insist that the Arabic renaissance, which can only flourish if it is essentially religious, requires that women return to their so-called God-given roles. According to many, women's work can be tolerated only in case of necessity, which is typically understood to be economic circumstances. This opinion is partially based on a Qur'anic verse that is addressed exclusively to the "house" (or family) of the Prophet Muḥammad; it is a command to his wives to avoid excessive socializing, as in the verse, "Stay at home" (Q.33:33). Generally speaking, the main objection to women's work comes from concerns that a woman's duties as mothers and the responsibilities required by a professional lifestyle cannot be balanced. Al-Sha'rāwī claims, in his interpretation of Q.33:33, that women who repeatedly leave their homes have "no use inside their homes";[40] this he contrasts with good housewives who have no time to go out. According to traditional critics, women's right to work is not a Qur'anic right but an economic necessity, and it is better not to consider it if the woman is "supported by her father or husband, or if she has money to spend from for the rest of her life."[41] Even as women's participation in public life in the Arab and most of the Islamic world has become a fact, traditionalists never stopped using slippery slope arguments to criticize religiously committed Muslim women who work by claiming that women's work is an imported Western fashion that can cause "male unemployment and moral deterioration."[42]

This leads us to question the Qur'anic view of women's active participation in the work place: Is it prohibited or allowed only for necessities or is it an unconditional right for women? In the Qur'anic story of Moses, he meets two women, who are commonly believed to be the daughters of Prophet Shu'ayb (the biblical Jethro). According to the story, the two women were watering their animals among the shepherds when Moses first saw them. They explained to Moses that they were doing this difficult work because their father was an old man. Moses offered his help and they invited him to meet their father, who suggested that Moses, as a reward for his help, could marry one of the man's daughters.

This story is typically used by critics of women's work as evidence for its prohibition. These critics base this view on Moses's immediate offer to help; the premise being that he was alarmed to see two women working. In fact, I suggest that the story can be interpreted in the opposite way; one of the women suggested hiring Moses. This indicates that they could afford to hire someone to help. "One of the women said, 'Father, hire him: a strong, trustworthy man is the best to hire'" (Q.28:26). Although the arrangement was made for one of the daughters to marry Moses for his labor, this does not negate the fact that the initial offer—as the daughter proposed—was to hire Moses and not have her father propose a marriage between them.

This Qur'anic story is about two virtuous women working in a male-dominated work environment. The fact that the two women were two daughters of a prophet should cause us to reconsider the argument against the permissibility of women's work; clearly it was not considered shameful or inappropriate for chaste women. First, the fact that they proposed to hire Moses indicates that at the time, they were taking care of the work themselves until they find someone to hire. Second, they worked among men in an environment in which the genders were mixed—which is a red line for mainstream Muslim traditionalists—but according to the Qur'anic text, this was appropriate and permissible.

While economic hardship constitutes one reason to justify women's right to work, traditionalists treat this as the only reason for women's participation in the workplace. The traditionalists' insistence on minimizing the role of women in public life, by making their right to work strictly and exclusively conditional on economic hardship is based on cultural norms and is not based on what we find in the Qur'an. The argument that work is only acceptable for women whose economic circumstances require their income ignores the fact that working is not only a way to secure basic life necessities but is also an essential part of one's self-esteem, confidence, and often happiness. Some scholars who insist on viewing women's work as a one-dimensional economic activity reveal that their understanding of work does not go beyond its superficial link to material values, which are not authentic Islamic values; or, that their evaluation of the right to work is entirely sexist, it is a right exclusive to men. If work is one way to provide the community of believers the chance to become true deputies of God on earth, as the Qur'an clearly established as the reason for human existence (Q.2:30), why should women be excluded from participating in that mission?

To support this gender-based division of labor that limits women to work within the home—cooking, cleaning, childcare, and other service-related tasks, Muslim women are continually reminded of their sacred and valuable role as mothers. They are told that there is no reason to consider any other serious endeavor in life, or they risk losing the balance between their household responsibilities and their role as mothers. In an effort to make this argument more convincing, scientific and psychological studies are typically used to prove that women are biologically designed only to be mothers. While "women's duties" are highlighted, men's "domestic responsibilities" are completely overlooked. In this sexist power struggle, designed to ensure the continuity of women's unpaid domestic labor, concepts of motherhood and fatherhood are reduced to the biological level. Bell Hooks quite accurately comments on this tendency,

> Men will not share equally in parenting until they are taught, ideally, from childhood on, that fatherhood has the same meaning and significance as motherhood. As long as women or society as a whole see the mother/child relationship as unique and special because the female carries the child in her body and gives birth, or makes this biological experience synonymous with women having a closer, more significant bond to children than the male parent, responsibility for child care and childrearing will continue to be primarily women's work. Even the childless woman is considered more suited to raise children than the male parent because she is seen as an inherently caring nurturer. The biological experience of pregnancy and childbirth, whether painful or joyful, should not be equated with the idea that women's parenting is necessarily superior to men's.[43]

The fact that men cannot become pregnant, give birth, and breastfeed does not mean that they should not be fully involved in the lives of their children from the moment they are born, or even before that, to the same extent that women are. The process of building a strong masculine role model can only be done successfully if it starts early enough to be an integrated part of the development of the cognitive, behavioral, and linguistic abilities of children. As I noted in my discussion of polygyny, motherhood and the related duties are typically listed by those in favor of polygyny as an excuse for men to seek better sexual outlets with new wives. Even events like welcoming a new baby into a family, when a woman is desperately in need of emotional as well as actual physical care and support, are used to justify polygyny—because of the temporary interruption of women's sexual activity. Such arguments raise questions not only about the husband's duty toward his wife after she gives birth (when women are commonly more vulnerable to postpartum depression), but also about such a distorted view of fatherhood.

The gender-based division of work reduces the concept of fatherhood to a primitive one-dimensional biological level, which degrades the father's feelings for his child to a mere "extension of the love he feels about the mother of the child"[44]; such views are deeply sexist and inconsistent with the Qur'an's full recognition of the humanity of both women and men.

Motherhood, like fatherhood, is a role that a woman may have in life, along with many other roles; it is not and cannot be a "fundamental project"[45] for men or for women. Motherhood is one among many social roles a woman may have during her lifetime. She may be a good mother, just as she may be a faithful wife, a devoted sister, a loving daughter, or even a helpful neighbor. But this role as a good mother, for example, does not, by itself, overlap with her other roles. Motherhood and fatherhood are social roles that should not be confused with other social roles, but most importantly, should not be confused with professional roles.

For centuries, women in the Islamic world have been trapped in a vicious circle. I do not deny the gains Muslim women in the Arab world have made; in fact, they have been given opportunities to participate in a number of professions. Real reforms have successfully elevated the economic status of Arab and Muslim women. What is troubling though is the fact that these rights were not the result of a reconsideration of Islam and its views. On the contrary, modern religious scholars are highly suspicious of these secular reforms (just as religious figures were centuries ago) and only tolerate the reforms without any meaningful attempt to review or re-examine religious arguments; rather these figures remain suspicious of religiously committed women who try to redefine what it means to be a modern Muslim woman.

The time has come for religiously committed Muslim women to reclaim their rights, not through the backdoor but by challenging the patriarchal authorities that hijacked Islam through their interpretations of women's rights and responsibilities. Muslim women who engage in careers are psychologically harassed with questions about their neglect of their so-called God-given responsibilities, yet I argue that, according to the Qur'an, they are in fact more faithful to God's plans. Women who are supported by their husbands, fathers, brothers, or any male figure in the family and prefer that option to aspiring to economic independence are not fulfilling God's will, contrary to the views of traditional clerics. The advice that women should pray and wait for a good husband who will provide for her is false and misleading; while it is normal to dream of having a family and a harmonious marriage, nothing (certainly not Islam) should stop a woman from becoming educated, discovering her talents, and working in a field that fulfills her. Islam does not envision marriage and child-rearing as the only goal of a woman's life, it is, rather, one aspect of a fulfilled life.

Women's Economic Independence as Wives

Economic independence is a key aspect of women's liberation. As we see in the following section, the Qur'an by acknowledging *ajr*—which I explain in this section—clearly acknowledges and grants economic independence to every woman, including women who decide to stay home and devote their time to their husbands, their children, and domestic labor. This reconsideration of the Qur'anic text supports economic independence as an essential right for women, even when it is not strictly linked to labor outside the home. In this section, I argue that women's work in the home, which has been universally and historically unrecognized as paid work, is acknowledged in the Qur'an as work that should be compensated.

So, what is *ajr*? The Qur'an acknowledges financial responsibilities in marriage. First, is the *ṣidāq*, which the Qur'an clearly defines as a one-time gift, paid to the bride before marriage and before she takes on any responsibilities. Second, *ajr* is what I argue a husband must (continuously) pay his wife after marriage, for what she provides as a wife and a mother. In other words, while *ṣidāq* is a one-time gift, given when the marriage contract is approved, *ajr* is a continuous financial compensation that a woman receives during her marital life, for domestic work, and other physical tasks. This compensation is ongoing—it lasts as long as the marriage, and for a period after a divorce takes place, and in cases when a divorced woman is pregnant or nursing.

Unfortunately, this distinction between *ajr* and *ṣidāq* was completely eliminated by traditional and even by modern exegetes, who treat the two words in the Qur'an loosely, as if they are interchangeable and refer to the same thing. This lack of differentiation between the two terms is rarely questioned. In one attempt to investigate the difference between the terms, Maha al-Tinawī argues that *ṣidāq* is a marriage gift specific for widows[46] and *ajr* is a marriage gift that is not restricted to any category.[47]

To clarify this confusion, I explore the Qur'anic text. First, we find *ṣidāq* (the one-time gift at marriage) mentioned in, "Give women their bridal gift upon marriage" (Q.4:4). This verse clearly defines *ṣidāq* as a one-time gift for the bride, which the bride has the right to forfeit. The fact that this financial responsibility is referred to as a gift excludes the possibility that it was earned or that it is given in exchange for work. The linguistic root (ṣ-d-q) that links *ṣidāq* to *ṣadaqa*, which refers to charity, is further confirmation that *ṣidāq* is a gift. Second, we find *ajr*. To be able to fully understand *ajr* and distinguish it from *ṣidāq* we must examine the way the word *ajr* is generally used in the Qur'anic text. The Qur'anic text uses the word to refer to compensation in the afterlife for the good deeds of one's worldly life; sometimes, it refers to compensation or salary in exchange for hired work. In all these cases, in the Qur'anic text *ajr* is related to the performance of a task or a job. *Ajr* always comes as a compensation in the Qur'an and is not granted freely; on the contrary, *ṣidāq* only appears once and means "giving for no requital."[48] When *ajr* appears in the Qur'an, it is always related to effort that deserves reward, in this worldly life or in the afterlife, as in the following verses: Q.2:62, Q.2:112, Q.2:262, Q.2:277, Q.3:136, Q.3:171, Q.3:179, Q.4:40, Q.4:67, Q.4:74, Q.4:100, Q.5:9, Q.6:90, Q.7:113, Q.7:170, Q.8:28, Q.9:22, Q.9:120, Q.11:11, Q.11:29, Q.11:115, Q.73:20, Q.64:15, and others. Therefore, when the same word *ajr* is used in a marital context, it must refer to a situation in which compensation is given for some form of work. In other words, it must refer to the Qur'anic acknowledgment of women's domestic work, like cleaning, cooking, serving, and other related responsibilities, like giving birth, nursing, and child-rearing.

Both *ajr* and *ṣidāq* are considered the Qur'anic criterion, required for a marriage to be sound and legal, "and there is no blame upon you if you marry them after you commit yourselves to their due marriage compensation (*ajūruhunna*)" (Q.60:10).[49] But while both *ajr* and *ṣidāq* are considered a condition for marriage, *ajr* is a financial compensation associated with wives' labor. For example, "So for whatever you enjoy [in marriage] from them, give them their due marriage compensation (*ajūruhunna*) as an obligation" (Q.4:24).[50] In this verse, giving *ajr* (pl. *ajūr*), which closes the conditional sentence, is a compensation for what men "enjoy" in marriage. In this case, the fact that the verb for "enjoy" is in the past tense is a clear reference to sexual pleasure, which according to Islamic norms is only lawful after the marriage contract is completed and the *ṣidāq* is paid, and contradicts any understanding that *ajr* is synonymous with *ṣidāq*. We can easily understand from Q.4:24 that *ṣidāq* precedes *ajr*.

In Q.4:25 we read, "So marry them with the permission of their people and give them their due compensation (*ajūrahunna*) according to (*ma'rūf*)" (Q.4:25).[51] In this verse, *ajr* also refers to a requirement for the marriage to be legal or sound. But in addition, the verse adds the obligation that such a payment is made to wives; it is an obligation to follow the *ma'rūf* rule—as previously discussed.[52] This means that the payment of *ajr* can vary according to what is appropriate and accepted. In another verse, we find *ajr* precisely used to refer to what the husband must pay his divorced wife in the event she is pregnant or nursing when he divorces her, "If they nurse for you give them their due marriage compensation (*ajūruhunna*)" (Q.65:6).[53] In this particular verse, the term *ajr* cannot refer to a bridal gift, since the verse deals with ending, not initiating, the marriage. This example proves my argument against the interchangeability of the terms *ajr* and *ṣidāq*. According to the traditional interpretation of Q.65:6, *ajr* was interpreted as a reference to the husband's financial responsibility to spend on his divorced wife if she was pregnant or nursing a child at the time of divorce. While I agree that the verse is confirmation that the divorced wife has the right to be financially supported during her pregnancy or while nursing, I disagree that this financial right is new and only due to a wife in the case of divorce. On the contrary, I argue that the right asserted in Q.65:6 should not be viewed as the *initiation* of a new right but as the *continuation* of an already established marital right that does not expire in two cases, namely, pregnancy and nursing.[54] In other words, a man has an obligation to spend on his wife and to pay her *ajr* and this responsibility is canceled three months after divorce, unless the wife is pregnant or nursing. By way of support, note that in Q.4:24, Q.4:25, Q.5:5, and Q.60:10, the term *ajr* refers to financial responsibilities of husbands in cases other than divorce.

As we can see, both Q.4:24 and Q.65:6 assert *ajr* as financial compensation in marriage, compensation that is required for the marriage to be sound.

Unfortunately, this understanding of the verses has been lost in traditional exegetical assessments, which interpret *ajr* in Q.4:24 as a reference to *ṣidāq* or the premarriage gift, and interpret *ajr* in Q.65:6 as a reference to the payment after divorce. Interestingly, according to these interpretations,[55] both verses grant financial rights to women outside marriage, either before or after, and deny them these rights while married. In contrast to this interpretation, I argue that *ajr* refers to a financial right within marriage, that is, one that is separate from *ṣidāq* (as *ṣidāq* is prior to the marriage), and unlike *ṣidāq*, *ajr* is an ongoing compensation. In addition, it is worth noting that Q.65:6 confirms the right of a divorced woman to *ajr* if she is pregnant or nursing, that is, it is a declaration of the continuity of this compensation during these specific times (even outside marriage), not the initiation of a new right that married women do not have.

It is important to note the following about my argument for *ajr*: first, this argument for *ajr* is entirely compatible with the Qur'anic concept of marriage, which I have previously explained "as a concept not based on servitude, but on compassion and cooperation."[56] Second the main source of the rejection of this argument might spring primarily from its unconventionality; re-evaluating women's domestic labor in this way and compensating women for it is unprecedented. However, if compensating women financially for domestic work seems like an extreme act, perhaps we need to consider why we so vehemently insist that women's unpaid domestic labor makes sense. Ironically, negating the value of women's work at home and treating it as free labor is a unique issue about which Western feminists and Islamic traditionalists seem to agree on—both maintain that this domestic labor does not count. Consequently, women's domestic labor does not secure women any real economic independence. Although Western feminists and Muslim traditionalists take a similar position, they respond to this commonly held assumption in opposite ways. Western feminists recognized the problematic aspects of women's unpaid domestic labor, and so, in order to secure women's economic independence, they insisted that labor outside the house was the only "positive work"[57] and the basic right that will empower women inside and outside the home. Unfortunately, Western feminists did not foresee that in arguing for this, they gained women the right to work outside the home, but this came in addition to women's work inside the home. Thus, we have a situation in which women work in almost every industry and are paid (almost universally) less than men (because of the patriarchal system that established and is in full control of the labor market), and women still have the same responsibilities in the home (for which they are still not recognized or paid).

At the other end of the spectrum, Islamic traditionalists, who are also fully convinced that women's domestic work should be unpaid, argue that women must be fully devoted wives and mothers and deny any right to economic independence. These two groups equally keep using *argumentum ad populum* arguments to support their assumptions about indoor labor and ignore the fact that for many women this domestic work represents a lifetime commitment that cannot simply be neglected. This domestic work should be recognized, especially in extraordinary cases, for example, for families of disabled children or those with special needs. While it is far from the ideal situation, women may make the choice to prioritize their domestic responsibilities and should be compensated for it.

Third, while I assert the Qur'anic approval of *ajr* as a Qur'anic right, I leave out the details of how to calculate *ajr* because I have chosen to remain faithful to a methodology of following the Qur'an. As we see in the Qur'an, women's economic independence is a fundamental right that should not be contingent on or limited to labor outside the home. Women who decide to prioritize domestic work should be financially compensated for doing this. As I noted, this argument will be challenged, simply because in the history of economic development, women's domestic work has never been considered "real" work, that is, work worthy of financial compensation; therefore, it is difficult to calculate all the specifics. How would we objectively estimate the value of women's domestic work? What is the merit of the effort invested? How should husbands' and other household help be calculated? While it is true that women's domestic work was never treated or evaluated as a financially rewardable job, the fact that historically people have not considered it as such does not mean that it does not merit consideration.

The Qur'an is general and universal, as this enables different communities to figure out the details according to their diverse needs. My suggestion is an invitation to consider the economic, social, and legal details; these should be left for experts to determine. As I noted, the epistemic desire to create a full theory to explain everything should not motivate us, as scholars, to add details to what is mentioned in the Qur'an in a general way. If I do this, I will be doing what I have criticized others for doing (in what I refer to as the "excessive exegetical narrativization of the Qur'an").

Fourth, I do not dismiss the possibility that compensating women for domestic labor might take the form of collective responsibility that the believing community should consider. Because while the commandment to give wives their *ajr* is personally addressed to divorcing husbands (as in Q.65:6) and in one case is personally addressed to the Prophet (as in Q.33:50), the same commandment to give women their *ajr* is addressed to the community of believers (as in "you who believe" in Q.4:25 and in Q.60:10). Whether compensation for domestic labor should be considered a personal obligation of husbands, as a condition for the soundness of their Islamic marriage contracts, or as a legal right for women who live in "believing communities,"—whatever this term might mean now—is another problematic aspect that this proposal does not attempt to answer. At one point, al-Ghanūshī argued in favor of a government compensation for housewives, one that would be given to women the way scholarships are paid to students, since "both types of dedication provide the society future service."[58]

Fifth, *ajr* or compensation for women's domestic labor in marriage is an argument that is closely related to the historical role women have always held. *Ajr* is a financial compensation for a physical and psychological (domestic) commitment, which means that the evaluation of *ajr* is dependent on the society; in some societies, wives and husbands share domestic responsibilities, and in other societies men may invest more domestic commitment than women. However, this should not lead to the total elimination of *ajr* because of the decline of women's domestic labor, since, women, according to the Qur'anic criterion, are to be compensated even for pregnancy and nursing and other biological aspects of life that men cannot share with women.

Finally, it is important to note that my argument in favor of compensating women for domestic work is not a negation of my overt preference for women's work outside the home, and my belief that, in general, this is the best way for women to find both economic security and fulfillment. Rather, I assert two elements: first, women have the right to economic independence as a practical realistic necessity that can and should be secured regardless of circumstances. Second, women's right to be compensated for domestic work is a legal necessity if we seek to re-establish real justice. Because although *ajr* works to secure women's economic independence, and justly and fairly recognizes women's devotion to domestic work, this option should remain a second choice. It is not and will never be the best choice for a woman to consider, particularly when other options are available, first because *ajr*, as we see, depends on what the husband can afford; and second, because ultimately, work (for both men women) is more than just economic sufficiency. Fulfillment based on work is a fundamental aspect of human nature, deeply embedded in the fabric of our humanity; people are fulfilled by striving for excellence. In my view, securing economic independence from a woman's domestic work should be a last option for women, in the absence of better choices. It secures the wife's dignity but does not address her needs as a full human being, help her discover her talents, or develop her personality; a woman should not depend on her husband and children to justify her "existence through them."[59]

Based on my understanding of the Qur'an, it is simply not true that Muslim women's God-given responsibility is to stay home and not engage in an independent career, unless they are obliged to do so. I argue that the option of remaining at home and only engaging in domestic work is not even the preferred alternative; it is just one option of many others that women might consider; therefore, the Qur'an makes it an obligation for men to financially compensate their wives. *Ajr* is without doubt a practical consideration for women who may, under the pressure of their responsibilities, give up (temporarily or permanently) their careers; I believe economic independence is necessary for all humans—men and women; economic independence is also the only guarantee that no woman might become trapped in marriage for mere financial reasons.

In sum, this acknowledgment is not an encouragement or even a recommendation for a certain lifestyle that limits women to domestic work; *ajr* is a just compensation for a sacrifice that some women may choose to make or even for the extra indoor responsibilities. In addition, *ajr* is a reminder for men that their wife's decision to stay at home should be financially compensated and not taken for granted as their right and as an obligation for women. A woman who gives up her economic security to dedicate herself to domestic responsibilities should have the alternative financial security that *ajr* is supposed to provide, at least in part. This argument for *ajr* as a compensation for the domestic work and marital responsibilities of married women provides them with a degree of economic security and ensures a more just evaluation of their role as housewives and mothers.

In contrast to the culturally constructed concepts, the Qur'an clearly states that women are not created *from* men, and even more importantly, they are not created *for* men, and are not assigned a sacred duty to serve men. Both men and women enter into marriage as equal and autonomous partners; therefore, when women serve men and maintain their domestic lives they must not do so out of obligation, rather they should be financially compensated for domestic work.

In this section, I argue that every woman should have an independent budget, whether from her own income, inheritance, or from her work as a housewife, or from both; this is the route to dignity, financial security, and independence. The Qur'an offers solutions to women's lack of financial independence because it recognizes that financial dependence is the cause of much of women's vulnerability. A woman without financial security is at the mercy of a husband who may mistreat her in some way or opt for a second wife. A woman who works and has financial independence can freely choose to marry and be an equal partner in that marriage, which will be based on mutual respect and equality. The Qur'an grants women the right to economic independence, and insists on a customized system of compensation within marriage, one that variably, yet justly, acknowledges women's domestic labor. A woman who devotes her time to this work, as we see, has the right to financial compensation. This compensation, which the Qur'anic text refers to as *ajr*, is based on an agreement and dependent on what the husband is able to provide. As we see, *ajr*, like *ṣidāq* or the one-time gift given at marriage, are both left to be evaluated and determined individually.

To sum up this chapter, women's rights and agency are guaranteed in the Qur'an, which acknowledges women's religious agency (as *Maryam* was a prophet), their political agency (for example, in the case of the Queen of Sheba), and finally, women's economic agency (from her right to work and from her right to domestic labor compensation in numerous verse that refer to *ajr*).

NOTES

1. Farīd al-Anṣārī, *Simā' al-mar'a fī l-Islām* (Meknes: Alwān Maghribiyya, 2003), 25.
2. Barlas, "Qur'anic Hermeneutics," 149.
3. This section was originally published as an article: Abla Hasan,"The Qur'anic story of Mary: Does rethinking the text support women prophethood?" *Ar-Raniry* 3, no. 1 (2016).
4. Translated by Abla Hasan. The insertion of "truly" in Abdel Haleem's translation is not faithful to the text.
5. al-Sha'rāwī, *Tafsīr al-Sha'rāwī*, 1453.
6. al-Ṭabarī, *Jāmi' al-bayān*, 2:254.
7. al-Faḍl b. al-Ḥasan al-Ṭabarsī, *Majma' al-bayān* (Beirut: Dār al-Murtaḍa, 2006), 2:235.
8. al-Rāzī, *al-Tafsīr al-kabīr*, 8:47.
9. 'Alī b. Muḥammad al-Māwardī, *al-Nukat wa-l-'ayūn* (Beirut: Dār al-Kutub al-'Ilmiyya, 2010), 1:390.
10. al-Qurṭubī, *al-Jāmi' li-aḥkām al-Qur'ān*, 5:127.
11. Ibn Ḥazm al-Andalusī, *al-Faṣil fī l-milal wa-l-ahwā' wa-l-niḥal* (Cairo: Maktabat al-Salām al-'Ilmiyya, 1923), 4:11.
12. Rāshid al-Ghanūshī, *al-Mar'a bayn al-Qur'ān wa-waqi' al-muslimin* (London: Moroccan Center of Research and Translation, 2000), 34.
13. Stowasser, *Women in the Qur'an*, 77.
14. al-Qurṭubī, *al-Jāmi' li-aḥkām*, 1:108.
15. al-Qurṭubī, *al-Jāmi' li-aḥkām*, 13:436.
16. al-Sha'rāwī, *Tafsīr al-Sha'rāwī*, 1469.
17. Muḥammad Amīn al-Shanqīṭī, *Aḍwā' al-bayyān* (Riyadh and Mansoura: Dār al-Faḍīla and Dār al-Hādī l-Nabawī, 2005), 632.

18. Fāṭima Huda Najā, *al-Mustashriqūn wa-l-mar'a al-muslima* (Alexandria: Dār al-Īmān, 1991), 13.

19. Maryam Bakhtyar and Akram Rezaei, "Female Leadership in Islam," *International Journal of Humanities and Social Science* 2, no. 17 (September 2012), 266.

20. This section was originally published as an article: Abla Hasan, "The Queen of Sheba: Would Rethinking the Qur'anic Story Support Female Public Leadership In Islam?" *Analize*, 21, no. 7(2016).

21. According to the Qur'anic story, Solomon rejected the gift.

22. Nevin Reda, "From Where Do We Derive 'God's Law'? The Case of Women's Political Leadership: A Modern Expression of an Ancient Debate," in *Feminism and Islamic Perspectives: New Horizons of Knowledge and Reform*, ed. Omaima Abou Bakr (Cairo: Women and Memory Forum, 2013), 122.

23. al-Qurṭubī, *al-Jāmi' li-aḥkām*, 16:139.

24. Ibid.

25. al-Ṭabarī, *Jāmi' al-bayān*, 5:555.

26. Muḥammad Ḥusayn al-Ṭabāṭabā'ī, *al-Mīzān* (Beirut: al-A'lamī, 1997), 15:352.

27. Ibid.

28. Maḥmūd b. 'Abdallāh al-Alūsī, *Rūḥ al-ma'ānī* (Beirut: Dār al-Kutub al-'Ilmiyya, 2010), 10:185.

29. al-Bukhārī, *Saḥīḥ al-Bukhārī*, 1086, hadith no. 4425.

30. This archaic word can be used to describe an animal like a zebra or a person lacking grace.

31. al-Māwardī, *al-Nukat wa-l-'ayūn*, 4:208.

32. Stowasser, *Women in the Qur'an*, 65.

33. Ali, *The Position of Women*, 122.

34. Qasim Amin, *The Liberation of Women and the New Woman* (Cairo: American University in Cairo Press, 2000), 6.

35. Nawāl al-Sa'dawī, *al-Untha hiya al-aṣl* (Arabic Books, 1974), 216 [ebook].

36. Muṣṭafā Maḥmūd, *Fī l-ḥub wa-l-haya* (Cairo: Dār al-Ma'ārif, 1966), 12.

37. al-Ghanūshī, *al-Mar'a*, 76.

38. Jamāl al-Bannā, *al-Mar'a al-muslima*, 19.

39. Ibid., 128.

40. al-Sha'rāwī, *Tafsīr al-Sha'rāwī*, 12021.

41. Hind al-Khūlī, *'Amal al-mar'a* (Damascus: Dār al-Fārābī, 2001), 297.

42. Muḥammad Zīnū, *Rasā'īl al-tawjihāt al-islāmiyya* (Riyadh: al-Sumi'ī, 1997), 345.

43. Bell Hooks, *Feminist Theory from Margin to Center* (Boston: South End Press, 1984), 137.

44. Ibrāhīm Zakariyā, *Mushkilat al-ḥubb* (Cairo: Dār Miṣr, n.d.), 86.

45. de Beauvoir, *The Second Sex*, 508.

46. Maha al-Tinawī, *Mā malakat aymānukum* (Damascus: al-Ahālī, 2011), 99.

47. I reject this view for including an external non-Qur'anic suggestion.

48. Riḍā, *Ḥuqūq al-nisā'*, 23.

49. Translated by Abla Hasan.

50. Translated by Abla Hasan.

51. Translated by Abla Hasan.

52. Probably this male financial obligation in marriage is what explains why a female gets half of what a male gets in inheritance as we read in (4:11).

53. Translated by Abla Hasan.

54. As noted, during the *'idda*, which typically lasts three months, women still deserve to be paid *ajr*.

55. Like the interpretations of al-Rāzī, al-Bayḍāwī, al-Suyūṭī, al-Sha'rāwī, and many others.

56. Abou El Fadl, *Speaking in God's Name*, 52.

57. de Beauvoir, *The Second Sex*, 550.

58. al-Ghanūshī, *al-Mar'a*, 75.

59. Ibid., 550.

Conclusion

My goal in this book is not to claim an apodictic approach but to pave the way for future similar examinations of the Qur'anic text. I must emphasize my commitment to rationality and to avoiding a systematic error that I have found in so many traditional Islamic-oriented approaches to Qur'anic studies, namely, the claim of epistemic certainty that excludes and terminates all other opinions. To avoid the very mistake I criticize others for making, I am careful not to claim that this book is, or can be, a decisive, definite, or final way of reading the Qur'anic text, because the gap between our human attempts to understand the text and the essential transcendentalism of the divine is a fact that will always dominate our unrealistic search for an absolute epistemic theological truth. This book is simply one attempt of many to unearth the overlooked Qur'anic message of female empowerment, a message that has been lost in the cacophony of historical interpretations, which, despite their variety, are variably but clearly engaged, in a way or another, in a historical process of an unjustifiable masculinization of the religious text.

More importantly, this book, in essence, aims to join the new reform movement in the Islamic world, a movement that has been painstakingly orchestrated by many enlightened and brave scholars. Today, reformers are increasingly rethinking religious taboos that were restricted to the elite and calling into question the unjust accusations of blasphemy that earlier reformers faced for rethinking traditional interpretations.

Not long ago, many Muslims in the Arab world did not have access or the ability to understand the real Islam—they could only appeal to their imams or shaykhs. In the postcolonial modern Arab world the narrow social environments and the challenging economic conditions in which ordinary Muslims lived in for so long meant that reading was a luxury that the majority had neither the time nor the budget for. Today, Muslims around the globe can click one button and have access to the largest libraries, the rarest manuscripts, and most importantly, they can have an access to institutionally banned voices. Meena Sharify-Funk elaborates on these rapid changes by saying,

> By providing an open forum in cyberspace, the internet has become a highly pluralistic arena for Islamic thinking, networking, and campaigning. As a medium, however, the internet is neutral, providing scope for progressive and traditionalist as well as radical discourses. Websites arguing for dialogue and 'rethinking' exist in juxtaposition with those that embrace illicit violence as a means of implementing anti-pluralistic Islamic interpretations and identities. By providing a forum for such diverse voices – voices that have often been repressed or driven underground in specific national contexts – the internet simultaneously undermines traditional authority and provides amplification for a variety of different voices that are competing for authority. At the same time, the internet democratizes and provides a forum for voices that are not necessarily democratic. It pluralizes and even fragments identity while allowing space for totalizing, revisionist political projects.[1]

Given these unprecedented historical changes, in an era when voices of the intellectual opposition and socially unrepresented minorities can no longer be silenced, facing the challenges by answering the pending questions is a priority. More importantly, these global changes, including but not limited to the democratization of knowledge and the free accessibility of information, have launched an unprecedented countdown for the monolithic domination of *tafsīr bi-l-ma'thūr* (heritage-based interpretation) schools of exegeses and Islamic jurisprudence.

My goal in this book is not to deny that premodern Muslim scholars were devoted and sincere in their efforts but to assert that we must continue to contribute to the intellectual structure; this structure must be built with the accumulated knowledge of scholars. The retrospective investigation of the past (as I use many medieval commentaries) is necessary, first to bridge the rift brought about by a history of misinterpreting the divine text; second because of the current, unsatisfactory status of hermeneutical based Qur'anic studies; and third, for the increasing need for purifying the Islamic heritage and the need to distinguish what can be treated as cultural, accidental, and temporary from what is truly Qur'anic, religious, and everlasting. Unfortunately, many have left the past unexamined; this is evident in the way many—even in academia—still depend on traditional *argumentum ad populum* based outcomes and are satisfied to recycle the same views, without rethinking or questioning their current validity.

The Qur'an fully acknowledges and strongly affirms women's humanity and equality. This equality is confirmed from the beginning, from the story of creation itself. In addition, by clarifying the deficiency I refer to as the "excessive exegetical narrativization of the Qur'an," I explain the exegetical process which ended by an unjust shifting of the blame to Eve in the famous story of Adam and Eve. Gender equality is affirmed in worldly responsibilities, in terms of religious merit, her rewards in the afterlife and in marriage which is strictly identified in the Qur'an as a sacred relationship between two equal human beings. Yet this affirmation does not prevent an exegetical reconstruction of the concept of *qiwāma*, which was reinterpreted from being a male duty, to being a divine assertion of male superiority. By clarifying the confusion caused by the "male addressee fallacy" we can understand *qiwāma* as a duty, not an assertion of male superiority. The "male addressee fallacy" is the key also to unlock the semantic mystery of Q.4:34. The Qur'an does not commend domestic violence or wife beating as many wrongly interpret the verse. The interpretation I provide for Q.4:32 which views the provision for and responsibilities related to *qiwāma* as a duty that can earn men a divine reward helps clarify the misinterpretation of the concept of "degree" which is an outcome of what I refer to as the flaw of "exegetical contextomy." This supports an interpretation of the concept of degree in Q.2:288 as a duty rewarded to men, specific to divorce. By way of clarifying "the fallacy of relative reform," "the exegetical contextomy fallacy," "the authoritative ascendancy of early religious scholars," "the use of the hadith to invalidate the Qur'anic text," and "the fallacy of exegetical semantic satiation" I distinguish "Islamic polygyny" from "Qur'anic polygyny," which appears in the Qur'anic text as conditional, gender egalitarian, and precisely codified. *Hijāb* as I explain is the visual face of Muslim women, a religious duty, and a symbol of a liberal Islamic feminist philosophy. Finally, by rethinking "the so-called authoritative ascendancy of early religious scholars" we unlock the Qur'anic confirmations of women's full religious, political, and economic agency. This includes women's right to work, education, public authority positions, prophethood, and *ajr*, which refers to a continuous marital financial obligation.

Finally, this book comes as a response to the Qur'anic repeated invitations to "reflect" (Q.16:11), a function and a responsibility that defines us as humans. But more importantly, a responsibility that constitutes the essential prerequisite to understand the Qur'an and to turn it from an abstract book to a practical guidance. Hisham Altalib (b. 1940) beautifully elaborates on the importance of this worldly human mission as he says,

> Some people think that since we have the perfect code of life in the Qur'an we can just go ahead and apply it to our life without thinking. Allah gave us a brain to use in the understanding and application of our faith. This is what makes us different from animals. We are not the fastest, the biggest, the strongest, or the tallest of creatures. But we are the 'brainiest' of them all![2]

In addition, the book indirectly addresses one essential theological question about the nature of God. Because, revealing the lost gender-egalitarian message of the Qur'an doesn't only constitute a core part of any modern academic discussion about Islam as a religion and about the status of Muslim women; in addition, rethinking the Qur'an as a gender-egalitarian book is closely related to our understanding of God. If we start from the unanimously agreed upon Islamic premise that the Qur'an is the literal word of God, then exploring gender egalitarianism in the Qur'an is one logical way of answering the theological question: Is God just? Or is he gender biased? In addition, exploring gender egalitarianism in the Qur'an can help resolve the logical self-contradiction between the Qur'anic repeated affirmations of God's justice as we read, "He does not wring anyone by as much as the weight of a speck of dust" (Q.4:40) and the human-based conceptualization of the Qur'an as a patriarchal book. Unlocking gender egalitarianism in the Qur'an can help us reconcile the full and the unconditional adoption of gender equality in verses like (Q.33:35) with the traditional patriarchal understanding of verses like (Q.2:228). If the question "Who is God?" is—as it should always be—an everlasting open question, then, every attempt to answer it should be continuous, free, and ongoing as long as there is someone asking that question. Rethinking the Qur'an's gender egalitarianism constitutes one way, if not the best way, to explore God's gender egalitarianism because "by their fruit you will recognize them. Do people pick grapes from thornbushes, or figs from thistles?" (Mt. 7:16)[3]

NOTES

1. Meena Sharify-Funk, *Encountering the Transnational: Women, Islam and the Politics of Interpretation* (Burlington: Ashgate Publishing, 2013), 105.
2. Hisham Altalib, *Training Guide for Islamic Workers* (Herndon, VA: International Institute of Islamic Thought, 1981), 91.
3. www.biblegateway.com.

Bibliography

'Abd al-Raḥmān, 'Ā'isha. *Nisā' al-nabī*. Beirut: Dār al-Kitāb al-'Arabī, 1979.

'Abd al-Raḥmān, 'Ā'isha. *al-Qur'ān wa-qaḍayā al-insān*. Cairo: Dār al-Ma'ārif, 1999.

'Abdel Haleem, Muhammad. *The Qur'an*. New York: Oxford University Press, 2010.

'Abdel Haleem, Muhammad. *Understanding the Qur'an: Themes and Style*. London: I.B.Tauris, 2011.

Abou-Bakr, Omaima (ed.). *Feminism and Islamic Perspectives: New Horizons of Knowledge and Reform*. Cairo: Women and Memory Forum, 2013.

Abou-Bakr, Omaima. *Gender Perspectives in Islamic Tradition*. Edited transcript of talk given at the Second Annual Minaret of Freedom Institute Dinner. Gaithersburg, MD, 26 June 1999. Online: http://www.minaret.org/gender.htm.Abou El Fadl, Khaled. *Speaking in God's Name: Islamic Law, Authority and Women*. New York: Oneworld, 2014.

Abou El Fadl, Khaled, Deborah Chasman, Joshua Cohen, and Noah Feldman. *Islam and the Challenge of Democracy: A Boston Review Book*. Princeton, NJ: Princeton University Press, 2004.

Abu-Lughod, Lila. *Do Muslim Women Need Saving?* Cambridge, MA: Harvard University Press, 2013.

Abū Zayd, Naṣr Ḥāmid. *Dawa'ir al-khawf*. Beirut: al-Markaz al-Thaqāfī l-'Arabī, 2004.

Abū Zayd, Naṣr Ḥāmid. *Ishkāliyat al-qirā'a wa-āliyyat al-ta'wīl*. Beirut: al-Markaz al-Thaqāfī l-'Arabī, 2005.

Abū Zayd, Naṣr Ḥāmid. *Mafhūm al-naṣṣ*. Beirut: al-Markaz al-Thaqāfī l-'Arabī, 2014.

Ahmed, Leila. *Quiet Revolution: The Veil's Resurgence, From the Middle East to America*. New Haven, CT and London: Yale University Press, 2011.

al-'Alawī, Hādī. *Fuṣūl 'an al-mar'ā*. Beirut: Dār al-Kunūz al-Adabiyya. 1996.

Ali, Kecia. *Marriage and Slavery in Early Islam*. Cambridge, MA: Harvard University Press, 2010.

Ali, Kecia. "On Critique and Careful Reading." *Journal of Feminist Studies in Religion* 32, no. 2 (2006): 121–6.
Ali, Kecia. "Rethinking Women's Issues in Muslim Communities." In *Taking Back Islam: American Muslims Reclaim Their Faith*, edited by Michael Wolfe, 91–99. Emmaus, PA: Rodale Press, 2002.
Ali Khan, Liaquat. "Jurodynamics of Islamic Law." *Rutgers Law Review* 61, no. 2 (2009): 231–93.
Ali, Syed Mohammed. *The Position of Women in Islam: A Progressive View*. Albany: State University of New York Press, 2004.
Altalib, Hisham. *Training Guide for Islamic Workers*. Herndon, VA: International Institute of Islamic Thought, 1981.
al-Alūsī, Maḥmūd b. *'Abdallāh. Rūḥ al-ma'ānī*. Beirut: Dār al-Kutub al-'Ilmiyya, 2010.
Amer, Sahar. *What Is Veiling?* Chapel Hill: University of North Carolina Press, 2014.
Amin, Qasim. *The Liberation of Women and the New Woman*. Cairo: American University in Cairo Press, 2000.
al-Anṣārī, Farīd. *Simā' al-mar'a fī l-Islām*. Meknes: Alwān Maghribiyya, 2003.
al-'Aqqād, 'Abbās Maḥmūd. *al-Mar'a fī l-Qur'ān*. Cairo: Nahḍat Miṣr, 1980.
Arkoun, Mohammed. *Ayna huwa al-fikr al-Islāmī l-mu'aṣir*. Beirut: al-Saqui, 1995.
Arkoun, Mohammed. *al-Qur'an: min al-tafsīr al-mawrūth ilā tahlīl al-khiṭāb al-dīnī*. Beirut: Dār al-Tali'a, 2005.
'Aṭiyya, Ṣaqr. *Fatāwa wa-aḥkām li-l-mar'a al-muslima*. Cairo: Wahba, 2006.
'Atr, Nūr al-Dīn. *Mādha 'an al-mar'a?* Damascus and Beirut: al-Yamama, 2003.
al-'Awa, Salwa. "Linguistic Structure." In *The Wiley Blackwell Companion to the Qur'an*, edited by Andrew Rippin and Jawid Mojaddedi, 61–81. Chichester, W. Sussex, UK: Wiley-Blackwell, 2017.
al-'Aẓīm, *Ṣādiq Jalāl. Fī l-ḥubb wa-l-ḥubb al-'uthrī*. Baghdad: Dār al-Mada, 2002.
al-'Azīzī, Khadīja. *al-Usūs al-falsafiyya li-l-fikr al-nasawī l-gharbī*. Beirut: Bisan, 2005.
al-Bahi, Muḥammad. *al-Fikr al-Islāmī l-ḥadīth wa-ṣilathu bi-ista 'mār al-gharbī*. Cairo: Wahba, 1964.
Bakhtiar, Laleh. *The Sublime Qur'an*. Chicago: Kazi Publishers, 2007.
Bakhtyar, Maryam and Akram Rezaei. "Female Leadership in Islam." *International Journal of Humanities and Social Science* 2, no. 17 (Sept. 2012): 259–67.
al-Bannā, Ḥasan. *al-Mar'a al-muslima*. Cairo: Dār al-Kutub al-Salafiyya, 1986.
al-Bannā, Jamāl. *Jawāz imāmat al-mar'a li-l-rijāl*. N.p.: Dār al-Shurūq, 2010.
al-Bannā, Jamāl. *al-Mar'ā bayn taḥrīr al-Qur'ān wa-taqīd al-fuqaha'*. Cairo: Dār al-Fikr al-Islāmī, 1998.
Barazangi, Nimat Hafez. *Woman's Identity and the Qur'an: A New Reading*. Gainesville: University Press of Florida, 2004.
Barlas, Asma. *Believing Women in Islam*. Austin: University of Texas Press, 2002.
Barlas, Asma. "Qur'anic Hermeneutics and Sexual Politics." *Cardozo Law Review* 28, no. 1 (2006): 143–51.
Baumeister, Roy. *Is There Anything Good About Men? How Cultures Flourish by Exploiting Men*. Oxford: Oxford University Press, 2010.
Al-Bihiri, Islām. *Zawāj al-nabī min 'Ā'isha*. Giza: al-Yawm al-Sābi', 2008.

Bin A'bada, Samah. "Asma al-murābit baḥitha jarī'a tarfūd al-tammiz al-ijtima'ī wa-l-irqī wa-l-dīnī." *al-Arab [Newspaper]*. October 20, 2013.
al-Biqā'ī, Burhān al-Dīn. *Naẓm al-durar*. Cairo: Dār al-Kitāb al-Islāmī, 1984.
al-Bishrī, Ṭāriq. *al-Tajadd al-ḥaḍārī*. Beirut: Arabic Network for Research and Publishing, 2015.
Bouhdiba, 'Abd al-Wahhāb. *al-Islam wa-l-jins*. Beirut: Riyāḍ al-Rayyes, 2001.
Brown, Jonathan. "Did the Prophet Say It or Not?" *Journal of the American Oriental Society* 129, no. 2 (2009): 259–85.
al-Bukhārī, Muḥammad. *Ṣaḥīḥ al-Bukhārī*. Damascus and Beirut: Dār Ibn Kathīr, 2002.
al-Bustānī, Buṭrus. *Udabā' al-'Arab fī l-jāhiliyya wa-ṣadr al-Islām*. Beirut: Dār Ṣādir, 1953.
Chan-Malik, Sylvia. "A Space for the Spiritual." *Amerasia Journal* 40, no. 1 (2014): 17–33.
Chaudhry, Ayesha. *Domestic Violence and the Islamic Tradition*. Oxford: Oxford University Press, 2013.
Clark, Russell and Elaine Hatfield. "Gender Differences in Receptivity to Sexual Offers." *Journal of Psychology and Human Sexuality* 2, no. 1 (1989): 39–55.
De Beauvoir, Simone. *The Second Sex*. New York: Vintage Books, 2010.
Demir, Sehmus. "On Modernity, Islamic World and Interpretation of Qur'an." *Ekev Academic Review* 12, no. 37 (September 2008): 97–119.
Denffer, Ahmad von. *'Ulum al-Qur'an: An Introduction to the Sciences of the Qur'an*. Leicestershire: Kube Publishing, 2011.
Donner, Fred. "The Historical Context." In *The Cambridge Companion to the Qur'an*, edited by Jane McAuliffe. Cambridge and New York: Cambridge University Press, 2007.
Dworkin, Andrea and Catharine MacKinnon. *Pornography and Civil Rights: A New Day for Women's Equality*. Minneapolis, MN: Organizing Against Pornography, 1989.
El-Desouky, Ayman. "Between Hermeneutic Provenance and Textuality: The Qur'an and the Question of Method in Approaches to World Literature." *Journal of Qur'anic Studies* 16, no. 3 (2014): 11–38.
Engineer, Asghar Ali. *The Rights of Women in Islam*. New York: Sterling Publishers, 1992.
Esposito, John. *Women in Muslim Family Law*. Syracuse University Press, 1982.
Figo, 'Abd al-Salām. *al-Qir'a al-mu'aṣira li-l-nuṣūṣ al-shar'iyya*. Cairo and Mansoura: Dār al-Kalīma, 2016.
Geissinger, Aisha. *Gender and Muslim Construction of Exegetical Authority: A Rereading of the Classical Genre of Qur'an Commentary*. Leiden: Brill, 2015.
al-Ghaḍbān, Munīr. Aḍwa' *'alā tarbiyyat al-mar'a al-muslima*. Cairo: Dār al-Kutub al-Salafiyya, 1986.
al-Ghanūshī, Rāshid. *al-Mar'a bayn al-Qur'ān wa-waqi' al-muslimin*. London: Moroccan Center of Research and Translation, 2000.
Grabe, Shelly and Janet Shibley Hyde. "Body Objectification, MTV, and Psychological Outcomes among Female Adolescents." *Journal of Applied Social Psychology* 39, no. 12 (2009): 2779–86.

Haddad, Yazbeck and John L. Esposito. *Islam, Gender, and Social Change*. New York and Oxford: Oxford University Press, 1998.

Hādī, Riyāḍ and Niḍāl Māl Allāh. "Manhajiyyāt Ibn Isḥāq fī tadwīn al-sīra al-nabawiyya." *Majalat al-'Ulūm al-Islāmiyya* 6, no. 12 (2012). Online: http://islamicscience.uomosul.edu.iq/files/files/files_5893070.pdf. Accessed April 9, 2018.

Ḥamād, Suhila Zayn al-'Abidīn. "Zawāj al-qāṣarāt wa-āyā wa-llaytī lam yaḥḍna" [Minor Marriage and the Verse: Those Who Did Not Menstruate]. *al-Medina*, February 5, 2016.

Ḥarb, 'Alī. *al-Ḥubb wa-l-fanā'*. Beirut: Dār al-Manāhil, 1990.

Hassan, Riffat. "Feminism in Islam." In *Feminism and World Religions*, edited by Arvind Sharma and Katherine K. Young. Albany: State University of New York Press, 1999.

Hassan, Riffat. *Her Voice Her Faith*. Edited by Arvind Sharma and Katherine K. Young. Boulder, CO: Westview Press, 2003.

Hassan, Riffat. "What Islam Teaches about Ethics and Justice." An Interview with Riffat Hassan. *U.S. Catholic* 61, no. 5 (1996): 14–19.

al-Ḥaydarī, Ibrāhīm. *al-Niẓām al-abawī wa-mushkilat al-jins 'inda al-'arab*. Beirut: Dār al-Sāqī, 2011.

Hidayatullah, Aysha. *Feminist Edges of the Qur'an*. Oxford: Oxford University Press, 2014.

Hidayatullah, Aysha. "Muslim Feminist Birthdays." *Feminist Studies in Religion* 27, no. 1 (March/April 2011): 119–22.

Ho, Christina and Dreher Tanja. *Beyond the Hijab Debates: New Conversations on Gender, Race, and Religion*. Newcastle upon Tyne, UK: Cambridge Scholars Publishing, 2009.

Hooks, Bell. *Feminism is for Everybody*. Cambridge, MA: South End Press, 2000.

Hooks, Bell. *Feminist Theory from Margin to Center*. Boston: South End Press, 1984.

Ibn 'Abbās, 'Abdallāh. *Tanwīr al-miqbās min tafsīr Ibn 'Abbās*. Beirut: Dār al-Kutub al- 'Ilmiyya, 1992.

Ibn 'Ajība, Aḥmad b. Muḥammad. *al-Baḥr al-madīd fī tafsīr al-Qur'ān al-majīd*. Cairo: Maṭāba' al-Miṣriyya al-'Āmma li-Kitāb, 1999.

Ibn 'Āshūr, Muḥammad b. al-Ṭāhir. *al-Taḥrīr wa-l-tanwīr*. Tunis: al-Dār al-Tunisiyya, 1984.

Ibn Bāz. *Nūr 'alā l-darb*. Riyadh: al-Riyāsa al-'Āma li-l-Buḥūth al-'Ilmiyya wa-l-Iftā', 2011.

Ibn Ḥazm al-Andalusī. *al-Faṣil fī l-milal wa-l-ahwā' wa-l-niḥal*. Cairo: Maktabat al-Salām al-'Ilmiyya, 1923.

Ibn Kathīr, Ismā'īl b. 'Umar. *Tafsīr al-Qur'ān al-'aẓīm*. Riyadh: Dār Ṭayyiba, 1999.

Ibn Māja, Abū 'Abdallāh Muḥammad b. Yazīd. *Sunan Ibn Māja*. Cairo: Dār Iḥyā' al-Kutub al-'Arabiyya, n.d.

Ibn Nabī, Malik. *Mushkilat al-afkār fī l-'alām al-Islāmī*. Damascus: Dār al-Fikr, 1979.

Ibn Nabī, Malik. *al-Ẓāhira al-qur'āniyya*. Damascus: Dār al-Fikr, 1979.

Ibn Qudāma, 'Abd al-Raḥman. *al-Sharḥ al-kabīr*. Aleppo: Dār al-Kitāb al-'Arabī.

'Isā, Ibrāhīm. *Afkār muhadada bi-l-qatal*. Cairo: Maṭāba' Sitār bi-Ras li-l-Ṭibā'a wa-Nashr, 1993.

al-Jābirī, Muḥammad. *Madkhal 'ilā al-Qur'ān al-karīm*. Vol. 1. Beirut: Markaz Dirasāt al-Wiḥda al-'Arabiyya, 2006.
al-Joueli, Nasr. "Contemporary Interpretations of Qiwamah." In *Feminism and Islamic Perspectives: New Horizons of Knowledge and Reform*, edited by Omaima Abou-Bakr, 165–76. Cairo: Women and Memory Forum, 2013.
al-Jundī, Anwar. *al-Mar'a al-muslima fī wajh al-tahddiyyat*. Cairo: Dār al-I'tisām, 1979.
Kahf, Mohja. "From Her Royal Body the Robe was Removed." In *The Veil: Women Writers on Its History, Lore, and Politics*, edited by Jennifer Heath, 27–43. Berkeley: University of California Press, 2008.
Katz, Marion. *Women in the Mosque*. New York: Columbia University Press, 2014.
al-Khudarī, Muḥammad. *Min asrār ḥurūf al-jar fī l-dhikr al-ḥakīm*. Cairo: Wahba, 1989.
al-Khūlī, Hind. *'Amal al-mar'a*. Damascus: Dār al-Fārābī, 2001.
Lazreg, Marnia, *Questioning the Veil: Open Letters to Muslim Women*. Princeton: Princeton University Press, 2009.
Leaman, Oliver. *The Qur'an: An Encyclopedia*. London: Routledge, 2006.
Leirvik, Oddbjørn. "Modern Islamic Approaches to Divine Inspiration, Progressive Revelation, and Human Text." *Studia Theologica* 69, no. 2 (2015): 101–25.
Mackinon, Catharine. *Feminism Unmodified*. Cambridge, MA: Harvard University Press, 1987.
Maguire, Daniel C. and Sadiyya Shaikh. *Violence Against Women in Contemporary World Religions*. Cleveland, OH: Pilgrim Press, 2007.
Maḥmūd, 'Abdallāh. *Nihayat al-mar'a al-gharbiyya: bidayat al-mar'a al-'arabiyya*. Cairo: Dār al-Kutub al-Salafiyya, 1986.
Maḥmūd, Muṣṭafā. *Fi l-ḥub wa-l-haya*. Cairo: Dār al-Ma'ārif, 1966.
Maḥmūd, Muṣṭafā. *Min asrār al-Qur'an*. Cairo: Dār al-Ma'ārif, 1977.
Malamuth, Neil. "Sexually Explicit Media, Gender Differences and Evolutionary Theory." *Journal of Communication* 46, no. 3 (1996): 8–31.
Mawdudi, Abul A'la. *Four Key Concepts of the Qur'an*. Leicester: Kube Publishing, 2013.
al-Māwardī, 'Alī b. Muḥammad. *al-Nukat wa-l-'ayūn*. Beirut: Dār al-Kutub al-'Ilmiyya, 2010.
Mernissi, Fatima. *al-Harīm al-siyāsī*. Damascus: Dār al-Hasad, 1987.
Mernissi, Fatima. *Mā wara' al-ḥijāb*. Casablanca: al-Fanak, 2005.
Mernissi, Fatima. *Scheherazade Goes West*. New York: Washington Square Press, 2001.
Mernissi, Fatima. *The Veil and the Male Elite*. Translated by Mary Jo Lakeland. New York: Basic Books, 1991.
Mir-Hosseini, Ziba. "Beyond 'Islam' vs. 'Feminism.'" *IDS Bulletin* 42, no. 1 (January 2011): 67–77.
Mir-Hosseini, Ziba. "Classical Fiqh, Contemporary Ethics and Gender Justice." In *New Directions in Islamic Thought: Exploring Reform and Muslim Tradition*, edited by Kari Vogt and Christian Larsen, 77–88. New York: I.B. Tauris, 2011.
Mir Hosseini, Ziba. "Muslim Women's Quest for Equality: Between Islamic Law and Feminism." *Critical Inquiry* 32, no. 4 (2006): 629–45.

al-Miṣrī, 'Abd al-Wahhāb. *Qadiyyat al-mar'a*. Giza: Nahḍat Miṣr, 2010.

Moad, Omar Edward. "Honored Since Adam: Islam and the Value of Human Freedom." In *Yaqeen*. October 23, 2017. Online: yaqeeninstitute.org.

Muslim, Abū al-Ḥusayn 'Asākir al-Dīn. *Saḥīḥ Muslim*. Riyadh: Dār Ṭayyiba, 2006.

Najā, Fāṭima Huda. *al-Mustashriqūn wa-l-mar'a al-muslima*. Alexandria: Dār al-Īmān, 1991.

Nurmila, Nina. *Women, Islam and Everyday Life: Renegotiating Polygamy in Indonesia*. New York: Routledge, 2009.

Nussbaum, Martha. "Objectification." *Philosophy and Public Affairs* 24, no. 4 (1995): 249–91.

Pakeeza, Shahzadi and Chishti Asghar. "Critical Study of the Approaches to the Exegesis of the Holy Qur'an." *Pakistan Journal of Islamic Research* 10 (2012): 19–26.

Qaramī, Amāl. *al-Ikhtilāf fi l-thaqafa al-'arabiyya al-islāmiyya*. Beirut: Dār al-Madar al-Islāmī, 2007.

al-Qurṭubī, Muḥammad b. Aḥmad. *al-Jāmi' li-aḥkām al-Qur'ān*. Beirut: al-Risāla, 2006.

Rahmaan, Yasiin. "Feminist Edges of Muslim Feminist Readings of Qur'anic Verses." *Journal of Feminist Studies in Religion* 32, no. 2 (2016): 142–8.

Ramī, Layla. *Mawqi' al-mara' al-nakhbūayi fī mujtama' al-risāla*. Doha: Idārat al-Buḥūth al-Dirāsāt al-Islāmiyya, 2011.

al-Razī, Fakhr al-Dīn Muḥammad b. 'Umar. *al-Tafsīr al-kabīr*. Beirut: Dār al-Fikr, 1981.

Reda, Nevin. "From Where Do We Derive 'God's Law'? The Case of Women's Political Leadership: A Modern Expression of an Ancient Debate." In *Feminism and Islamic Perspectives: New Horizons of Knowledge and Reform*, edited by Omaima Abou Bakr, 119–36. Cairo: Women and Memory Forum, 2013.

Riḍā, Rashīd. *Ḥuqūq al-nisā' fī l-Islām*. Beirut and Damascus: al-Maktab al-Islāmī, 1984.

Riḍā, Rashīd. *Tafsīr al-manār*. Egypt: Dār al-Manār, 1947.

Riley, Robin L. *Depicting the Veil: Transnational Sexism and the War on Terror*. London: Zed Books, 2013.

Rumminger, Jana, Mulki al-Sharmani, and Ziba Mir-Hosseini. *Men in Charge: Rethinking Authority in Muslim Legal Tradition*. London: Oneworld, 2015.

Russell, Diana. *Making Violence Sexy*. New York: Teachers College Press, 1993.

Ruthven, Malise. *Islam in the World*. Oxford and New York: Oxford University Press, 1984.

al-Sa'dawī, Nawāl. *al-Untha hiya al-aṣil*. Arabic Books, 1974. ebook.

al-Sa'dī, 'Abd al-Raḥmān b. Nāṣir. *Taysīr al-Karīm al-Raḥmān*. Beirut: al-Risāla, 2002.

Saeed, Abdullah. *The Qur'an: An Introduction*. London: Routledge, 2008.

Sa'īd, 'Abd al-Sattar Fatḥallāh. *al-Ghazū l-fikrī wa-l-ṭayarāt al-mu'adiyya li-l-Islām*. Mansoura: Dār al-Wafa, 1988.

Said, Edward. *Orientalism*. New York: Vintage Books, 1979.

Saleh, Walid. *The Formation of the Classical Tafsir Tradition*. Leiden: Brill, 2004.

Saleh, Walid. "Hermeneutics." In *The Wiley Blackwell Companion to the Qur'an*, edited by Andrew Rippin and Jawed Mojaddedi, 389–405. Hoboken, NJ: Wiley-Blackwell, 2017.

al-Sanadī, Abū Muḥammad ʻAbd al-Qādir. *Raf‘ al-janna amam jilbāb al-mar'a al-muslima fī l-kitāb wa-l-sunna*. Riyadh: Dār al-Kitāb wa-Sunna, 1996.

Sardar, Ziauddin. *Reading the Qur'an: The Contemporary Relevance of the Sacred Text of Islam*. Oxford and New York: Oxford University Press, 2011.

al-Sarrani, Abeer and Alaa Alghamdi. "Through Third World Women's Eyes: The Shortcomings of Western Feminist Scholarship on the Third World." *Analize* 2 (2014): 1–6. Online: www.analize-journal.ro/library/files/alaa.pdf. Accessed April 9, 2018.

Seedat, Fatima. "Islam, Feminism, and Islamic Feminism: Between Inadequacy and Inevitability." *Journal of Feminist Studies in Religion* 29, no. 2 (2013): 25–45.

Shah, Niaz. *Women, the Koran and International Human Rights Law: The Experience of Pakistan*. Leiden: Brill, 2006.

Shaḥrūr, Muḥammad. *Fiqh al-mar'a*. N.p.: al-Ahali, 2000.

Shaḥrūr, Muḥammad. *Nahw awsūl jadīda li-l-fikr al-Islāmī*. Damascus: al-Ahali, 2000.

Shaḥrur, Muḥammad and Andreas Christmann. *The Qur'an, Morality and Critical Reason: The Essential Muhammad Shahrur*. Leiden and Boston: Brill, 2009.

al-Shanqīṭī, Muḥammad Amīn. *Aḍwā' al-bayyān*. Riyadh and Mansoura: Dār al-Faḍīla and Dār al-Hādī l-Nabawī, 2005.

al-Sha‘rāwī, Muḥammad Mutwalī. *Tafsīr al-Sha ‘rāwī*. N.p.: Akhbār al-Yawm, 1991.

Sharīa‘tī, ‘Alī. *Mas'ūliyyāt al-mar'a*. Beirut: al-Amīr, 2007.

Sharify-Funk, Meena. *Encountering the Transnational: Women, Islam and the Politics of Interpretation*. Burlington: Ashgate Publishing, 2013.

al-Sharmani, Mulki. "Islamic Feminism: Transnational and National Reflections." *Approaching Religion* 4, no. 2 (December 2014): 83–94.

al-Shaykh, Mamdūḥ. *al-Islāmiyyūn wa-l-‘ilmāniyyūn*. Beirut and Amman: Dār al-Bayyāriq, 1999.

Sidani, Yusuf. *Muslim Women at Work: Religious Discourses in Arab Society*. Cham: Palgrave Macmillan, 2017.

Soroush, Abdolkarim. "The Changeable and the Unchangeable." In *New Directions in Islamic Thought: Exploring Reform and Muslim Tradition*, edited by Kari Vogt, Lena Larsen, and Christian Moe. New York: I.B. Tauris, 2011.

Souaiaia, Ahmed E. *Contesting Justice: Women, Islam, Law, and Society*. Albany: State University of New York Press, 2008.

Stanciu, Elena-Larisa and Bjørn Christensen. "Controlling Women's Bodies: The Black and Veiled Female Body in Western Visual Culture. A Comparative View." *Analize* (2014). Online: www.analize-journal.ro/library/files/stanciu.pdf. Accessed April 9, 2018.

Stowasser, Barbara. *Women in the Qur'an, Traditions and Interpretation*. New York: Oxford University Press, 1994.

Sultan, Jasim. *al-Turāth wa-ishkaliyyathu al-kubrā*. Beirut: Arab Network for Research and Publishing and Tamkin, 2015.

al-Suyūṭī, ‘Abd al-Raḥmān b. al-Kamāl. *al-Durr al-manthūr*. Cairo: Markaz Ḥajar, 2003.

Swami, Viren, Jusnara Miah, Nazerine Noorani, and Donna Taylor. "Is the Hijab Protective? An Investigation of Body Image and Related Constructs among British Muslim Women." *British Journal of Psychology* 12, no. 105 (2014): 352–63.

al-Ṭabarī, Muḥammad b. Jarīr. *Jāmi‘ al-bayān*. Beirut: Mu’assasa al-Risāla, 1994.
al-Ṭabāṭabā’ī, Muḥammad Ḥusayn. *al-Mīzān*. Beirut: al-A‘lamī, 1997.
al-Ṭabarsī, al-Faḍl b. al-Ḥasan. *Majma‘ al-bayān*. Beirut: Dār al-Murtaḍa, 2006.
al-Tinawī, Maha. *Mā malakat aymānukum*. Damascus: al-Ahālī, 2011.
Venker, Suzanne and Phyllis Schlafly. *The Flipside of Feminism: What Conservative Women Know and Men Can’t Say*. New York: WND Books, 2011.
Wadud, Amina. “Can One Critique Cancel All Previous Efforts?” *Journal of Feminist Studies in Religion* 32, no. 2 (2016): 130–4.
Wadud, Amina. *The Qur’an and Women*. New York: Oxford University Press, 1999.
al-Wasīṭ. Cairo: al-Shurūq al-Dawaliyya, 2004.
Yusuf, B.O. “Feminism in the Shade of the Qur’an.” *Journal of Nigerian Association of Arabic and Islamic Studies* 15, no. 1 (2000).
Zadeh, Travis. “Quranic Studies and the Literary Turn.” *Journal of the American Oriental Society* 135, no. 2 (April 2015): 329–42.
Zakariyā, Ibrāhīm. *Mushkilat al-ḥubb*. Cairo: Dār Miṣr, n.d.
al-Zamakhsharī, Maḥmūd b. *‘Umar. al-Kashāf*. Beirut: Dār al-Ma‘rīfa, 2009.
Ziāda, May. *Baḥithat al-badiyya*. Beirut: Mu’asassat Nawfil, 1983
Zīnū, Muḥammad. *Rasā’īl al-tawjihāt al-islāmiyya*. Riyadh: al-Sumi‘ī, 1997.

Subject Index

About the Author

Abla Hasan is an associate professor of practice of Arabic language and culture at the University of Nebraska-Lincoln (UNL). She completed her PhD in philosophy of language from the UNL in 2013, and her MA in philosophy, as a Fulbright grantee, from the UNL in 2009. Dr. Hasan obtained her BA in philosophy from Damascus University/Syria in 2000, followed by a diploma of high studies from Damascus University in 2001. She is a native speaker of Arabic. She teaches Arabic language and culture at UNL, and she is the program's coordinator and undergraduate adviser. Her current teaching and research focus on Qur'anic studies, Islamic feminism, gender and sex in the Arab world, and Arabic studies. She has published with Analize, Ar-Raniry, the Journal of Information Literacy, Disputatio, Al-Manarah, E-logos, and other peer-reviewed international journals. She is married to Hassan Saleh and a mother to Zein, Yman, and Taym saleh.

Made in the USA
Coppell, TX
16 November 2021

65864936R00111